DECISION MAKING AND ACCOUNTING: CURRENT RESEARCH

Edited by

Shane Moriarity
The University of Oklahoma

and

Edward Joyce
The University of Minnesota

1984

Composition	Alice Watkins
Typesetter	Pat Wickham
Printer	University of Oklahoma Printing Service
Publisher	The University of Oklahoma, Center for Economic and Management Research
Cover Design	John Carl Van Horn

Copies of **Decision Making and Accounting: Current Research** may be purchased from:

The Center for Economic and Management Research
College of Business Administration
The University of Oklahoma
Norman, OK 73019

The price per copy is:

Academics and students	$11.95
All others	$14.95

Oklahoma residents, please add 5% sales tax. A 20% discount is allowed on orders of 10 or more copies.

TABLE OF CONTENTS

Foreword

This volume contains the proceedings of a conference held at the University of Oklahoma on December 8, 9, 1983. The papers were selected from a group of nearly twenty submissions received in answer to several "calls for papers." The papers were chosen on the basis of quality, relevance to the announced topic and diversity (we avoided having two or more papers on very similar topics). The result was a very interesting program.

We were fortunate to have an excellent group of disscusants for the papers. The discussants were requested to emphasize the avenues for further research suggested by the paper they discussed. Our intent was to try to stimulate new ideas, particularly for graduate students. Of course the discussants were encouraged to be critical, but we did ask that they also be constructive in their criticisms.

The authors of the papers were allowed to revise their papers after the conference, whereas the discussants were not. We requested that authors not change their paper in such a manner as to doviate a specific criticism, however, when a discussant mentioned that a point in the original paper was unclear, the authors frequently did attempt to clarify the point in the revision. Hence discussant's comments on clarity may no longer seem appropriate.

A major source of funding for this and succeeding conferences comes from the sale of proceedings for previous conferences. We appreciate all attempts by our friends and colleagues to make the availability of these proceedings known to the widest possible audience.

We thank all of the participants for their interest and help in making this volume possible. We invite readers to submit papers for, and/or attend, future conferences on topics yet to be announced.

Clifton Brown
University of Arizona

Confidence in Causal Reasoning and Evidence Search for Performance Evaluation

This paper was funded, in part, by the Department of Accountancy at the University of Illinois and by Coopers & Lybrand.

Most managerial decisions involve diagnostic or predictive procedures. Diagnosis in managerial decision-making involves attributing particular circumstances as causes of past events and assessing the validity of those attributions. Prediction in managerial decision making involves forecasting the occurrence of future events under particular circumstances and assessing the validity of those forecasts. Given repetitive situations, predictions and diagnoses may be cyclically interconnected. For example, a company's sales budget may begin with prediction, but after a period of time the actual sales occur and, when different from budget, diagnosis must be made in an effort to understand the cause of such difference. Subsequently, the cycle begins again with prediction of a new sales budget.

This paper is concerned with management control of operations as a result of performance reports and evaluations. Diagnostic procedures, therefore, were the focus of this study. A major impact of managerial accountants within businesses is on the design and operation of managerial information systems and on the training of managers to utilize these systems. Knowledge of managers' diagnostic processes is essential to accomplish the objectives of effective system design and adequate manager training.

In particular, this study employs standard cost variances as reports of operating performances requiring diagnosis prior to formulation of control actions. Subjects assumed roles as middle managers of a manufacturing company and were asked to evaluate a series of variance reports on subunits within their area of responsibility. These evaluations consisted of assigning likelihoods to possible causes of the variances, and reporting confidence in the likelihood assessments. For each variance, the subjects selected four items of evidence from a provided list that they would desire to know most in determining the actual cause of the variance.

Diagnosis will have little, or negative, value to managers when the degree of confidence in it is unknown or is substantially biased. This paper reports the results of the confidence judgments.[1]

The following section of this paper develops a conceptual framework for diagnosis in the control of processes and for confidence in judgment. This section is followed by sections describing the research design, the experiment, and analyses and results. A final section discusses the results together with their implications and limitations.

CONCEPTUAL FRAMEWORK

Diagnosis in Control of Processes

Diagnosis in the control processes is represented in Figure 1. The process (objective of control) produces particular events (process outcomes) which require diagnosis (attribution of causes) prior to taking action (evaluation and control of the process).

Recognition of the event. Within a formal accounting system the dissemination of a standard cost variance report implies an event which, at least institutionally, is recognized as an indication of operating performance over a specific period of time. For managers with day-to-day interaction with the operating process this report may not contain new information (i.e., the recognized event may not have been the variance report, but rather the actual operations which produced the given variance). However, for middle managers who do not have day-to-day interaction with the operating process the variance report may be an initial indication of recent operating efficiency.

Initial attribution of cause. Based either on experience with the process or on some information received prior to or contemporaneously with the variance report, the manager will make an initial attribution of the variance's cause. The initial attribution of cause may involve counterfactual reasoning [Einhorn and Hogarth, 1981] in which the manager thinks of the ways in which the variance can occur both with and without being caused by the attributed circumstances. Counterfactual reasoning implies the use of the availability heuristic [Tversky and Kahneman, 1973].[2]

Search for evidence. Depending on the nature of the event and the degree of confidence in the initial causal attribution, the manager will search for evidence to confirm or disconfirm the attributed cause as the actual cause. Insignificant variances would be attributed to random variation and a search for evidence would not be a cost beneficial action, whereas significant variances would be attributed to some non-random cause and a search for evidence may be a cost beneficial action [Brown, 1981; Brown, forthcoming]. The extent of the initial evidence search may be inversely related to the manager's confidence in the initial causal attribution.

Re-attribution of cause. Depending on the results of the evidence search, the manager may re-attribute the variance's cause. Sufficiently disconfirming evidence may prompt the manager to search for additional evidence. The additional search could continue until sufficient confirming evidence is obtained, ignoring the disconfirming evidence, or until a set of circumstances consistent with the evidence is attributed to be the variance's cause.[3]

FIGURE 1

Diagnosis in the Control of Processes

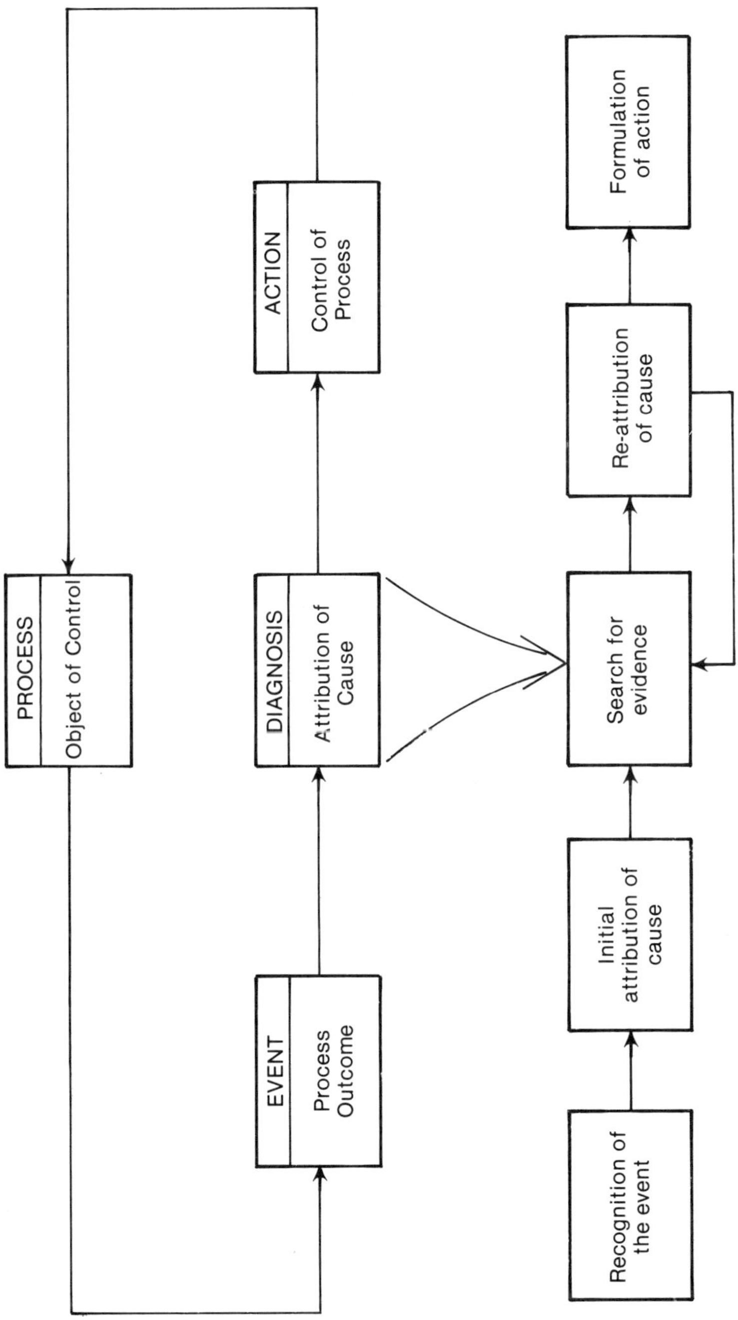

Formulation of actions. Depending on the final attribution of the variance's cause and on the degree of confidence in this attribution, the manager will formulate some set of actions to be taken. The objective of these actions will be to improve control over the process and its costs by either taking corrective measures or gaining a better understanding of the process itself. Gaining a better understanding of the process will allow the manager to better train his subordinates and to better structure the process and its environment.

Confidence in Judgment

Confidence in judgment under uncertainty has been primarily examined in terms of the appropriateness ("goodness") of probability assessments [Oskamp 1962]. This attribute of probability assessment has more recently been labeled calibration [Lichtenstein, Fischhoff, and Phillips 1982]. These approaches examine the relation between subjects' probability assessments and the proportions of true propositions over a large number of instances. An individual is considered to be overconfident when, for all propositions assigned a given probability, the proportion that is true is less than the probability assigned. Conversely, an individual is considered to be underconfident when the proportion that is true is greater than the probability assigned. The most common result in research employing these concepts of confidence is that people tend to be overconfident in their judgments [Lichtenstein, Fischhoff, and Phillips 1982; Nisbett and Ross 1980; Einhorn and Hogarth 1978; Fischoff, Slovic, and Lichtenstein 1977; Lichtenstein and Fischhoff 1977].

Most of the overconfidence results have been obtained using general-knowledge judgments. Some studies, however, have extended these results using other types of judgments. Overconfidence has been found in forecasts and planning judgments (Fischhoff and MacGregor [1982]; Hogarth and Makridakis [1981]), in self-appraisals of job performance (Thornton [1980]), and in strategic business problem solving (Stumpf and Zand [1981]).

Within this study, confidence was interpreted as a second-order probability assessment. Confidence was the subjective probability (or belief) that an assessment of a cause likelihood (the first-order probability) was an accurate assessment. Tversky and Kahneman [1973] demonstrated that subjective assessment of event likelihood is partially determined by the availability of the events (i.e., the ease with which the events are imagined or remembered). Mehle et al. [1981] found that the availability of unspecified hypotheses partially explained overconfidence in the probability of specified hypotheses. Koriat, Lichtenstein, and Fischhoff [1980] found that subjects required to list reasons contradicting their answers to general-knowledge questions reduced their overconfidence.

Translating to situations requiring diagnosis (i.e., causal explanation), Brown [1983] demonstrated that the subjective assessment of cause likelihood is partially determined by the availability of both the causes and the events. The subjective ease of explanation should serve to strengthen confidence in causal judgments.

H1: Managers will tend to report greater confidence in

judgments of cause likelihood when given a common variance and the initial attribution is to a common cause, than when given an uncommon variance and the initial attribution is to an uncommon cause.

Numerous information processing biases have been identified with the acquisition of information (c.f., Hogarth [1980]). Selective perception includes such biases as structuring problems based upon one's experience, seeking information consistent with one's views, and disregarding conflicting evidence. Also a form of selective perception, the extent of confidence in an initial causal attribution may affect the search for evidence. Given increased confidence in causal judgments, individuals may tend to seek less evidence concerning the maintained explanation.

H2: Managers who have greater confidence in their causal attributions will tend to have lesser preference for evidence relevant to their attributed cause.

H3: Managers who have lesser confidence in their causal attributions will tend to have greater preference for evidence relevant to their attributed cause.

RESEARCH DESIGN

Experimental Task

The subjects were asked to assume the role of an assistant manager for an electronic communications equipment manufacturing division. Within this role the subjects were presented with a series of standard cost variance reports for assembly departments within their division. Evaluations of the variance reports were made with the long-run objective being to assess the quality of control being exercised by the managers of each assembly department.[4]

The type of standard cost variance reported was a labor efficiency variance stated in terms of favorableness. A favorable labor efficiency variance was one in which the absolute difference between the actual assembly labor hours worked and the standard assembly labor hours allowed for output achieved was less than or equal to 10 percent of the standard hours allowed. All other variances were labeled as unfavorable.

Within this task the information available to the subjects came from two sources. The first source was information from past experience and was presented to the subjects in the form of a background information pamphlet. This pamphlet described the role the subject was being asked to assume, the company and its manufacturing processes, the accounting control system, and the subject's task and objectives within the experiment.

The second source of information was the variance report and information contemporaneously available with this report. The variance report (see Appendix A), consisted of the variance favorableness and a list of four possible causes of the variance. Information contemporaneously available with this report depended upon the specific between-subjects treatment combination. Table 1 indicates the information contemporaneously available with the variance report for each of the four between-subjects treatment combinations.

The subjects were asked to respond to a series of evaluations on each department's labor efficiency variance report. First, they were asked how likely they believed each of the four possible causes were to have been the actual cause of the department's reported labor efficiency variance. Second, they were asked how confident they were that their estimates of likelihood were accurate. Finally, they were asked to select, in rank-order, four items of evidence from a provided list (see Appendix B) that they would desire to know most in determining the actual cause of the department's labor efficiency variance.

TABLE 1

Information Available With the Variance Report

Item	Availability			
Between-Subjects				
Event (variance) Priors	G	G	N	N
Cause Priors	G	N	G	N
Within-Subjects				
Event Favorableness	G	G	G	G
Event Commonness	G	G	N	N
Cause Commonness	G	N	G	N
Nature of Cause	G	G	G	G

G = Given N = Not Given

Experimental Design

The experimental design was a 2^2 x 2^4 repeated measures design with two between-subjects variables, each at two levels, and four within-subjects variances, each at two levels. The two between-subjects variables were event (variance) priors (either given or not given) and cause priors (either given or not given). The four within-subjects variables were event favorableness (either favorable or unfavorable), event commonness (either common or uncommon), cause commonness (either common or uncommon), and nature of cause (either specific person or general other).

Operationalization of Variables

Cause likelihoods were elicited from subjects using 100 point scales (see Appendix C). The cause likelihood scale ranged from most unlikely (-100), to equally likely as unlikely (0), and from equally likely as unlikely to most likely (100). Cause likelihoods were scaled by dividing each estimate by a factor of 10 (which reduced the likelihood scale to [-10, 10]).

Confidence in cause likelihood assessments was defined in terms of the perceived degree of accuracy. Subjects were asked the extent to which they believed that their cause likelihood assessment was within plus or minus five percent of the true cause likelihood. Confidence was reported by the subjects using 100 point scales (see Appendix C). The confidence scale ranged from minimum confidence (0) to maximum confidence (100). Reported confidence was scaled by dividing each estimate by a factor of 10 (which reduced the confidence scale to [0, 10]).

The subjects indicated, in rank order, the four items of evidence they most desired to know from a provided list of 16 items of evidence (see Appendix B). The selected items of evidence were converted into a between-subjects group measure of evidence preference using the following arcsin transformation [Snowball and Brown 1979].

$$EP_{ij} = ½ \left[\text{ARCSIN} \sqrt{\frac{R_{hij}}{M_j + 1}} + \text{ARCSIN} \sqrt{\frac{R_{hij} + 1}{M_j + 1}} \right],$$

where EP_{ij} = preference for evidence relevant to the causal hypothesis consistent with the ith within-subjects condition (i = 1, 16) of the jth between-subjects Group (j = 1, 4).

R_{hij} = number of subjects assigning a rank of h (h = 1, 4) to an item of evidence relevant to the causal hypothesis consistent with the ith condition of the jth Group.

M_j = total number of subjects in the jth between-subjects Group.

The possible range of EP_{ij} is from .1263 (lowest preference) to 1.4445 (highest preference).

Both common events and common causes had base rate (prior) probabilities equal to 75 percent. Both uncommon events and uncommon causes had base rate (prior) probabilities equal to 25 percent. Circumstances involving the department manager (the assistant division manager's subordinate) and those involving the assembly workers (the department manager's subordinates) were defined as specific person causes. Circumstances involving workload scheduling (between departments) and direct material qualities were defined as general other causes.

THE EXPERIMENT

Subjects

The subjects were undergraduate and master's level graduate students enrolled in the business school of a large state university. A total of 64 volunteer subjects participated in the experiment.[5]

The subjects were randomly assigned to the four between-subjects treatment combinations with the restriction that the four cell sizes remained equal. Upon assignment to a treatment condition each subject received the background information pamphlet.

Procedures

The experiment was conducted in two phases, an experiment phase occurring immediately following a training phase. Both phases were conducted in group sessions of two to ten subjects in size.

The training phase. Training within all treatment conditions consisted of additional written instructions, a period of time in which subjects could ask questions, and two practice labor efficiency variance cases. In each case the subject was provided with a labor efficient variance report together with information consistent with the subject's assigned treatment condition. There was no feedback following either of the training phase cases.

The experiment phase. The experimental phase consisted of obtaining the subjects' response to four labor efficiency variance cases. The four cases were structured to be factoral combinations of the four within-subjects variables (event favorableness, event commonness, cause commonness, and cause nature). Feedback was not given to the subjects during this phase. Immediately following the experiment phase the subjects completed a post-experimental questionnaire.

ANALYSES AND RESULTS

Hypothesis 1

Hypothesis 1 was tested using a $2^2 \times 2^4$ repeated-measures ANOVA with confidence in cause likelihood as the dependent variable. The independent variables were those listed in Table 1. Within this model the hypothesis is contained within a significant event priors x cause priors x event commonness x cause commonness interaction ($F = 6.7542$; 1,56 d.f. and $p < .025$; $\omega^2 = .003$ with the model $R^2 = .094$) which is graphically represented in Figure 2. Although the interaction was significant within the between-subjects treatment in which subjects were given both event and cause priors, hypothesis 1 was supported only by direction and not by significance. That is, average confidence within the common event and cause combination was larger than average confidence within the uncommon event and cause combination, but not significantly larger. The interaction significance results from the subjects reporting higher confidence within the common event and uncommon cause and the uncommon events and common cause combinations.

Hypotheses 2 and 3

Hypotheses 2 and 3 were tested using the Pearson product-moment correlation coefficient with confidence in cause likelihood and evidence preference as the correlates. Within this model the hypotheses would jointly predict a significant inverse relation between confidence and evidence preference.

The correlation coefficient over all between-subjects treatments was negative, but not significant ($r = -.128$; $t = 1.016$ with 62 d.f.). However, within the between-subjects treatment in which both event and cause priors were given to the subjects the correlation coefficient was significantly negative ($r = -.674$; $t = 3.418$ with 14 d.f., $p < .01$ one-tailed).

FIGURE 2

Event Priors x Cause Priors x Event Commonness x Cause Commonness Interaction on Confidence in Cause Likelihood Assessment

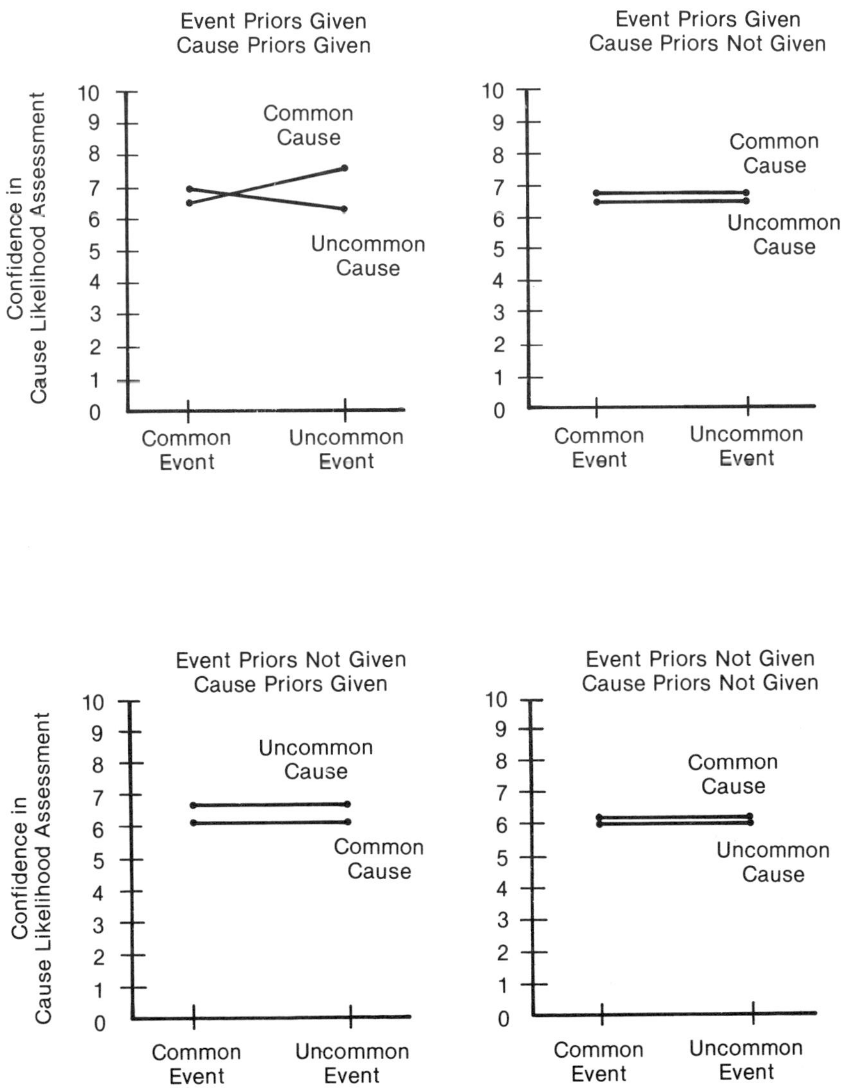

Additional Results

Cause likelihood and confidence. Using the Pearson product-moment correlation coefficient the relationship between cause likelihood assessments and confidence in cause likelihood assessments was examined. Over all between-subjects treatments the correlation coefficient was significantly negative ($r = -.192$; $t = 6.047$ with 958 d.f., $p < .001$ one-tailed).

Event favorableness. Employing a model similar to the one used to test hypothesis 1 except that the two independent variables cause commonness and cause nature (each at two levels) were replaced with the variable cause likelihood rank (at four levels), the interaction event favorableness and rank of cause likelihood had a significant effect on confidence in cause likelihood assessments ($F = 5.201$; 3 and 168 d.f., $p < .005$; $\omega^2 = .001$ with the model $R^2 = .827$). Presented in Figure 3, confidence was higher when the variance was unfavorable than when the variance was favorable, but significantly different only for the third and fourth ranked cause likelihood assessments (the lower ranks). The rank of cause likelihood has a significant main effect on confidence in cause likelihood assessments ($F = 1481.347$; 3 and 168 d.f., $p < .001$). This effect accounted for most of the explained variation within the model ($\omega^2 = .768$ with the model $R^2 = .827$).

Event and cause priors. Both event priors and cause priors had a significant main effect within the models used to test hypothesis 1 and event favorableness (event priors $F = 16.385$ with 1 and 56 d.f., $p < .001$, $\omega^2 = .005$; cause priors $F = 5.864$ with 1 and 56 d.f., $p < .025$, $\omega^2 = .001$). Confidence in cause likelihood assessment was greater when event priors were given (6.742) and when cause priors were given (6.648) than when event priors were not given (6.275) and when cause priors were not given (6.369).

Overall variation. Although the likelihood scale was twice the length of the confidence scale, the variance of cause likelihood assessments was better than 4.5 times that of the confidence in cause likelihood assessments (12.996 versus 2.863). This would indicate greater subject consensus for confidence than for likelihood assessments.

DISCUSSION

Event and Cause Commonness

The test of hypothesis 1 indicated a significant event commonness by cause commonness interaction on confidence in cause likelihoods for the between-subjects treatment in which event and cause priors were given to the subjects. As this treatment was the only one in which event and cause commonness was known by the subjects (through the priors), the lack of effect within the other treatments was a check on the commonness manipulation validity.

The interaction was of the form in which higher confidence was reported within the common event/uncommon cause and the uncommon event/common cause conditions than within the other two event/cause commonness conditions. Brown [1983] demonstrated that conditions with mixed event/cause commonness were assigned significantly lower likelihoods than conditions with similar event/cause commonness. Additional results above indicated a significant inverse correlation between cause likelihood and confidence in cause likelihood. These results are consistent with the hypothesis that subjects within this situation were more confident of what was *not* the cause than what was the cause of the variances.

Event Favorableness

Confidence in cause likelihoods was higher for unfavorable variances than for favorable variances, but significantly higher only for the two causes with the lowest likelihood assessments. This result would be consistent with the belief that unfavorable variances generally result from a few specific circumstances, whereas favorable variances generally result from the joint occurrence of many circumstances. Interestingly, this effect was not on cause likelihood, but rather on confidence in cause likelihood.

FIGURE 3

Event Favorableness x Cause Rank Interaction on Confidence in Cause Likelihood Assessment

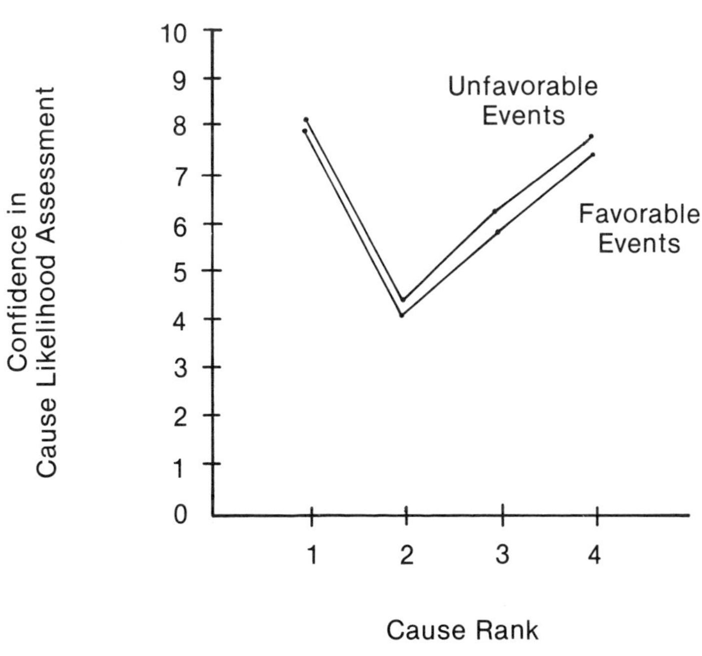

Prior Probabilities as Information

The prior probabilities defined the degree of commonness of the events and possible causes. Information concerning the degree of commonness was employed by the subjects in reporting confidence in their cause likelihood assessments. In situations where event and cause priors were given to the subjects, the subjects reported higher confidence for conditions with mixed event/cause commonness than for conditions with similar event/cause commonness. Further, a significant correlation between confidence in cause likelihoods and evidence preference existed within the event and cause priors given treatment, but not over the other between-subjects treatments.

The lower confidence reported when the event priors and/or the cause priors were not given to the subjects modifies the general hypothesis proposed in Brown [1983], that as information richness within a decision situation declines, the importance of the available individual items of information increases.[6] The modification would be that although available information importance increases as information richness decreases, overall confidence in judgment decreases as well.

Limitations

A major limitation to the generalizability of results would be the use of student subjects within a hypothetical performance control environment. These subjects lacked prior training and experience with performance control/evaluation in business contexts.

The reduction of possible causes of labor efficiency variances to four in number and the assumption that these causes were independent of each other is an additional limitation to the generalizability of results. Within an actual performance control/evaluation situation the number of possible causes would be much larger, would not be necessarily independent of each other, and would not be explicitly stated.

Future Research

This paper examined judgment confidence in the initial stages of the diagnostic process within performance evaluation and control. Future research should examine the other stages of the diagnostic process: evaluation of evidence, re-attribution of cause, and formulation of actions. Further, future research should address the limitations of this paper. Of particular importance would be the use of natural subjects within experimental environments based upon their natural environments. Additional avenues of future research would be the manipulation of information system variables such as the validity of evidence sources, conflicting evidence, as well as the information report format, frequency, and level of information aggregation.

NOTES

[1]The results of the likelihood assessments and the evidence selections are reported in Brown [1983].

[2]Also relevant to this diagnostic category is recent work in attribution theory (Kruglanski *et al.* [1978]; Kruglanski [1980]; Kelly and Michela [1980]). The fundamental assumption of attribution theory is that the layman's approach to diagnosis is basically similar to a logico-scientific approach to diagnosis.

[3]Searching for confirming evidence and/or ignoring disconfirming evidence has been labeled a confirmation bias (Nisbett and Ross [1980]; Libby [1981]).

[4]The quality of control was defined in terms of the standard cost variance performances being satisfactory to division management. Subjects were instructed that to accomplish such evaluations they should be interested in gaining an understanding of the circumstances that cause good control and good performance as well as the circumstances that cause poor control and poor performance. The subjects were told that this knowledge would allow the division to better train its department managers and to better structure the assembly environment.

[5]The subjects included 41 males and 23 females. Two subject selection criteria were employed: 1) completion of an intermediate level managerial accounting course and 2) an overall grade point average of at least 3.0 on a 5.0 scale.

[6]Information richness was defined to be a function of the quantity and quality (validity) of the information available to decision makers in a particular situation.

REFERENCES

Brown, C., "Effects of Dynamic Task Environment on the Learning of Standard Cost Variance Significance," *Journal of Accounting Research,* forthcoming.

____________, "Causal Reasoning and Evidence Search in Performance Evaluation," Unpublished manuscript, (University of Illinois at Urbana-Champaign, 1983).

____________, "Human Information Processing for Decisions to Investigate Cost Variances," *Journal of Accounting Research* (Spring 1981), pp. 62-85.

Einhorn, H.J. and R.M. Hogarth, "Uncertainty and Causality in Practical Inference," Unpublished manuscript, (University of Chicago, 1981).

____________, "Confidence in Judgment: Persistence of the Illusion of Validity," *Psychological Review* (1978), pp. 395-416.

Fischhoff, B., P. Slovic, and S. Lichtenstein, "Knowing with Certainty: The Appropriateness of Extreme Confidence," *Journal of Experimental Psychology: Human Perceptions and Performance* (1977), pp. 552-564.

____________ and D. MacGregor, "Subjective Confidence in Forecasts," *Journal of Forecasting* (1982), pp. 155-172.

Hogarth, R. *Judgment and Choice,* (Wiley & Sons, 1980).

____________ and S. Makridakis, "Forecasting and Planning: An Evaluation," *Management Science* (1981), pp. 115-138.

Kelly, H.H. and J.L. Michela, "Attribution Theory and Research," *Annual Review of Psychology* (1980), pp. 457-501.

Koriat, A., S. Lichtenstein, and B. Fischhoff, "Reasons for Confidence," *Journal of Experimental Psychology; Human Learning & Memory* (1980), pp. 107-118.

Kruglanski, A.W., "Lay Epistemo-Logic-Process and Contents: Another Look at Attribution Theory," *Psychological Review* (1980), pp. 70-87.

__________, I.Z. Hamel, S.A. Maides, and J.M. Schwartz, "Attribution Theory as a Special Case of Lay Epistemology," In *New Directions in Attribution Research,* J.H. Harvey; W. Ickes; and R.F. Kidd (editors), (Lawrence Erlbaum Associates, 1978).

Libby, R., *Accounting and Human Information Processing: Theory and Applications,* (Prentice-Hall, 1981).

Lichtenstein, S., B. Fischhoff, and L.D. Phillips, "Calibration of Probabilities: The State of the Art to 1980," In *Judgement Under Uncertainty: Heuristics and Biases,* D. Kahneman; P. Slovic; and A. Tversky (editors), (Cambridge University Press, 1982).

__________ and B. Fischhoff, "Do Those Who Know More Also Know More About How Much They Know?" *Organizational Behavior and Human Performance* (1977), pp. 159-183.

Mehle, T., C.F.Gettys, C. Manning, S. Baca, and S. Fisher, "The Availability Explanation of Excessive Plausibility Assessments," *Acta Psychologica* (1981), pp. 127-140.

Nisbett, R. and L. Ross, *Human Inference: Strategies and Shortcomings of Social Judgment,* (Prentice-Hall, 1980).

Oskamp, S., "The Relationship of Clinical Experience and Training Methods to Several Criteria of Clinical Prediction," *Psychological Monographs* (1962), (28, Whole No. 547).

Snowball, D. and C. Brown, "Decision Making Involving Sequential Events: Some Effects of Disaggregated Data and Dispositions Toward Risk," *Decision Sciences* (1979), pp. 527-546.

Stumpf, S. and D. Zand, "Participant Estimates of the Effectiveness of Judgmental Decisions," *Journal of Management* (1981), pp. 77-87.

Thorton, G., "Psychometric Properties of Self-Appraisals of Job Performance," *Personnel Psychology* (1980), pp. 263-271.

Tversky, A. and D. Kahneman, "Availability: A Heuristic for Judging Frequency and Probability," *Cognitive Psychology* (1973), pp. 207-32.

APPENDIX A

Performance Evaluation Trial

Ian's department had an unfavorable labor efficiency variance for Month 3. Over the last five years 25% of this department's labor efficiency variances have been unfavorable. Possible causes of an unfavorable labor efficiency variance include:

A. Actual workload schedule less than normal volume. Over the last five years 75% of the actual workload schedules within Ian's department have been less than normal volume.†

B. Actual raw material quality less than standard. Over the last five years 25% of the actual raw material quality within Ian's department have been less than standard.†

C. Actual assembly worker training/skill level less than standard. Over the last five years 75% of the actual assembly worker training/skill levels within Ian's department have been less than standard.†

D. Ian's managerial efforts and abilities less than standard. Over the last five years Ian's managerial efforts and abilities have been less than standard 25% of the time.†

†These frequencies have been determined without taking into account the nature (favorable or unfavorable) of the variances involved.

I. Evaluation of Possible Causes

Prior to receiving evidence, how likely do you believe each of the four possible causes are to have been the actual cause of this department's unfavorable labor efficiency variance for Month 3? How confident are you that your estimates of likelihood are accurate (within ±5% of the true likelihoods)?

II. Selection of Evidence

Select four items of evidence (from the provided list) that you would desire to know most in determining the actual cause of this department's unfavorable labor efficiency variance for Month 3. Rank order your choices indicating the item you desire to know first, second, third, and fourth.

APPENDIX B

Available Items of Evidence

List of Available Evidence Concerning Possible Causes Of Labor Efficiency Variances

Item Number	Item of Evidence
	A. Workload Schedule
	The department's normal volume workload schedule and actual workload schedule for the month of the variance and for the six months prior to that month, *and* a report of the estimated frequency *within the department* over the last five years of the joint occurrence (i.e., *both* the type of variance and the circumstance occurring at the same time) of:
1	Favorable variances and actual workload schedules greater than or equal to normal volume.
2	Favorable variances and actual workload schedules less than normal volume.
3	Unfavorable variances and actual workload schedules greater than or equal to normal volume.
4	Unfavorable variances and actual workload schedules less than normal volume.
	B. Raw Material Quality
	The department's raw material quality standard and report of actual raw material quality for the month of the variance and for the six months prior to that month, *and* a report of the estimated frequency *within the department* over the last five years of the joint occurrence (i.e., *both* the type of variance and the circumstance occurring at the same time) of:
5	Favorable variances and actual raw material quality greater than or equal to standard.
6	Favorable variances and actual raw material quality less than standard.
7	Unfavorable variances and actual raw material quality greater than or equal to standard.
8	Unfavorable variances and actual raw material quality less than standard.
	C. Assembly Worker Training/Skill
	The department's standard number of weeks on the job for assembly workers and

report of actual number of weeks on the job for assembly workers as of the month of the variance and as of each of the six months prior to that month, *and* a report of the estimated frequency *within the department* over the last five years of the joint occurrence (i.e., *both* the type of variance and the circumstance occurring at the same time) of:

9 Favorable variances and actual number of weeks on the job greater than or equal to standard.

10 Favorable variances and actual number of weeks on the job less than standard.

11 Unfavorable variances and actual number of weeks on the job greater than or equal to standard.

12 Unfavorable variances and actual number of weeks on the job less than standard.

D. Department Manager's Managerial Efforts and Abilities

The ranking of the department manager's labor efficiency performances relative to the division's other department managers for the month of the variance and for the six months prior to that month *and* a report of the estimated frequency *within the department* over the last five years of the joint occurrence (i.e., *both* the type of variance and the circumstance occurring at the same time) of:

13 Favorable variances and the department manager's labor efficiency performance rankings greater than or equal to the median ranking for all department managers.

14 Favorable variances and the department manager's labor efficiency performance rankings less than the median ranking for all department managers.

15 Unfavorable variances and the department manager's labor efficiency performance rankings greater than or equal to the median ranking for all department managers.

16 Unfavorable variances and the department manager's labor efficiency performance rankings less than the median ranking for all department managers.

PLEASE USE THEIR RESPECTIVE NUMBERS WHEN REFERRING TO THESE ITEMS OF EVIDENCE

APPENDIX C

Subject Response Scales

I. EVALUATION OF POSSIBLE CAUSES

Please Draw Slash(/) Marks Through The Following Scales At the Appropriate Points

_____ MOST LIKELY CAUSE

_____ SECOND MOST LIKELY CAUSE

_____ THIRD MOST LIKELY CAUSE

_____ LEAST LIKELY CAUSE

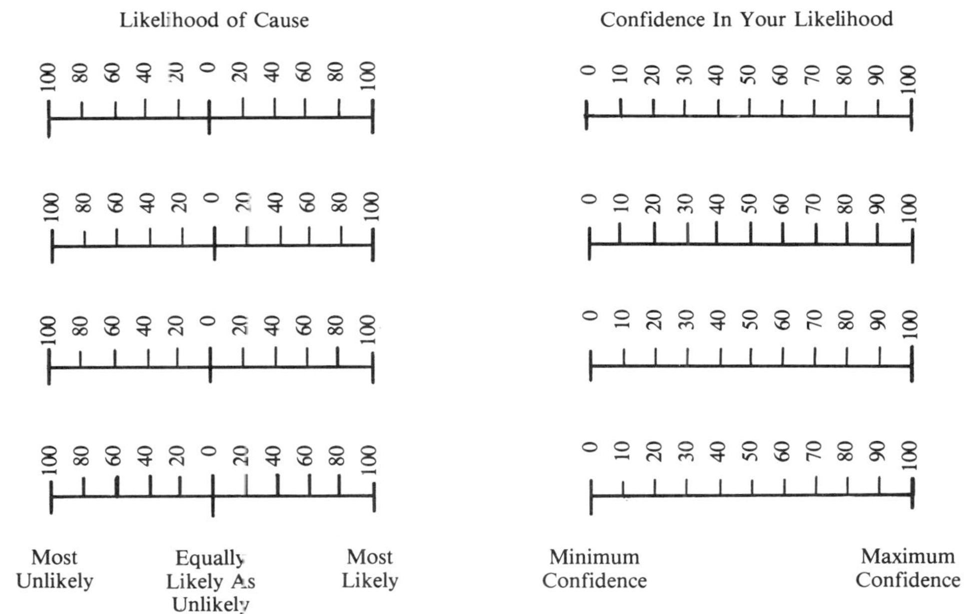

PLEASE INDICATE YOUR SELECTIONS USING THE *LETTERS* FROM THE LIST OF POSSIBLE CAUSES

Appendix C (continued)

II. SELECTION OF EVIDENCE

_____ ITEM OF EVIDENCE DESIRED *FIRST*

_____ ITEM OF EVIDENCE DESIRED *SECOND*

_____ ITEM OF EVIDENCE DESIRED *THIRD*

_____ ITEM OF EVIDENCE DESIRED *FOURTH*

↑ PLEASE INDICATE YOUR SELECTION USING THE *NUMBERS* FROM THE LIST OF AVAILABLE EVIDENCE

Adrian Harrell
University of South Carolina

Discussant's Comments on:

"Confidence in Causal Reasoning and Evidence Search for Performance Evaluation"

Brown [1984], in his paper, "Confidence in Causal Reasoning and Evidence Search for Performance Evaluation," presents an interesting attempt to examine the cognitive processes managers employ in response to the information presented in variance reports. The design of the experiment was elaborate and the data analysis procedures appeared to be appropriate for the situations involved. This does not, however, mean the experiment was without potential flaws, some of which were acknowledged by the author. Let us consider some of the potential flaws which might cause one to question what the results of the experiment imply for managerial accounting.

The individuals who served as experimental subjects were not managers; they were university students majoring in business. Although it is appropriate in some circumstances for students in academic environments to be used as surrogates for more mature adults in business environments [e.g., Ashton and Kramer, 1980; Harrell and Stahl, 1984], no rationale is provided by the author to support the use of the relatively inexperienced students employed as subjects in the experiment as surrogates for experienced managers. The nature of the subjects is particularly critical, for the experiment seems to assume its subjects have some knowledge of the working environment of a relatively large organization, experience which the students who served as subjects apparently did not have. Accordingly, it is difficult to justify any generalization of the results of the experiment to working managers. This flaw could, of course, be eliminated with the use of working managers as subjects.

The experimental task the students completed does not appear to be representative of the real-world task it attempts to portray. It appears to be unrepresentative in several ways. First, the variance report provided to the subjects is unlike any variance report described in any cost or managerial accounting textbook known to me. It is also unlike any variance report I have observed to be used in practice. Typically, a "favorable" variance is defined as when substantially fewer resources are actually consumed than were expected to be consumed. An "unfavorable" variance is defined as when substantially more resources are actually consumed than were expected to be consumed. In most instances, organizational incentive systems seek to reward the supervisors responsible for favorable cost variances and to fail to reward (or even punish) the supervisors responsible for unfavorable variances. Since the subjects had all completed a cost accounting course, one would presume they had some knowledge of these usual relationships. In the experiment, a "favorable" variance is defined as when the resources actually consumed do not exceed an amount 10 percent greater than budgeted consumption and are no less than an amount 10 percent less than budgeted consumption. This range apparently is designed to allow for chance fluctuations. In addition, however, it implies that the firm will reward those supervisors whose actual consumption of resources is approximately the same as the amount budgeted. Does this imply the supervisor responsible for his department consuming 25 percent less resources than budgeted would not be considered to have incurred a "favorable" variance? This is a very different approach than is suggested in most textbooks and is most often used in practice. No rationale for any potential benefits to be gained from the new approach is provided and none are apparent.

An "unfavorable" variance is defined in the experiment as when (1) the resources actually consumed are less than an amount 10 percent below the budget or when (2) the resources actually consumed are more than an amount 10 percent larger than the budget. In many organizations, an "unfavorable" variance of the first type might result in the responsible supervisor receiving positive rewards (e.g., a promotion or a salary increase), while an "unfavorable" variance of the second type might result in the responsible supervisor's eventual unemployment. Within the circumstances of the experiment, how can the subjects know which of these "unfavorable" variances is involved? Did the subjects, who had all completed at least one cost accounting course and consequently had some knowledge of variance reports, readily accept a system of variance reports in which a supervisor who is responsible for consuming substantially fewer resources than budgeted is identified as causing an "unfavorable" variance to exist? Libby [1981] has admonished researchers to make their experimental tasks realistic. More realism could eliminate this criticism of the experiment.

There is still another way in which the decision making circumstances of the experiment appear to be unrepresentative of the environment in which a working manager usually functions. Most supervisors are aware of how their superiors will react when large unfavorable variances are presented in variance reports. In most instances, supervisors anticipate their superior's questions and provide an explanation of the cause of the unfavorable variance. This explanation is either a part of the variance report or else accompanies the variance report. With this in mind, the decision task faced by the typical working manager appears to be somewhat different than the task faced by the subjects of the experiment. The typical working manager must initially decide whether he believes the supervisor's explanation of what caused an unfavorable variance to be true, exaggerated, or false. Only in the latter two (probably infrequent) situations would it be necessary to make guesses about other potential explanations for the unfavorable variance. The experimental subjects were, however, required to make such judgments without the benefit of the explanation a supervisor would usually provide to a working manager. Providing such an initial explanation would, of course, avoid this criticism. Doing so might, however, also change the results of the experiment.

To summarize, it appears that (1) the subjects probably are not acceptable surrogates for working managers, (2) the variance report used in the experiment is unlike any variance report described in textbooks or used in practice and (3) the experimental task differs from the usual environment in which working managers function.

Despite these criticisms, the paper was, however, well-written and the experiment appears to have been well-executed. Consequently, one must ask: "How serious are these flaws?" A response to this question must depend upon the researcher's objectives when performing the study. If the study was intended to be an applied experiment in psychology which aimed at examining the cognitive responses of students who completed a series of challenging intellectual problems, these flaws are probably not important, for the research appears to have accomplished this objective. If, however, the study was intended to provide an explanation of how working managers in actual organizations behave when presented with traditional variance reports which contain substantial unfavorable variances, one must question whether the author's objectives were achieved.

A question not addressed by Brown [1984] is whether a manager's cognition is the most important factor to be considered in understanding his reaction to variance reports. Many might argue that understanding the motivational aspects of this situation should be at least as important as understanding a manager's cognitive processes if one is to understand his behavior. Some recent methodological and measurement developments [e.g., Harrell and Stahl, 1981, 1984a, 1984b; Stahl and Harrell, 1981, 1982, 1983] which employ behavioral decision theory to study human motivation make it practical to identify many of the factors which motivate a manager's responses in situations such as the one examined in this study.

Research such as that examined in this comment is desirable and should be encouraged. Despite the flaws which make it difficult to relate the results to real-world circumstances, new insights into the cognitive processes of individuals were provided.

REFERENCES

Ashton, R. and S. Kramer, "Students as Surrogates in Behavioral Accounting Research," *Journal of Accounting Research* (Spring 1980), pp. 1-15.

Brown, C., "Confidence in Causal Reasoning and Evidence Search for Performance Evaluation," in S. Moriarity and E. Joyce (Eds.), *Decision Making and Accounting: Current Research,* (University of Oklahoma, Center for Economic and Management Research, 1984), pp. 1-18.

Harrell, A. and M. Stahl, "A Behavioral Decision Theory Approach for Measuring McClelland's Trichotomy of Needs," *Journal of Applied Psychology* (1981), pp. 242-247.

Harrell, A. and M. Stahl, "Modeling Managers' Effort-Level Decisions for a Within-Persons Examination of Expectancy Theory in a Budget Setting," *Decision Sciences* (forthcoming in January 1984a).

Harrell, A. and M. Stahl, "McClelland's Trichotomy of Needs Theory and the Job Satisfaction and Work Performance of CPA Firm Professionals," *Accounting, Organizations and Society* (forthcoming in 1984).

Libby, R., *Accounting and Human Information Processing: Theory and Applications* (Prentice-Hall, Inc., 1981).

Stahl, M. and A. Harrell, "Modeling Effort Decisions with Behavioral Decision Theory: Toward an Individual Differences Model of Expectancy Theory," *Organizational Behavior and Human Performance* (1981) pp. 303-325.

Stahl, M. and A. Harrell, "The Evolution and Validation of a Behavioral Decision Theory Measurement Approach to Achievement, Power and Affiliation," *Journal of Applied Psychology* (1982) pp. 744-751.

Stahl, M. and A. Harrell, "Using Decision Modeling to Measure Second-Level Valences in Expectancy Theory," *Organizational Behavior and Human Performance* (August 1983).

Robert H. Ashton
New York University

Discussant's Comments on:

"Confidence in Causal Reasoning and Evidence Search For Performance Evaluation"

Brown has produced a very interesting study based on a rather complicated experimental task. My comments on the study will fall into three areas. First, I will try to characterize the general nature of the study to show where I think it fits in the behavioral decision making literature in accounting. Second, I will summarize what I see as the most important results of the experiment. In studying the paper, I found that rearranging the results, and the various linkages among them, helped me to better understand exactly what the findings were. Finally, I will provide a critical evaluation of certain aspects of the study. I hope these comments will be useful to Brown as he continues his research program in the variance investigation area.

To characterize the basic nature of the study, I would describe it as involving two of the traditional paradigms of human information processing research—the probabilistic judgment and predecisional behavior paradigms. However, the study extends these well-known paradigms by overlaying on them some elements of another paradigm—attribution theory. Brown uses this extended framework to study people's confidence in their own likelihood assessments for certain causes of favorable and unfavorable variances. In so doing, he builds on the confidence literature in psychology, which has developed rapidly in the past few years as researchers have probed the reasons for, and implications of, people's confidence in their own judgments. Brown is especially concerned with the impact that confidence can have on the search for additional information that might be desired before a decision is made and an action taken.

While the main focus of the study differs from most behavioral decision making research in accounting, the basic structure of the study does not. In fact, the study's structure bears a close resemblance to the typical study in this area described by Einhorn more than seven years ago at the University of Chicago conference on human information processing in accounting. Einhorn observed that the typical experimental judgment task is well defined, the necessary information is given and is perfectly reliable, and the range of hypotheses to be considered is restricted. In contrast, judgment tasks in the real world may be ill defined, information search may be necessary, information may not be perfectly reliable, and hypothesis formation may occur within a wide range of possibilities.

In the present study, the subjects played a passive role by responding to a very structured task in which a small number of possible variance causes were explicitly stated, the prior probabilities that they were the actual causes were provided, the causes were assumed to be independent of each other, and a list was provided of the types of additional information for which one might "search." Thus, while some aspects of the study go beyond the traditional approach employed in this type of research, several other aspects of the study do not.

To summarize the study's results, note that the subjects' degree of confidence in their cause likelihood assessments was found to be inversely related to the strength of expressed preference for additional information relevant to the possible causes, as hypothesized by Brown. Note also that confidence in cause likelihood assessments was inversely related to the magnitude of the cause likelihood assessments. Putting these two results together, one of the principal findings of the study is that greater likelihood assessments are associated with less confidence in those assessments, which is, in turn, asssociated with greater preference for additional information. Likewise, lower likelihood assessments are associated with greater confidence and with less preference for additional information. These relationships between likelihood assessments and confidence, and between confidence and information preference, are the key findings of the study.

Other results presented in the paper make it clear that the findings with respect to confidence are moderated in four ways: (1) Confidence is greater for unfavorable variances than for favorable variances. (2) Confidence is greater when the prior probabilities of the variance and the causes are provided to the subjects than when they are not provided. (3) Confidence is greater when the prior probability of *either* variance *or* the cause is high and the prior probability of the other is low, than when the priors of the variance and the cause are both high or both low. (4) Confidence is greater for causes that are thought to be most likely and least likely, than for causes for which intermediate levels of likelihood are assessed.

Relating all of this to the preference for additional information, the results suggest that such preference will be less when (1) the variance is unfavorable, (2) the priors of the variance and the causes are given, (3) the priors of the variance and the cause are not both high or both low, and (4) the cause in question is not thought to be either the most likely or the least likely of the possible causes under consideration. The preference for additional information will be greater when the opposite of these conditions obtains.

At this point, I will offer some evaluative comments on the research. In any study as complicated as this one, it is always possible to find some problem areas that might need attention. Basically, however, the study was designed, conducted, and analyzed very well. The presentation of the study could have been improved in some places by a more complete description of the relationships among the various findings and potential implications. The current presentation, although streamlined and generally quite good, is a bit too lean in a few places.

Aside from considerations of design, analysis and presentation, a positive feature of the study is that Brown did a good job of developing a *reason* for studying confidence, instead of simply noting that other people have studied it too or arguing that he found the topic interesting. As I mentioned earlier, the reason has to do with the relationship between confidence and information search.

One concern I have with the study is the way Brown operationalized information search. When one searches for information in a variance investigation (or other) context, both the type and the amount of information sought are likely to vary under different sets of conditions. The study, however, deals only with the type of information desired, and not with the amount. Moreover, Brown's surrogate for information search is a measure of information *preference,* and is not a direct measure of search itself. Thus, Brown has captured only a portion of the overall notion of information search.

One might argue that a measure of the strength of information preference, as used by Brown, would be highly associated with a more direct measure of information search. Such an argument ignores the cost of the information, however, and this brings up another concern I have with Brown's study; that is, the information is implicitly assumed to be costless. Of course, in a real variance investigation setting the information would not be costless, and to the extent that the various types and amounts of information were differentially costly, one's information preferences, information search, and the relationship between preferences and search might be affected (assuming some budget constraint).

Raising the issue of information cost prompts the Rational Economic Man inside me to ask whether there is an optimal set of information (in an expected utility sense) that the subjects should have chosen in the experiment. A related question has to do with whether some types of available information were more relevant than others in terms of understanding the cause(s) of a variance, and, if so, whether the relevance of the information could have been taken into account in the data analyses. Furthermore, if the concern for the optimal type or amount of information is taken back one step in the variance investigation process, a question can be raised as to whether there is an optimal amount of confidence that the subjects should have had in their initial causal attributions. I think the answer to this question is not in the context of the present study, but the notion of the appropriateness of one's confidence is something Brown may want to consider in future work.

My remaining comments relate to additional information I would have liked to have seen presented in the paper. First, what do the central tendencies and distributions of the likelihood and confidence assessments look like? Given the complex nature of the experimental task and the subjects' lack of experience with variance investigation problems, my guess is that the confidence assessments were lower than the likelihood assessments, and that the latter reflected a great deal of variability across subjects. (This conjecture is partially supported by some data presented in the paper.) Second, did the subjects appear to "anchor" their likelihood assessments on the priors (.75 and .25) that were given for the variance and the causes? Again, given the complexity of the task and the subjects' lack of experience, this would seem to be a reasonable response strategy. Answers to these two questions might help one understand why the subjects rated likelihood and confidence as they did. Finally, why is the second-ranked cause associated with such a low level of confidence (see Fig. 3) relative to the first-, third- and fourth-ranked causes? This result implies that preferences for additional information will be greatest for causes ranked as second most likely. This seems like an odd result, and I would have liked to have seen an examination of it.

In summary, I think Brown's paper is a good beginning toward understanding the relationships among cause likelihood assessments, confidence and information search in variance investigation decisions. Before the full implications of this research can be understood, however, additional work will be needed on information search, re-attribution of causes and formulation of decisions and actions, as will research involving expert subjects who are experienced in this decision setting.

William S. Waller
William L. Felix, Jr.
University of Arizona

Cognition and the Auditor's Opinion Formulation Process: A Schematic Model of Interactions Between Memory and Current Audit Evidence

The public auditor provides a service to society by an opinion on the client's financial reports. This opinion is generated by an opinion formulation process, which has been described elsewhere [e.g., Felix and Kinney 1982]. However, the frameworks previously used to describe this process tend to lack an organizing principle(s) which allows for descriptions of the structure and process of expert judgment in auditing at both global and decomposed levels. Also, these frameworks were inconsistent with human information processing capabilities and constraints.

This paper presents the rudiments of a descriptive model of the auditor's opinion formulation process, which may have some potential as a framework for future empirical research. The model represents the auditor's opinion formulation process as a special case of schematic information processing, employing the schema construct from cognitive psychology as an organizing principle. More specifically, the model attempts to integrate the following notions. First, the dual role of audit evidence is to reduce the auditor's uncertainty in two of its facets: (1) a "first-order" uncertainty about whether the client's financial statements contain a material error and (2) a "second-order" uncertainty about whether a set of audit evidence provides adequate support for a conclusion about the "first-order" uncertainty. Reducing the "first-order" uncertainty may be seen as the "opinion-forming" role of audit evidence, while reducing the "second-order" uncertainty may be seen as the "opinion-justifying" role of audit evidence. These roles obviously are not independent. Second, current audit evidence and the auditor's knowledge structures (schemata) in memory are interdependent in at least two ways: (1) the auditor's knowledge structures control the search for and assimilation of current audit evidence and (2) the auditor's knowledge structures in a sense *are* current audit evidence.[1]

The paper is organized as follows. The second section presents a characterization of the dual role of audit evidence. The third section discusses the search for and assimilation of current information from a cognitive psychology perspective, noting some distinctions that pertain to the organization of human memory and some effects that knowledge structures in memory have on current information processing. The fourth and main section presents a model of the auditor's opinion formulation process, which incorporates the characterization of the dual role of audit evidence and theoretical constructs from cognitive psychology to provide a basis for describing interdependencies between current audit evidence and the auditor's knowledge structures. The fourth section also notes a number of issues for future empirical research on the auditor's opinion formulation process. The fifth section contains some concluding remarks.

THE ROLE OF AUDIT EVIDENCE

The role of audit evidence in the opinion formulation process is to reduce the auditor's uncertainty. The manner in which audit evidence reduces uncertainty can be characterized by a number of useful analogies: (1) The auditor is a quasi-scientist who obtains and evaluates evidence in order to test a specific hypothesis (e.g., an assertion in the client's financial reports) [Mautz and Sharaf, 1962]. The degree to which the evidence confirms or corroborates the hypothesis can be seen as a measure of uncertainty reduction [Carnap, 1945; Popper, 1965]. (2) The auditor is a quasi-logician who attempts to prove, or establish inductive support for, the "ultimate proposition" that the financial reports present fairly the client's financial position, results of operations and changes in financial position [Toba, 1975; Kissinger, 1977]. The weight of the evidence E with respect to the ultimate proposition P, $w(P|E)$, can be seen as a measure of uncertainty reduction. (3) The auditor is a quasi-statistician who combines pre-audit evidence or knowledge, in the form of a prior probability distribution, with current audit evidence, in the form of a likelihood function, to produce a posterior probability distribution [Felix, 1974 and 1976; Kinney, 1975]. The change from priors to posteriors can be seen as a measure of uncertainty reduction. While such analogies should not be accepted uncritically as descriptive models, they can provide insights into the role of audit evidence in the auditor's opinion formulation process and help researchers to frame empirical questions as well as to prescribe methods for improving practice [Waller and Jiambalvo, in press].

The analogy to be used in the present paper differs somewhat from those mentioned above. Under our characterization, the auditor collects and processes evidence E in order to reduce uncertainty in two of its facets: $R = Bel(M|E)$ and $S = Bel(R|E)$, where M is a material error in the client's financial reports and $Bel(.|.)$ is an evidential support or belief support function [Shafer, 1976; Keynes, 1921; Einhorn and Hogarth, 1982; see also Cohen, 1977, and Chesley, 1982]. The auditor's goal is to collect and process E such that $R \leqslant R^*$, $S \geqslant S^*$, and $C \leqslant C^*$, where R^* is the maximum allowable audit risk, S^* is the minimum allowable justification for a conclusion about audit risk, C is the cost of E, and C^* is the maximum allowable cost of E. The gist of the characterization is to propose that (1) in collecting and processing current audit evidence, the auditor must be concerned implicitly or explicitly with R (which represents the auditor's "first-order" uncertainty about M), S (which represents the auditor's "second-order" uncertainty about R) and C (the cost of evidence) and (2) E drives R, S and C, usually jointly but at times severally. It should be noted that the judgment/decision variables M, R, R*, S, S*, C and C* are subjectivist constructs and their values need not be numerical. Also, we do not mean to assert that R and S necessarily conform to some *a priori* axiomatic system.

The distinction between R and S can be rationalized in a number of ways. One way is to think of the auditor's opinion formulation process as an act of categorization. Society rewards the auditor for accurately categorizing firms into those with $R \leqslant R^*$ and those with $R > R^*$. In a sense, S measures the degree to which the evidence supports the auditor's categorization, and S must be equal to or greater than S* in order for the auditor to satisfy society's demand for his or her service. Another way is to suggest that the usefulness of a probability (i.e., degree of belief) statement depends on the information upon which it is based as well as its numerical value. For example, the usefulness of the statement "there's a 50 percent chance that the surgical operation will save person X's life" may differ depending on whether it is made by a surgeon, a first-year medical student or an uniformed bettor who blindly applies the principle of non-sufficient reason [see Black, 1967]. Contrary to the view that probabilities differ "only in value...a probability is a probability is a probability" [Phillips, 1973, p. 21; see also Raiffa, 1968], individuals often perceive differently numerically equal probabilities which are based on different amounts or types of information, and these differences in perception sometimes influence decision behavior [Ellsberg, 1961; Becker and Brownson, 1965; Beach and Wise, 1969; Yates and Zukowski, 1976; Crocker, Mitchell and Beach, 1978]. To the extent that the product of an audit is viewed as a probabilistic rather than determinate conclusion about the state of the world [DeAngelo, 1981], the auditor must be concerned about S as well as R.

Taking this characterization a step further, *useful* audit evidence may be defined as information processed by the auditor that affects R and/or S (ignoring C). Useful audit evidence can include information that is currently collected and processed (e.g., bank confirmation inquiries) and information that was previously collected, processed and stored in external memory (e.g., last year's working papers) or internal memory (e.g., the auditor's knowledge of the client's industry) and is retrieved for use in the current audit situation. In short, the E that drives R and S can vary greatly in form and content.

This characterization of the dual role of audit evidence is used in the model of the auditor's opinion formulation process presented later. Before presenting the model, the next section notes three useful distinctions regarding human memory (short-term memory vs. long-term memory, episodic memory vs. semantic memory, and declarative knowledge structures vs. procedural knowledge structures) and discusses the effects that knowledge structures in memory have on the search for and assimilation of current information (schematic information processing).

KNOWLEDGE STRUCTURES IN MEMORY AND CURRENT INFORMATION

Short-term Memory vs. Long-term Memory

Short-term memory can be functionally defined as the information content or set of "chunks" that is directly available for cognitive processing at a given instant of time [Newell and Simon, 1972]. Short-term memory is "working memory" in that its contents comprise the knowledge currently in use. For a cognitive process to be effective, the knowledge or information required by the process must be in short-term memory. However, the capacity of short-term memory is very small—limited to only a few (perhaps four to seven) chunks at a given instant [Simon, 1974 and 1976]. Although the efficient chunking of information can provide some flexibility in this constraint, it is reasonable to conclude that the limited capacity of short-term memory is essentially invariant across cognitive tasks and generally has profound effects on cognitive performance [Newell and Simon, 1972].

Long-term memory refers to the capacity to store knowledge for use at an unspecified future time [Bourne, Dominowski and Loftus, 1979]. Unlike short-term memory, long-term memory has no practical capacity constraint [Newell and Simon, 1972]. Many models of long-term memory exist in the cognitive psychology literature and model-building continues to be very active [Simon, 1979; Wickelgren, 1981]. For present purposes, it will be useful to represent long-term memory in terms of a "text" of stored information (specifically, the "text" consists of a network of nodes, which contain knowledge or information, and relations, which link the nodes) and an "index" which provides routes of accessibility to the "text" information.[2]

Episodic Memory vs. Semantic Memory

Many cognitive theorists distinguish two long-term memories; episodic memory and semantic memory [Tulving, 1972 and 1983; Puff, 1979; however, see Wickelgren, 1981]. Episodic memory contains information about autobiographic experiences which are associated with a particular time and place. Semantic memory contains general knowledge that does not depend on a particular time and place—for example, meanings of words, rules of grammar, and general knowledge about the world and how it works. An auditor's personal experiences such as "Yesterday, I designed the audit program for accounts receivable on the audit of Z Company" would be stored in episodic memory, whereas an abstract representation of the opinion formulation process applicable to many audits would be stored in semantic memory.[3]

Episodic memory and semantic memory are highly interdependent. The effects of semantic memory on episodic memory have been clearly demonstrated by many psychological studies. For example, in studies on eyewitness testimony [Loftus, 1975; Loftus and Zanni, 1975], in which subjects are asked to report on an event that they personally observed (e.g., a film of a car crash), subjects tend to produce recollections that are significantly distorted by semantic information (e.g., knowledge about traffic accidents in general). The effects of episodic memory on semantic memory, on the other hand, are fundamental to cognitive development—experiences stored in episodic memory are the basis upon which many cognitive structures in semantic memory are built [Waller and Felix, in press].

Declarative Knowledge vs. Procedural Knowledge

To be adequate, a model of memory must go beyond the issue of how knowledge about facts is represented in long-term memory, such that the processes that operate on that knowledge are also represented [Klatzky, 1980]. This consideration leads to the distinction between declarative knowledge and procedural knowledge. Declarative knowledge or "knowing that" consists of the facts one has in memory, whereas procedural knowledge or "knowing how" consists of the skills, including cognitive skills, one knows how to perform [Anderson, 1980].[4] Below, we refer to declarative knowledge structures as "template-schemata" and to procedural knowledge structures as "procedural-schemata." These structures are discussed in detail in the next subsection.

Schematic Information Processing

Following Bartlett [1932], Minsky [1975], Neisser [1976], Rumelhart and Ortony [1977], and Taylor and Crocker [1981], among many others, we propose that there are generic cognitive structures (i.e., schemata, singular form—schema) which organize knowledge in semantic memory and which play a fundamental role in all cognitive activity (e.g., perception, remembering, comprehension, explanation, prediction, formulating an opinion regarding a client's financial reports and so on). We adopt the view that "schemata truly are *the building blocks of cognition.* They are the fundamental elements upon which all information processing depends" [Rumelhart, 1980, p. 33].

When discussing schemata or related constructs (e.g., scripts [Abelson, 1976 and 1981], frames [Minsky, 1975; Kuipers, 1975], templates [Gibbins, in press], and prototypes [Rosch, 1977; Mervis and Rosch, 1981]), one faces a dilemma. Because the nature of knowledge structures in memory and their functioning in cognition are not yet well understood [Anderson, 1980; Rumelhart, 1980], one has the choice of either keeping the discussion vague and imprecise or attempting to explicate the nature and functioning of knowledge structures and, in all probability, turn out to be quite wrong. Consider a few examples of those who have taken the former approach.

> For the purposes of this article, we shall adopt a relatively broad definition of a schema that would be accepted by most researchers. Schemas are generic knowledge structures that guide the comprehender's interpretations, inferences, explanations, and attention [Graesser and Nakamura, 1982, p. 60].

> For the purposes of this review, we include almost any of the abstract hypotheses, expectations, organizing principles, frames, implicational molecules, scripts, plans, or prototypes that have been proposed as abstract mental organizing systems or memory structures in our use of the word "schema" [Hastie, 1981, p. 39].

> In the following discussion, we largely forsake any attempt at classifying or defining the possible structures [Nisbett and Ross, 1980, pp. 28-29].

The obvious problem with this approach is that the use of vague theoretical constructs makes it difficult, if not impossible, to derive empirical (i.e., refutable) propositions.[5] Given the present paper's purpose to present a descriptive model which may have some potential as a framework for future empirical research in auditing, below we follow the latter approach of being explicit but probably wrong.

Schematic information processing involves the interaction of two sorts of knowledge structures: template-schemata and procedural-schemata. The nature of template-schemata is as follows. There are template-schemata at all levels of abstraction and complexity, and narrower template-schemata (or subschemata) are embedded in broader template-schemata [Piaget, 1952; Neisser, 1976; Rumelhart and Ortony, 1977]. A template-schema is a network of nodes (which represent feature variables of concepts, objects and events) and relations which link the nodes [Minsky, 1975]. For the purpose of information storage in memory, a template-schema is a framework for organizing information about a concept or category of objects or events [Norman and Bobrow, 1975]. For the purpose of information assimilation, a template-schema is a format which specifies intelligible information and which is filled in during cognition [Neisser, 1976]. The process of filling in a template-schema is called instantiation [Rumelhart and Ortony, 1977]. Instantiating a template-schema involves the assignment of values to the nodes in its network [Minsky, 1975]. Associated with each node are modifiable sets of conditions and possible values. The sets of conditions and possible values are modifiable across applications of the template-schema to allow for current goals to influence the instantiation process and to allow for learning.

The set of conditions associated with a node influence the node's value assignment in three ways: (1) The conditions specify the kinds of values that can be assigned to the node (e.g., a thing, an event or a person). (2) The conditions require certain relations to hold between or among the values assigned to various nodes in the network; in effect, value assignments to one node can change the conditional probabilities for possible value assignments to another node. (3) The conditions specify default values for feature variables that are not observed during the instantiation process, and these default values are sensitive to value assignments for feature variables that are observed. Thus, the sets of conditions associated with nodes are of critical importance to schema-based inferences—the individual uses information that is "given" to instantiate partially the template-schema and, based on interrelationships and default values specified by the sets of conditions, goes beyond the information "given" to complete the template-schema's instantiation.

A highly versatile way to represent procedural-schemata is as hierarchies of "productions" or condition-action pairs [Newell and Simon, 1972; Newell, 1973]. A production consists of a set of conditions which, when met, lead to the implementation of the corresponding (mental or physical) action. More specifically, information in short-term memory is compared with the condition-component of a production at the top of a hierarchy of productions. If a sufficient match results, then the action-component of the production is implemented. If there is no immediate match, information in short-term memory is compared with the condition-component of a production lower in the hierarchy, until a match is made and some action-component is implemented.[6] It is important to note that comparisons with the condition-component of a production can involve either information from the environment or information from a partially or completely instantiated template-schema and that the action-component can involve an external action (e.g., information search in the environment) or internal action (e.g., assigning a value to a node of a template-schema). Also, as with template-schemata, the condition-components and action-components of productions in procedural-schemata must be modifiable to allow for current goals and learning.

Procedural-schemata perform at least three functions in their interaction with template-schemata: (1) activating a template-schema, (2) controlling the instantiation of a template-schema, and (3) testing the "fit" of a template-schema. The activation function involves a matching-up of information in short-term memory and components of a potentially applicable template-schema. Template-schema activation may be concept-driven (i.e., top-down) or data-driven (i.e., bottom-up) [Rumelhart, 1980]. Concept-driven processing is involved when a broad schema activates a narrower schema or subschema. For example, a schema for a common sequence of events, such as "dining at a restaurant," may activate a subschema embedded in it, such as "ordering a wine." Data-driven processing is involved when a datum or subschema activates a broader schema to which it relates. For example, an observation of broken pieces of glass strewn over a street intersection may activate a schema for traffic accidents to account for the presence of the glass.

In addition to performing the activation function, procedural-schemata provide plans for information search and the instantiation of template-schemata [Neisser, 1976; Hastie, 1981]. Controlling the instantiation of a simple template-schema may be a trivial function, since the order in which the schema's nodes are assigned values is likely to be unimportant. However, for a complex template-schema, because of constraining relationships among sets of conditions associated with various nodes of the schema, the order in which the nodes are assigned values may be crucial to the quantity and quality of information collected from the environment, or from other knowledge domains in long-term memory, and to the ultimate cognitive product (e.g., an explanation, a prediction or another sort of inference). Controlling the instantiation of a complex template-schema may require an equally complex procedural-schema, which provides plans for decomposing the instantiation process and for sequential information processing.

To our knowledge, there has been little research on the processes by which a template-schema's "fit" with the current situation is tested or evaluated. Most authors resort to analogies between evaluating the "fit" of a schema and scientific hypothesis-testing; for example:

> (W)hen a person uses a schema to comprehend some of the

> aspects of the situation, the schema constitutes a kind of theory about those aspects. Thus, in general, the process of comprehension can be regarded rather like the process a scientist goes through in testing a theory; evidence is sought which either tends to confirm it, or which leads to its rejection. Upon finding a theory which, to our satisfaction, accounts for observations we have made, we feel that we understand the phenomenon in question [Rumelhart and Ortony, 1977, p. 112].

While such analogies to hypothesis-testing may provide insights into the processes by which the "fit" of a template-schema is evaluated, they should not be accepted uncritically as descriptive. For present purposes, we propose that procedural-schemata perform the function of testing whether a template-schema's "fit" to the current situation is satisfactory. This function involves: (1) an early test of a template-schema's "fit," based on limited information, (2) more or less continuous (albeit much less intensive) monitoring of the template-schema's "fit" as instantiation proceeds, and (3) a final determination that the "fit" of the template-schema is satisfactory.

In sum, the effects that knowledge structures in memory have on the search for and assimilation of current information is represented in terms of schematic information processing, which involves the interaction of template-schemata and procedural-schemata. Template-schemata serve as a framework for organizing knowledge and as a format for information assimilation. Procedural-schemata perform the functions of activating template-schemata, controlling the instantiation of template-schemata, and testing the "fit" of template-schemata to the current situation.

A MODEL OF THE AUDITOR'S OPINION FORMULATION PROCESS

This section presents the rudiments of a descriptive model of the auditor's opinion formulation process, which represents the auditor's search for and assimilation of current audit evidence as a special case of schematic information processing driven by the goal of collecting evidence E such that $R \leq R^*$, $S \geq S^*$, and $C \leq C^*$. Two subsections follow. The first subsection presents the main components of the model and the second subsection "walks through" and describes the opinion formulation process in terms of these components, noting some issues for future research along the way.

Components of the Model

The auditor is proposed to have a network of interrelated template-schemata, which exist at many levels of complexity and abstraction. These template-schemata serve as frameworks that organize the auditor's knowledge as it relates to the opinion formulation process and serve as formats for the assimilation of current audit evidence. Associated with the auditor's template-schemata are procedural-schemata which perform the functions of activating, controlling the instantiation of and testing the "fit" of the template-schemata. These schema constructs could be used to describe the auditor's opinion formulation process at whatever level of detail desired. The discussion below focuses on the auditor's more abstract template-schemata and associated procedural-schemata.

The auditor is proposed to have a number of global template-schemata (GTS), each of which represents an entire audit at a high level of abstraction. A GTS is a network of nodes (which represent major elements or feature variables of the audit) and relations that link the nodes. Associated with each node are sets of conditions and possible values, which are modifiable across audits to allow for current goals and learning. The sets of conditions specify the kinds of values that can be assigned to the nodes, require certain relations to hold between or among the values assigned to various nodes, and specify default values for unobserved feature variables. Embedded in the GTS are many narrower template-schemata, each in itself being a network of nodes with modifiable sets of conditions and possible values. The schema-within-a-schema organization is a kind of problem decomposition, which is necessitated by the complexity of the opinion formulation process and constraints on the auditor's short-term or working memory.

It will require considerable future empirical research to explicate the auditor's GTS and related template-schemata in terms of their nodes, sets of conditions and possible values associated with their nodes, and relations between and among their nodes. It is tentatively proposed that the auditor's GTS includes nodes for the judgment/decision variables M, R, R*, S, S*, C and C*, and "summary" nodes for various elements of the audit (see Figure 1). These elements of the audit include: (1) client/environment factors (e.g., the client's geographic, economic and industrial setting, the nature of its operations, the competence and ethics of its management personnel, the personnel, equipment and procedures that constitute its accounting information system, and its financial reports), (2) users of the client's financial reports and the auditor's opinion, and (3) cost factors other than the cost of evidence (e.g., the cost of producing an incorrect unqualified opinion).

The relations between and among the nodes of the GTS are complex. For example, the nodes for M, R* and S* and the nodes for users and non-evidence cost factors must be linked such that value assignments to the user and cost nodes constrain the possible values for M, R* and S*. In other words, the auditor's judgments about materiality, the maximum allowable audit risk and the minimum allowable justification for a conclusion about audit risk all depend on the auditor's perceptions of how the report/opinion will be used and the cost of producing a wrong opinion. Similarly, the nodes for R and S and the nodes for client/environment factors must be linked such that value assignments to the client/environment nodes directly or indirectly constrain the possible values for R and S. Also, since some of the client/environment nodes represent feature variables that are not necessarily observed during the instantiation process, and thus have default values assigned to them (which are sensitive to value assignments for feature variables that are observed), and since these default values can in turn influence R and S, it is reasonable to say that the auditor's knowledge structures in a sense *are* current audit evidence.

The "summary" nodes for the various elements of the audit are also linked to narrower template-schemata which represent the elements in much greater detail. The auditor's assimilation of current audit evidence takes place for the most part in the context of these narrower template-schemata.

FIGURE 1

Components of Global Template-Schema

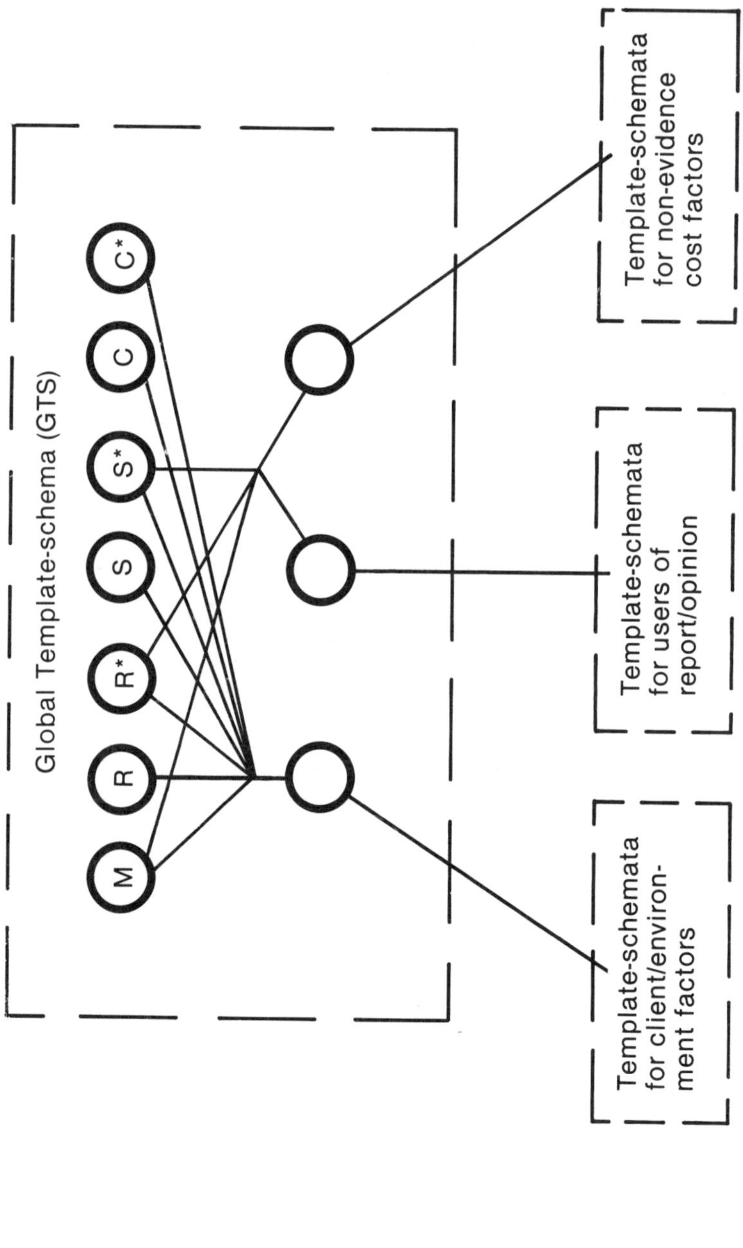

For example, it is proposed that, as a part of the opinion formulation process, the auditor decomposes the client's accounting information system and its output into transaction cycle/balance sets which are represented by template-schemata (see Figure 2). The template-schema(ta) for each transaction cycle/balance set i includes nodes for the decomposed judgment/decision variables m_i, r_i, r_i^*, s_i, s_i^*, c_i, c_i^*, *inter alia*. At the level of each transaction cycle/balance set i, the auditor's goal is to collect and process evidence E such that $r_i = Bel(m_i | E) \leqslant r_i^*$, $s_i = Bel(r_i | E) \geqslant s_i^*$ and $c_i(E) \leqslant c_i^*$. The decomposed judgment/decision variables m_i, r_i, r_i^*, s_i, s_i^*, c_i and c_i^* for each transaction cycle/balance set i are linked via the "summary" nodes in the GTS to M, R, R*, S, S*, C and C*. It may be noted that, given this decomposition, the instantiation of the GTS, and narrower template-schemata embedded therein, requires a hierarchical or "cascaded" inference process (cf. Peterson [1973]; Schum [1977]).

The auditor is proposed to have more than one GTS. One or more GTS might be applicable for "normal" audits while alternative GTS might be applicable for "problem" audits (e.g., those in which the potential for auditability problems, management fraud or bankruptcy is strong). The discussion here mainly concerns a normal audit GTS. However, two points regarding alternative GTS may be noted. First, one key difference between a normal audit GTS and a problem audit GTS is that the default value for R at the beginning of the opinion formulation process is likely to be much lower for the normal audit GTS, perhaps even less than R*. Second, it would be interesting for future research to examine cases in which the auditor's test of the "fit" of a normal audit GTS reveals a mismatch with the current situation. In such cases, depending on the point in the opinion formulation process at which the "goodness of fit" test is performed, the auditor might try to cope with the lack of good "fit" by replacing the normal audit GTS with a problem audit GTS or by attempting to adapt (perhaps without complete success) the partially instantiated normal audit GTS to the problem audit situation. Especially interesting is the issue of how, and possibly whether, the auditor re-interprets evidence collected prior to the "goodness of fit" test.

As noted above, the auditor is proposed to have procedural-schemata that perform the functions of activating template-schemata, controlling the instantiation of template-schemata, and testing the "fit" of template-schemata to the current audit situation. While the procedural-schema for activating a GTS is likely to be relatively simple, especially for recurring engagements, the procedural-schemata for controlling the instantiation of the GTS constitute plans for evidence collection and are likely to be extremely complex. Procedural-schemata for testing the "fit" of a GTS may also be complex, involving various "hypothesis-testing" strategies applied before, during and at the end of the audit engagement. These procedural-schemata are discussed further in the next subsection.

The Auditor's Opinion Formulation Process

For discussion purposes, we divide the opinion formulation process into four steps: (1) deciding to perform the audit, (2) gaining an understanding of the client and its environment (including a preliminary evaluation of internal accounting controls), (3) planning and execution of audit activities

FIGURE 2

Template-schemata for Client/Environment Factors

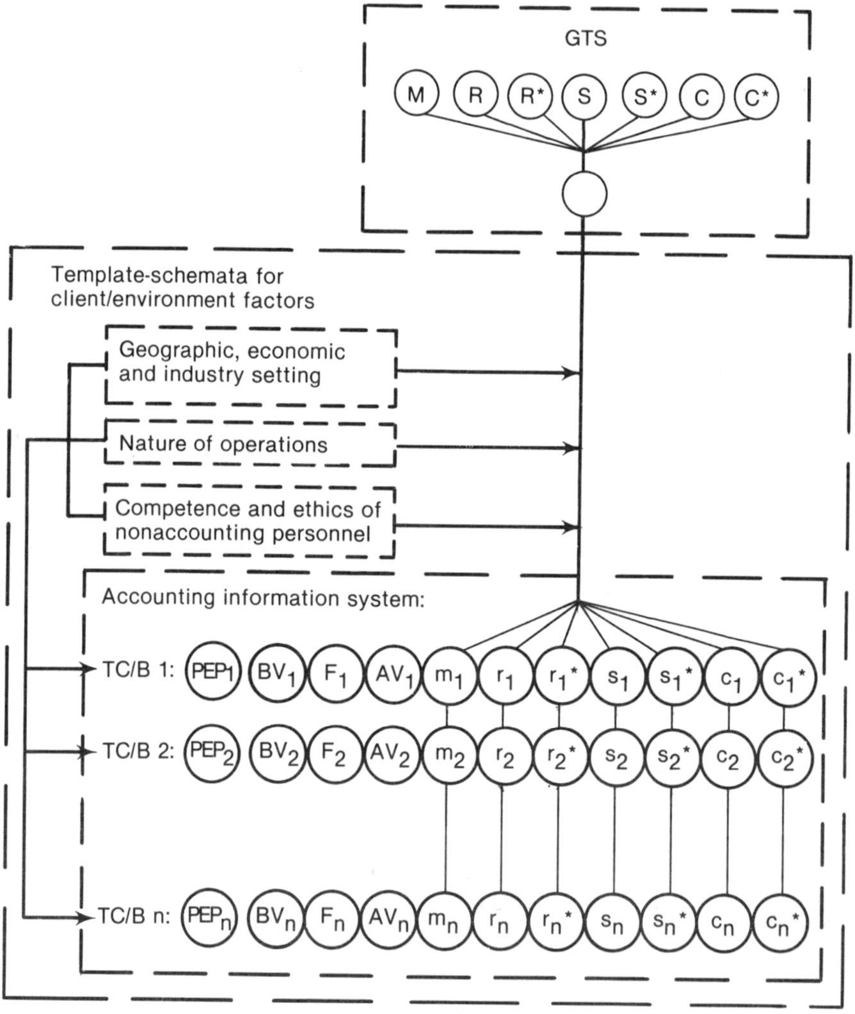

TC/B - transaction cycle/balance set
F - files for supporting documents
PEP - personnel, equipment, procedures
BV - book value(s)
AV - audit value(s)

(compliance tests and substantive tests) and (4) forming an opinion.

Decision to Perform the Audit. The auditor's opinion formulation process begins with either the decision to accept/reject a prospective client or the decision to continue/discontinue a recurring engagement. With respect to the decision to accept/reject a prospective client, the auditor tests the potential "goodness of fit" of a GTS to the current audit situation. For this purpose, the auditor is proposed to have a procedural-schema which controls the search for information that tentatively confirms or disconfirms the "fit" of a GTS. This procedural-schema may include inquiries of the client's management, reviews of prior period financial reports, inquiries of predecessor auditors, and perhaps obtaining reports from investigative agencies. An interesting issue for future research concerns the nature of the auditor's "hypothesis-testing" strategies indicated by this procedural-schema. Does the auditor's strategy involve the activation of a normal audit GTS and the search for information that tentatively confirms its "fit" to the current audit situation, or, does the auditor's strategy involve the activation of a problem audit GTS and the search for information that tentatively confirms (disconfirms) its "fit" and thereby disconfirms (confirms) the "fit" of a normal audit GTS? From a normative viewpoint, exclusive reliance on the former strategy may not be preferable because it renders the auditor vulnerable to a "confirmation bias" [Tweney, Doherty and Mynatt 1981; Waller and Felix in press]. It is expected that the auditor's procedural-schema for testing the "fit" of a GTS, at this early stage of the opinion formulation process, involves "hypothesis-testing" strategies that use both confirmatory and disconfirmatory information. With respect to the decision to continue/discontinue a recurring engagement, it is expected that the auditor engages in similar (albeit much less intensive) "hypothesis-testing" behavior. However, because it would be professionally difficult to justify the decision to discontinue an engagement with a financially weak client, relatively more weight would be placed on potential auditability and management fraud problems in the continue/discontinue decision than in the accept/reject decision, assuming a problem audit GTS is activated as a part of the auditor's "hypothesis-testing" strategy.

Regardless of whether the decision is to accept/reject a prospective client or to continue/discontinue a recurring engagement, the auditor must make an auditability assessment. An assessment of auditability is expected to require an *ex ante,* speculative test of the "fit" of a GTS to the current audit situation. In terms of the present model, the question of auditability rests upon the potential availability of some set of evidence E^a such that $R = Bel(M|E^a) \leqslant R^*$, $S = Bel(R|E^a) \geqslant S^*$, and $C(E^a) \leqslant C^*$. An assessment of auditability would appear to require the activation of a GTS and subschemata embedded therein, their partial instantiation using the limited amount of information available at the beginning of the opinion formulation process, the imagined completion of the instantiation process (based on interrelationships among nodes of pertinent template-schemata and default values specified by sets of conditions associated with these nodes), resultant predictions of the likely values for R, S and C, and comparisons of these predicted values with tentatively set values for R^*, S^* and C^*. It is reasonable to expect that assessments of auditability are much easier to perform for recurring engagements than for prospective clients.

Understanding the Client and Its Environment. Although for discussion purposes we treat the auditor's gaining an understanding of the client and its environment as a separate step in the opinion formulation process, it should be clear that this understanding or "learning" activity actually occurs throughout the auditor's opinion formulation process and, in the case of recurring engagements, extends back to prior years' audits. For example, a great deal of "learning" is likely to occur during the process of deciding whether to accept/reject a prospective client or to continue/discontinue a recurring engagement. In the present model, what distinguishes pre-decision-to-audit "learning" and post-decision-to-audit "learning" is that the former essentially involves evidence collection for the purpose of tentatively accepting or rejecting the hypothesis that there is an adequate "fit" of a GTS (in most cases, a normal audit GTS) to the current audit situation whereas the latter involves evidence collection conditioned on the tentative acceptance of that hypothesis. An important implication of this distinction is that, when the auditor begins the post-decision-to-audit "learning" step, it is likely that R either is low (perhaps less than R^*) or is expected to be low once foreseeable audit adjustments have been booked. In such cases, while it is possible that evidence collected after the decision-to-audit may increase or decrease R, it is expected that the major role of such evidence is to increase S to a value equal to or greater than S^*, subject to $C \leqslant C^*$.

In terms of schematic information processing, the auditor's gaining an understanding of the client and its environment involves the (continued) instantiation of template-schemata representing client/environment factors through the application of procedural-schemata. These procedural-schemata may include a variety of activities such as preliminary analytical review, analysis of the minutes of board and stockholder meetings, analysis of contracts and labor relations, a tour of facilities, reviewing relevant economic and industry literature, administering internal control questionnaires and discussions with client personnel. The template-schemata for client/environment factors represent the client's geographic, economic, and industrial setting, the nature of its operations, the competence and ethics of its nonaccounting personnel, and its accounting information system, including decompositions of the system in terms of transaction cycle/balance sets. The template-schema(ta) for each transaction cycle/balance set includes nodes that represent the personnel, equipment, and procedures that constitute the subsystem (including internal accounting controls), output from the subsystem (expected or actual book values and supporting documents), expected audit values, and the judgment/decision variables (see Figure 2).

Implicit in the organization of the auditor's template-schemata for client/environment factors is a number of "models." One "model" represents how the client's accounting information system *should* map economic activity into financial statement balances. Once values have been assigned to nodes for client/environment factors such as the client's economic setting and the nature of its operations, this "model" produces (or constrains the possible values of) expected audit values. Another "model" represents how the client's accounting information system *does* map economic activity into financial statement balances and produces (or constrains the possible values of) expected book values. Ultimately, the values assigned to the nodes for expected book values would be displaced by actual book values. Significant discrepancies between the expected audit values and expected (or actual) book values produced by these "models" are likely to impact r_i, the audit risk for transaction cycle/balance set i. Other "models" implicit in these template-schemata relate r_i with client/environment factors such as the economic setting and competence of management personnel (the effect on r_i due to these factors may be referred to as "inherent risk") and with components of the accounting information subsystem, including internal accounting controls (the effect on r_i due to these components may be referred to as "control risk"). An important task for future research is to explicate the variables and relationships that comprise these "models."

As the understanding or "learning" step proceeds and audit evidence is processed, it is expected that the values of s_i for the various transaction cycle/balance sets increase, approaching but not reaching s_i*. To attain $s_i \geqslant s_i^*$ would normally require the planning and execution of additional audit activity, i.e., compliance and substantive tests, which are discussed in the next subsection.

Planning and Execution of Audit Activity. Before discussing the planning and execution of audit activity, it is necessary to consider the relationship between the judgment/decision variables on global vs. decomposed levels of analysis. Unfortunately, this relationship is one of the most difficult parts of the opinion formulation process to model explicitly [Felix, 1980]. In terms of the present model, this issue concerns the relationship between the variables M, R, R*, S, S*, C and C* in the GTS and the variables m_i, r_i, r_i^*, s_i, s_i^*, c_i and c_i^* in the various transaction cycle/balance sets.

A variety of questions about this relationship could be pursued by future research. Are the values of the judgment/decision variables in the GTS updated continuously and automatically as the template-schemata for transaction cycle/balance sets are instantiated, or, is the updating done deliberately at certain specifiable points in the opinion formulation process? What are the rules for combining conclusions made at the decomposed levels of analysis (e.g., the conclusion that $r_i \leqslant r_i^*$ for transaction cycle/balance set i and $r_j \leqslant r_j^*$ for transaction cycle/balance set j) into conclusions at the global level of analysis (e.g., the conclusion that $R \leqslant R^*$). Explicating these rules is complicated by the fact that the auditor's knowledge about nonaccounting client/environment factors may have direct effects on R, S and C in addition to indirect effects through r_i, s_i and c_i (see Figure 2); that is, $R \neq \Sigma r_i$, $S \neq \Sigma s_i$ and $C \neq \Sigma c_i$. What are the rules for "allocating" M, R*, S* and C* to transaction cycle/balance sets? Again, the answer is not simple, since these "allocations" are in a sense incomplete; that is, $M \neq \Sigma m_i$, $R^* \neq \Sigma r_i^*$, $S^* \neq \Sigma s_i^*$ and $C^* \neq \Sigma c_i^*$.

It is expected that maintaining the relationship between the judgment/decision variables in the GTS and the decomposed judgment/decision variables in the template-schemata for transaction cycle/balance sets generally involves the use of intuitive or heuristic decomposition-combination rules, which are applied at specifiable points in the opinion formulation process. For example, it is expected that, at the end of the post-decision-to-audit "learning" step, as a prelude to planning audit activity, the auditor uses "bottom-up" information processing rules to update R, S and C, in light of current values of r_i, s_i and c_i for the various transaction cycle/balance sets.[7] (Revisions in M, R*, S* and C* may also occur as a result of post-decision-to-audit "learning" activity.) Once these revisions are complete, it is expected that the auditor uses "top-down" information processing rules to update m_i, r_i^*, s_i^* and c_i^* for each transaction cycle/balance set i, in light of current values of M, R*, S* and C*. These "top-down" revisions are in effect "allocations" of M, R*, S* and C* to transaction cycle/balance sets for the purpose of planning audit activity.

Given "allocations" of the judgment/decision variables from the global level to the decomposed level of analysis, the auditor is in a position to plan and execute specific audit activities pertaining to each transaction cycle/balance set. In the present model, the auditor is proposed to have procedural-schemata (i.e., hierarchies of productions or condition-action pairs) that represent plans for specific audit activity. The application of these procedural-schemata to the current audit situation constitutes the execution of such plans.

Several points about procedural-schemata may be noted. First, the selection or development of the procedural-schemata to be applied in a particular audit situation is not entirely *ad hoc*. Rather, the auditor is proposed to have "standardized" procedural-schemata for each transaction cycle/balance set, which are tailored to a particular audit situation through the addition/deletion of productions or through the modification of the condition-components or action-components of specific productions.[8] Second, at the level of transaction cycle/balance set i, the selection or development of the procedural-schemata is based on the expectation that the application of the procedural-schemata will produce evidence E such that $r_i = \text{Bel}(m_i \mid E) \leqslant r_i^*$, $s_i = \text{Bel}(r_i \mid E) \geqslant s_i^*$ and $c_i(E) \leqslant c_i^*$. Third, the procedural-schemata must contain mechanisms for comparing r_i with r_i^*, s_i with s_i^*, and c_i with c_i^* (so that the decision to continue/discontinue evidence collection can be made) and for updating r_i, s_i and c_i in light of collected evidence. An interesting question for future research concerns the nature of the updating process. How does the auditor make inductive inferences from the results of compliance and substantive tests to r_i and s_i? Does the updating process involve the deliberate re-assessment of r_i and s_i based on the specific evidence produced by the application of procedural-schemata, or, assuming that the produced evidence is positive with respect to the relevant audit objectives (e.g., completeness and authenticity), are there "automatic" changes in r_i and s_i consistent with expectations implicit in the evidence plan? Fourth, the application of the procedural-schemata for audit activity involves a form of sequential information processing in which the results from the application of one production can affect the application of a subsequent production (see footnote 6). An obvious example is the effect that the results of compliance tests can have on related substantive tests which are performed subsequently.

Figure 3 illustrates the application of a very simple procedural-schema for audit activity (ignoring costs). A production (P1) provides a mechanism for comparing r_i with r_i^* and s_i with s_i^*. If $r_i \leqslant r_i^*$ and $s_i \geqslant s_i^*$, then the search for audit evidence terminates; otherwise, productions for evidence collection (P2 and/or P3) are applied. P2 is applied first and the evidence that it produces can affect the application of P3. The applications of P2 and P3 may involve a variety of information stored in template-schemata for client/environment factors. The application of another production (P4) updates r_i and s_i in light of the evidence produced by the application of P2 and/or P3. If the evidence-based revisions in r_i and s_i do not satisfy $r_i \leqslant r_i^*$ and $s_i \geqslant s_i^*$, then additional productions would be applied.

Forming an Opinion. As noted above, it is expected that, after the execution of planned audit activity, the auditor uses "bottom-up" information processing rules to update R, S and C, in light of revised values of r_i, s_i and c_i for the various transaction cycle/balance sets. This aggregation process is necessary but not sufficient for completing the last step in the auditor's opinion formulation process. It is proposed that the auditor has a procedural-schema for a final test of the "fit" of the GTS to the current audit situation. This procedural-schema may include an analytical review of the financial reports, an evaluation of current litigation, and an examination of subsequent events that may affect the interpretability of the client's financial reports. Assuming that the application of this procedural-schema produces only confirmatory evidence for the "fit" of a normal audit GTS, it is expected that the auditor at this point has achieved the goal of $R \leqslant R^*$ and $S \geqslant S^*$ and, given these conclusions, will render a professionally acceptable report.

CONCLUDING REMARKS

The purpose of this paper has been to present the rudiments of a descriptive model of the auditor's opinion formulation process, which represents the auditor's search for and assimilation of current audit evidence as a special case of schematic information processing driven by the goal of efficiently collecting evidence in order to form and justify the conclusion that audit risk is acceptably low. Also a number of issues for future empirical research on the auditor's opinion formulation process were mentioned in the context of the model.

The model has at least three limitations. First, it ignores the increasing use of man-machine systems as a part of the audit process. It may be necessary in the future to expand our notions of knowledge structures and information processing to include interactions with the computer. Second, the model suppresses individual differences. The auditor's development of these knowledge structures depends on his or her personal intellectual endowment and experience, as well as on standardized training. Individual differences in knowledge structures can be expected within and across firms and within and across a given firm's functional levels. Third, the model uses an exclusively single-person perspective. However, it is obvious that most large audits involve co-ordinated teams. Although the team perspective is missing, it may be noted that a part of the problem is bringing about co-ordination among individuals is dealing with the fact that their knowledge structures differ. Perhaps future research based on cognitive models, such as the one presented here, will be of some use in understanding the nature of

FIGURE 3

Application of Procedural-Schema for Audit Activity

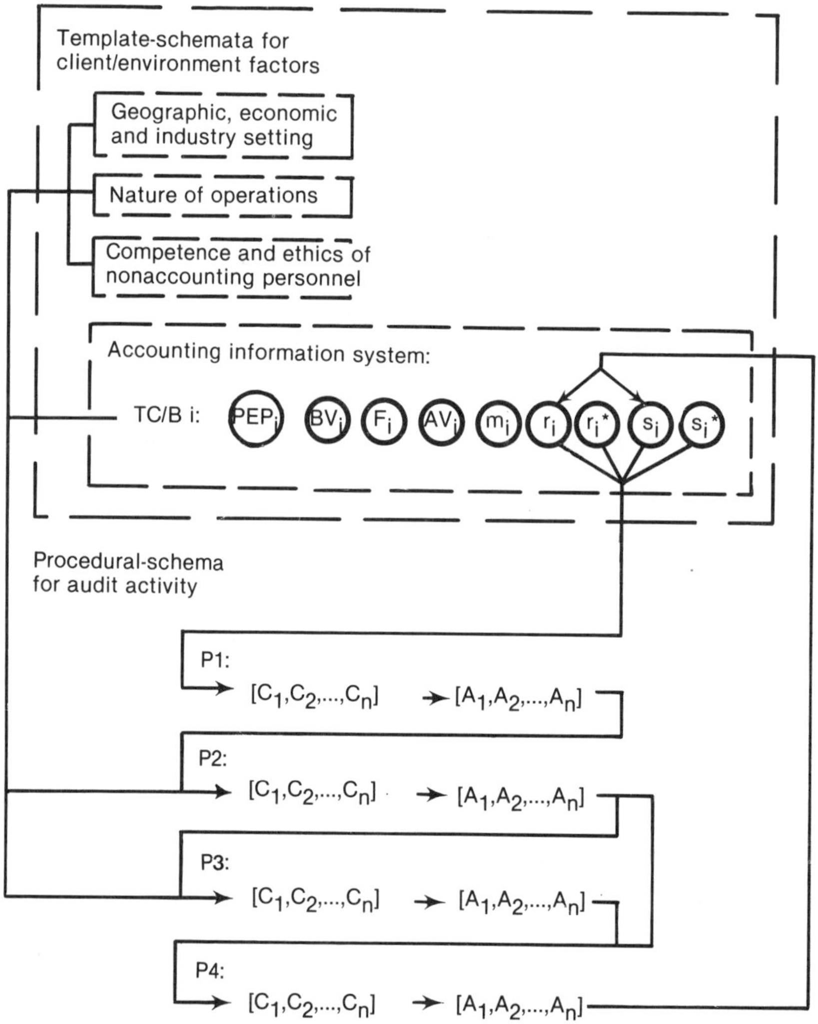

these differences in team members' knowledge structures and how they might be reduced, or otherwise exploited, to bring about more effective audits performed by audit teams.

The reader may have noticed that, contrary to many recent studies on audit judgment and decision making [see Joyce and Libby 1982; Felix and Kinney 1982], the present paper contained little discussion about the use of normative mathematical or statistical models for the purpose of evaluating the process or product of the auditor's judgments and decisions. The de-emphasis on normative models should not be taken as an implicit statement that evaluations of the auditor's judgments and decisions are unimportant or unnecessary. On the contrary, the ultimate objective is to prescribe ways to improve practice, and evaluation necessarily precedes meaningful prescription. However, building descriptive models is also an important research activity, because descriptive models may provide us with a better understanding of how auditors make judgments and decisions. Furthermore, to avoid confusion in our purposes and priorities, it may be prudent to postpone the imposition of evaluation frameworks until such an understanding has been gained, since understanding necessarily precedes meaningful evaluation and prescription.

NOTES

[1]A third interdependency is that the auditor's knowledge structures adapt to or accommodate current audit evidence, such that the ways in which the auditor's knowledge structures control the search for and assimilation of audit evidence change over his or her experience. This interdependency is discussed by Waller and Felix [in press].

[2]It is probably best not to suppose that short-term memory and long-term memory occupy different mental locations; instead, the two terms can refer to different aspects of the same location [Anderson, 1980]. When information is "retrieved" from long-term memory, it assumes an active state, rather than being transferred from one location to another. Thus, short-term memory or "active memory" consists of (1) nodes that hold new information which has not been encoded into long-term memory and (2) long-term memory nodes that hold previously encoded information and that have been temporarily activated.

[3]Some theorists would further distinguish a lexical network (or dictionary) for words and a semantic network for concepts [Collins and Loftus, 1975]. Thus, words and the concepts to which they refer have different nodes in long-term memory; and, each word node in the lexical network is linked to one or more concept nodes in the semantic network.

[4]Even more so than for the distinctions between short-term memory and long-term memory and between episodic memory and semantic memory, it is problematic as to where the line of demarcation between declarative knowledge and procedural knowledge should be drawn:

> (I)t is impossible to evaluate a representational system apart from the process that operates on it. Consequently, in modeling any cognitive process, there is always the problem of deciding how to partition that part of the knowledge system that is "process" from that part that is "data." Depending on the relative amounts of the system allocated to "process" and to "data," we have what Winograd (1975) has called "procedural" or "declarative" representational systems. Some authors have emphasized the "data," trying to have as few special-purpose procedures as possible; such a system is called *declarative.* Others have emphasized the processes involved and have largely embedded the knowledge of the system within these processes. These systems are generally called *procedural.* The issues involved in choosing one or the other of these strategies has been described by Winograd as the "declarative-procedural controversy" [Rumelhart and Norman, 1981, pp. 336-337].

[5]For other criticisms of the schema construct, see Fiedler [1982] and Alba and Hasher [1983].

[6]Newell [1973, p. 463] describes the application of a set of productions as follows.

> (S)tarting with an initially given set of data structures,...(t)hat production whose condition is true of the current data (assume there is only one) is executed, that is, the action is taken. The result is to modify the current data structures. This leads in the next instant to another (possibly the same) production being executed, leading to still further modification. So it goes, action after action being taken to carry out an entire program of processing, each evoked by its condition becoming true of the momentarily current collection of data structures.

[7]It is also expected that, after the execution of planned audit activity, the auditor again uses "bottom-up" information processing rules to update R, S and C, in light of revised values of r_i, s_i and c_i for the various transaction cycle/balance sets (see next subsection).

[8]The auditor also may have "standardized" procedural-schemata for audit activity that are industry-specific.

REFERENCES

Abelson, R., "Script Processing in Attitude Formation and Decision Making," in J. Carroll and J. Payne (eds.), *Cognition and Social Behavior* (Erlbaum, 1976), pp. 33-45.

Abelson, R., "The Psychological Status of the Script Concept," *American Psychologist* (1981), pp. 715-729.

Alba, J. and L. Hasher, "Is Memory Schematic?," *Psychological Bulletin* (1983), pp. 203-231.

Anderson, J., *Cognitive Psychology and Its Implications* (Freeman, 1980).

Bartlett, F., *Remembering: A Study in Experimental and Social Psychology* (Cambridge, The University Press, 1932).

Beach, L. and J. Wise, "Subjective Probability Estimates and Confidence Ratings," *Journal of Experimental Psychology* (1969), pp. 438-444.

Becker, S. and F. Brownson, "What Price Ambiguity? Of the Role of Ambiguity in Decision Making," *Journal of Political Economy* (1964), pp. 62-73.

Black, M., "Probability," in P. Edwards (ed.) *The Encyclopedia of Philosophy (*Macmillan, 1967), pp. 464-479.

Bourne, L., R. Dominowski, and E. Loftus, *Cognitive Processes* (Prentice-Hall, 1979).

Carnap, R., "The Two Concepts of Probability," *Philosophy and Phenomological Research* (1945).

Chesley, G., "Probabilistic Inference in Auditing: A Fresh Look," Unpublished Manuscript, Dalhousie University (1982).

Cohen, L., *The Probable and the Provable* (Oxford: Clarendon, 1977).

Collins, A. and E. Loftus, "A Spreading-Activation Theory of Semantic Memory," *Pscyhological Review* (1975), pp. 407-428.

Crocker, O., T. Mitchell, and L. Beach, "A Further Examination of Equivalence Intervals," *Organizational Behavior and Human Performance* (1978), pp. 253-261.

DeAngelo, L., *The Auditor-Client Contractual Relationship: An Economic Analysis* (Ann Arbor, MI: UMI Research Press, 1981).

Einhorn, H. and R. Hogarth, "Diagnostic Inference and Causal Judgment: A Decision Making Framework," Unpublished Manuscript, University of Chicago (1982).

Ellsberg, D., "Risk, Ambiguity and the Savage Axioms," *Quarterly Journal of Economics* (1961), pp. 643-669.

Felix, W., "A Decision Theory View of Auditing," *Contemporary Auditing Problems* (University of Kansas Press, 1974), pp. 63-71.

Felix, W., "Evidence on Alternative Means of Assessing Prior Probability Distributions for Audit Decision Making," *The Accounting Review* (October 1976), pp. 800-807.

Felix, W., "The Beginnings of the Audit Logic Process: A Decomposition of Beliefs," Manuscript Presented at the Fourth Duke Univerity Symposium (1980).

Felix, W. and W. Kinney, "Research in the Auditor's Opinion Formulation Process: State of the Art," *The Accounting Review* (April 1982), pp. 245-271.

Fielder, K., "Causal Schemata: Review and Criticism of Research on a Popular Construct," *Journal of Personality and Social Psychology* (1983), pp. 1001-1013.

Gibbins, M., "Propositions about the Psychology of Professional Judgment in Public Accounting," *Journal of Accounting Research* (in press).

Graesser, A. and G. Nakamura, "The Impact of a Schema on Comprehension and Memory," in *The Psychology of Learning and Motivation,* (1982), pp. 59-109.

Hastie, R., "Schematic Principles in Human Memory," in E. Higgins, P. Herman and M. Zanna (eds.), *Social Cognition* (Erlbaum, 1981), pp. 39-88.

Joyce, E. and R. Libby, "Behavioral Studies of Audit Decision Making," *Journal of Accounting Literature* (Spring 1982), pp. 103-121.

Keynes, J., *A Treatise on Probability* (Macmillan, 1921).

Kinney, W., "A Decision Theory Approach to the Sampling Problem in Auditing," *Journal of Accounting Research* (Spring 1975), pp. 117-132.

Kissinger, J., "A General Theory of Evidence as the Conceptual Foundation in Auditing Theory: Some Comments and Extensions," *The Accounting Review* (April 1977), pp. 322-339.

Klatzky, R., *Human Memory: Structures and Processes* (Freeman, 1980).

Kuipers, B., "A Frame for Frames: Representing Knowledge for Recognition," in D. Bobrow and A. Collins (eds.), *Representation and Understanding: Studies in Cognitive Science* (Academic, 1975), pp. 151-183.

Loftus, E., "Leading Questions and the Eyewitness Report," *Cognitive Psychology* (1975), pp. 560-572.

Loftus, E. and G. Zanni, "Eyewitness Testimony: The Influence of the Wording of a Question," *Journal of Verbal Learning and Learning Behavior* (1975), pp. 585-589.

Mautz, R. and H. Sharaf, *The Philosophy of Auditing* (American Accounting Association, 1961).

Mervis, C. and E. Rosch, "Categorization of Natural Objects," *Annual Review of Psychology* (1981), pp. 89-115.

Minsky, M., "Framework for Representing Knowledge," in P. Winston (ed.), *The Psychology of Computer Vision* (McGraw-Hill, 1975), pp. 211-277.

Neisser, U., *Cognition and Reality* (Freeman, 1976).

Newell, A., "Production Systems: Models of Control Structures," in W. Chase (ed.), *Visual Information Processing* (Academic, 1973), pp. 463-526.

Newell, A. and H. Simon, *Human Problem Solving* (Prentice-Hall, 1972).

Nisbett, R. and L. Ross, *Human Inference: Strategies and Shortcomings of Social Judgment* (Prentice-Hall, 1980).

Norman, D. and D. Bobrow, "On the Role of Active Memory Processes in Perception and Cognition," in C. Cofer (ed.), *The Structure of Human Memory* (Freeman, 1975).

Peterson, C., "Introduction to the Special Issue on Hierarchical Inference," *Organizational Behavior and Human Performance* (1973), pp. 315-317.

Phillips, L., *Bayesian Statistics for Social Scientists* (Nelson, 1973).

Piaget, J., *The Origins of Intelligence in Children* (International Universities Press, 1952).

Popper, K., *Conjectures and Refutations: The Growth of Scientific Knowledge* (Harper Torchbooks, 1965).

Puff, C., "Memory Organization Research and Theory: The State of the Art," in C. Puff (ed.), *Memory Organization and Structure* (Academic, 1979), pp. 3-17.

Raiffa, H., *Decision Analysis: Introductory Lectures on Choices under Uncertainty* (Addison-Wesley, 1968).

Rosch, E., "Classification of Real-World Objects: Origins and Representations in Cognition," in P. Johnson-Laird and P. Wason (eds.), *Thinking: Readings in Cognitive Science* (Cambridge University Press, 1977), pp. 212-222.

Rumelhart, D., "Schemata: The Building Blocks of Cognition," in R. Spiro, B. Bruce and W. Brewer (eds.), *Theoretical Issues in Reading Comprehension* (Erlbaum, 1980), pp. 33-58.

Rumelhart, D. and D. Norman, "Analogical Processes in Learning," in J. Anderson (ed.), *Cognitive Skills and Their Acquisition* (Erlbaum, 1981), pp. 335-359.

Rumelhart, D. and A. Ortony, "The Representation of Knowledge in Memory," in R. Anderson, R. Spiro and W. Montague (eds.), *Schooling and the Acquisition of Knowledge* (1977), pp. 99-134.

Schum, D., "The Behavioral Richness of Cascaded Inference Models: Examples in Jurisprudence," in N. Catellan (ed.), *Cognitive Theory* (Erlbaum, 1977), pp. 149-173.

Shafer, G., *A Mathematical Theory of Evidence* (Princeton University, 1976).

Simon, H., "How Big is a Chunk?," *Science* (1974), pp. 482-488.

Simon, H., "The Information Storage System Called 'Human Memory'," in M. Rosenzweig and E. Bennett (eds.) *Neural Mechanisms of Learning and Memory* (MIT Press, 1976), pp. 79-96.

Simon, H., "Information Processing Models of Cognition," *Annual Review of Psychology* (1979), pp. 363-396.

Taylor, S. and J. Crocker, "Schematic Bases of Social Information Processing," in E. Higgins, P. Herman and M. Zanna (eds.), *Social Cognition* (Erlbaum, 1981), pp. 89-134.

Toba, Y., "A General Theory of Evidence as the Conceptual Foundation in Auditing Theory," *The Accounting Review* (January 1975), pp. 7-24.

Tulving, E., "Episodic and Semantic Memory," in E. Tulving and W. Donaldson (eds.), *Organization of Memory* (Academic, 1972).

Tulving, E., *Elements of Episodic Memory* (Clarendon, 1983).

Tweney, R., M. Doherty, and C. Mynatt, *On Scientific Thinking* (Columbia University Press, 1981).

Waller, W. and W. Felix, "The Auditor and Learning from Experience: Some Conjectures," *Accounting, Organizations and Society* (in press).

Waller, W. and J. Jiambalvo, "The Use of Normative Models in Human Information Processing Research in Accounting," *Journal of Accounting Literature* (in press).

Wickelgren, W., "Human Learning and Memory," *Annual Review of Psychology* (1981), pp. 21-52.

Yates, J. and L. Zukowski, "Characteristics of Ambiguity in Decision Making," *Behavioral Science* (1976), pp. 12-25.

Frances L. Ayres
University of Oklahoma

Discussant's Comments on:

"Cognition and the Auditor's Opinion Formulation Process: A Schematic Model of Interactions Between Memory and Current Audit Evidence"

This paper purports to present a descriptive model of the auditor's opinion formulation process. The authors criticize prior models as "superficial" and in need of more structure and detail in order to support future empirical research. The model utilizes the cognitive psychology construct of schema to describe how auditors process and integrate information.

The basic idea of the model is that auditors use evidence to reduce uncertainty regarding the client's financial statements. They categorize this uncertainty into two types, a first order uncertainty relating to the auditor's belief that the audit contains material error (R), and a second order uncertainty regarding the auditor's belief that the evidence supports the opinion (S).

Auditors are assumed to search for and process information (evidence) using a schematic information processing model described as an interaction between "template schemata," or a framework for organizing facts or knowledge, and "procedural schemata." Procedural schemata are assumed to perform three functions; 1) activate template schemata, 2) control instantiation of template schemata, and 3) test the fit of template schemata to the current situation.

My comments on this paper fall into two general categories. First, I have some comments about the schema construct and its applicability to the auditor's opinion formulation process. Second, I have some comments about the model itself.

THE SCHEMA CONSTRUCT

The schema construct represents an attempt to impose structure on the "black box" of the human mind. A schematic theory of information process suggests that prior knowledge of events or process influences peoples' ability to learn additional information about events and to recall information. Furthermore it assumes that information that is inconsistent with a particular activated schema may either be ignored or altered to suit the schema.

A fair amount of evidence exists which suggests that a schematic process may apply to processing and recall of at least some types of information. For example, Cheisi, Spili and Voss [1979] found that, when presented with narratives about baseball situations, subjects with high knowledge of baseball recalled more of the narrative than low knowledge subjects. On a similar vein, Chase and Simon [1973] found that master chess players remembered a board layout better than novices when the layout was based on actual games. However, when the layout was random, the experts performed no better than the novices.

The various heuristics and biases such as representativeness, anchoring, and conservatism that have been observed in individuals' probability revisions might be viewed as consistent with the schemata construct. These behaviors suggest that individuals tend to place more weight on their initial position than a Bayesian revision process would suggest. One might argue from a schema theory perspective that this occurs because information inconsistent with the initial schema is ignored or altered.

Despite evidence supporting the schema construct, I have some reservations about its usefulness as a model of the auditor's opinion formulation process. I don't think that the schema construct is sufficiently advanced in cognitive psychology to apply it to such a complex area as the audit decision. The authors of this paper note that "the nature of knowledge structures in memory and their functioning in cognition are not yet well understood," yet they attempt to apply an assumed model of these structures to audit opinions.

Two major problems exist with the schema construct as it has been employed in cognitive psychology. First, no clear definition of schema has been agreed upon, and as a result much research involving schemas is difficult to interpret and compare. Support or lack of support for schema theories depends in large part upon the operational definition employed by the researcher. Furthermore, the predictions of schema theory are often contradictory. On one hand, prior knowledge appears to increase recall, and on the other hand schemas may hinder processing of information, either through failure to process information because of its lack of fit to an existing schema, or through confusion of "default" values with outcomes of actual events. Because of these problems, schema theory, in its current form is essentially untestable.

Second, there exist many unanswered questions regarding how schema operate. These questions relate to the process by which schema are activated, how schema interact with each other and how and to what extent schema affect behavior. Virtually all of the research and empirical support for schema theories relates to memory and text comprehension. Schematic models have not been tested to any extent in terms of evaluating interpersonal behavior and judgment. The step from memory recall and recognition to judgments and decision making is a major step that needs to be dealt with at a basic level before we can hope to apply the schemata construct to an area as complex as the auditor's opinion formulation process.

My concern is that the model formulated in this paper may be premature in imposing a structure on the auditors that may not exist. The results of empirical studies which attempt to test the model proposed in this paper must be viewed as simultaneously testing the schema construct. As a result, interpretation of the results may be difficult or impossible. Furthermore, I believe that the auditor's decision process is more complex than schema theory suggests. Alba and Hasher [1983, p. 255], in a review of the schema construct, conclude that, "We think it is clear that the stored record of any event is more detailed than the prototypical schema theories imply."

THE MODEL

The model developed in this paper conceptualizes the audit as an attempt to instantiate a global-template schemata (GTS) by searching for audit evidence up to some optimal point at which $R \leq R^*$, $S \geq S^*$ and $C \leq C^*$. R represents the auditor's belief that the client's statements contain material error. S is the auditor's subjective confidence about R, and C is the cost of audit evidence. I have some problems with the definitions of these variables. First, although R and S are presented as subjective belief functions the authors claim that, "Society rewards the auditor for accurately categorizing firms into those with $R \leq R^*$ and those with $R > R^*$," [Waller and Felix, p. 29]. This seems to suggest that R represents a "true" but perhaps unknown risk and R^* is determined by society.

Second, C is represented as the cost of audit evidence. As defined in the paper, the cost of misclassification seems to be missing from the model. A more complete model would view C as a probabilistic function incorporating costs other than audit evidence along with the auditor's assessment of their probable occurrence. These costs include, but are not limited to, potential legal liability in the event of management fraud or bankruptcy, and the cost of insufficient evidence, even assuming correct classification (e.g. a possible negative peer review). These costs may vary for different clients, and may impact the auditor's assessment of R^* and S^*.

The constraining factor in the model which limits the auditor's search for evidence appears to be C^*. That is, as the model is formulated, if $R > R^*$ or $S > S^*$ the auditor continues to search for evidence until they reach C^*. At this point, the auditor would render a qualified opinion. They argued that in a normal audit MTS the major role of the audit is to gather sufficient evidence that $S \geq S^*$ subject to C^*. What the model fails to address, and this is really the decision making point in the audit, is what factors other than C^* lead the auditor to cease the search for evidence and formulate an opinion. As long as S^* and R^* are achieved prior to reaching C^* this is not a problem (which may be the case for a normal audit). However, in a non-normal audit the auditor cannot achieve R^* or S^*. In this case I would not expect that the auditor would continue to search for supporting evidence until the cost constraint was met. What is needed is some factor in the model which could serve as a "critical point" in the audit leading the auditor to change from a strategy of searching for evidence to increase R and S to one designed to support an alternate conclusion, such as a qualified opinion.

This brings me to my final point regarding the model. The authors postulate that the auditor's model incorporates several macro-template-schemata, including one for a normal audit. The problem with this is that the model allows for activation of only one schema (initially that of a normal audit in most cases), hence it does not allow the auditor to simultaneously consider the normal and abnormal cases. This seems to me an oversimplification. In addition it assumes the auditor is not really interested in forming an opinion, but rather with verifying what is already known (or assumed). I would find more credible a concept that the auditor has basically one GTS for an audit and that values assigned to various nodes as the audit progressed would lead the auditor to determine whether the audit was normal or non-normal.

In conclusion, while this paper considers important issues and the authors are to be credited for attempting to model inside the "black box," I think that more work needs to be done in order to adequately describe the auditor's opinion formulation process. First, I don't think that the schemata construct is sufficiently developed to apply to a decision as complex as the auditor's opinion formulation process. If the construct is to be used, more work is needed at a basic level to determine to what extent knowledge is imbedded in schematic form and how schema affect behavior and judgment. Second, the decision variables in the model need to be clarified and expanded to include a more complete definition of the audit cost function.

REFERENCES

Alba, J. and L. Hasher, "Is Memory Schematic?" *Psychological Bulletin* (1983), pp. 203-231.

Chase, W.G. and H.A. Simon, "Perception in Chess," *Cognitive Psychology* (1973), pp. 55-81.

Chiesi, H.L., G.J. Spilich, and J.F. Voss, "Acquisition of Domain-Related Information in Relation to High and Low Domain Knowledge," *Journal of Verbal Learning and Verbal Behavior* (1979), pp. 257-274.

Fiske, S.T. and P. Linville, "What Does the Schema Concept Buy Us?," *Personality and Social Psychology* (December 1980), pp. 543-557.

Slovic, P. and S. Lichtenstein, "Comparison of Bayesian and Regression Approaches to Study of Information Processing in Judgement," *Organizational Behavior and Human Performance* (1971), pp. 649-744.

Waller, W.S. and W.L. Felix, Jr., "Cognition and the Auditor's Opinion Formulation Process: A Schematic Model of Interactions Between Memory and Current Audit Evidence," in S. Moriarity and E. Joyce (Eds.), *Decision Making and Accounting: Current Research,* (University of Oklahoma, Center for Economic and Management Research, 1984, pp. 27-48.

Robert Libby
University of Michigan

Discussant's Comments on:

"Cognition and the Auditor's Opinion Formulation Process: A Schematic Model of Interactions Between Memory and Current Audit Evidence"

First, I would like to commend the authors for choosing to write about the interaction between the auditor's memory store and current audit evidence. Except for Ron Weber's innovating [1980] *JAR* paper and the discussion in Chapter Four of my book, this important topic has been missing from the behavioral decision making literature in accounting. For me, this was the most interesting part of my book to write. Further, in doing so, I became convinced that, because of recent developments in accounting, cognitive psychology, and computers, we are in a unique position to make important theoretical and practical contributions in this area.

Some of you may not be as convinced as I of this point. Why should we study auditors' knowledge structures? I believe that the answer to this question is fairly straightforward. It is highly likely that accountants are paid, not only for their judgmental abilities, but for the task specific knowledge that they bring to the audit. In the past, we have examined the auditor's judgmental ability in the hope of developing aids to help overcome any discovered limitations. In the same fashion, if we better understand the manner in which audit knowledge is acquired, stored, and retrieved, we may be able to develop learning and decision aids to help the novice perform more like the expert—and possibly even to aid the expert. How can we approach these issues in our research? Just as we have done in our examinations of cognitive limitations, we must study what people in general learn and how they employ this knowledge, and then we can count on accountants to exhibit most of the same strengths and weaknesses as learners and retrievers of knowledge as the general population. We then must examine the unique aspects of the auditing domain to complete the picture. This is the general approach that Waller and Felix have taken in this paper.

The paper has two distinct parts: the second order probability model and the schematic memory model of the audit process. Since these two components are not particularly well integrated (e.g., there is no indication of how the posited memory structure results in the second order probability model), I feel that I can discuss them separately with no loss of coherence.

Second Order Probability Model

I would like to address the second order probability model first. This model is based upon Ellsberg's [1961] interesting observation that, contrary to the laws of probability, two formally equivalent probability distributions may be judged to be different. The cause of this paradox has been labeled ambiguity. The important question to address here is whether the concept of ambiguity has anything to contribute to a descriptive model of auditing. I believe that the answer to this question is yes and that this may be the most useful insight in the paper. The authors define the second order probability as the degree of support for a risk estimate. They then suggest that the usefulness of a probability depends on the information on which the estimate is based, as well as its numerical value. The original idea and experimental findings from which the notion of a second order probability was derived really only point out that uniform distributions are not cognitively well-behaved. This observation is not directly relevant to the audit situation. However, later interpretations of ambiguity are particularly useful here. Roberts [1963] suggests that we avoid ambiguity to avoid being second quessed. Toda and Shufford [1965] similarly suggest that we avoid ambiguity to avoid embarrassment and to justify our beliefs. These interpretations relate directly to the auditor's problem. *Generally Accepted Auditing Standards* provide a criterion for the evaluation of audit decisions based on the *justifiability* of our beliefs as opposed to their accuracy.

This is an important insight. However, it is appropriate here to ask whether you need the complexity of a second order probability model to include this insight into the audit model. Remember that if you accept the existence of second order probabilities, you must discard the whole of probability calculus for which we have no good replacement. Luckily, it is not necessary that we accept the second order probability model to include this insight into our model. The problem with the traditional audit risk model (e.g., SAS 39) is that we have been dealing with the wrong first order probability. Consider the following problem that the traditional model has trouble with. Suppose that I am the partner in charge of the IBM audit. My assessment of inherent risk is so low to start with that, without conducting any analytical review, tests of internal control, or substantive tests, my assessment of audit risk is *below* the threshold necessary for the issuance of a clean opinion. Accordingly, I should conduct no audit procedures. But will I choose this plan of action? Of course not. Why? Because if an error does come to light, after the fact, my peers and the judge will estimate the ex ante probability of error as having been *above* the criterion for a clean opinion. Put another way, I would not be able to *justify* my belief and avoid being *second guessed.* This problem is obviously related to hindsight bias. What audit strategy will I pursue? I will audit until my assessment of the probability of being judged to have been reasonable in issuing a clean opinion meets a criterion value ($R \geqslant R^*$ where $R = p(\text{judged reasonable/opinion, circumstances})$. This formulation appears to include the notion of ambiguity without the requirements of a second order probability model.

Schematic Memory Model

The second part of the paper presents a schematic memory model of the audit opinion formation process. At the beginning of the paper, the authors suggest that prior descriptions of the process have been superficial and need more structure and detail. They go on to suggest that they have chosen the route of being "explicit but probably wrong" to have the potential for supporting future empirical research. This is a fairly bold statement given the difficulty of the task that they have set out for themselves. The tone of these comments suggests that the authors are concerned with Fiedler's [1983] four criteria for using the schema construct experimentally:

(1) Testability—the schema must imply hypotheses that can be falsified empirically;
(2) Schema stimulus contrast—the implications of the schema must be different than the normative implications of the stimulus alone;
(3) Schema variation—the schema must be different if the individual's experiences or the context differ;
(4) Convergence—the schema must have more than one testable property.

Meeting these criteria are doubly important in an applied discipline to avoid accusations from practitioners that we are just applying new jargon to old ideas.

In evaluating the Waller and Felix model, I attempted to identify the basic organizing principles and then to evaluate the importance of their testable implications to auditing. In general terms, the authors suggest that an auditor first recognizes a pattern of client cues and classifies the pattern into one of a very small number of categories. Associated with each category is a macro-template-schema which has associated with it a number of narrower template schemata and associated procedural schemata, each which has nodes and relations. So the auditor approaches his client with a hierarchy of schemata. Eliminating the new terminology, this suggests that the auditor approaches a client with knowledge of the important attributes of audit clients and ways of gathering evidence to determine the values of these attributes and that this knowledge is organized in an unspecified hierarchical fashion. What does this description imply in terms of empirically observable behavior? Beyond a gross difference between an ignorant and an educated person's approach to an audit, I am not sure what this suggests. Even the implications of having two types of sub-schemata, template and procedural, are beyond me. It would appear that if we could develop the same predictions from a model with only a single type of sub-schema, we would prefer such a model based on its parsimony.

Next, I will turn to some of the more specific ideas in the model. The discussion of hypothesis testing strategies is particularly interesting. The ability to differentiate hypothesis testing strategies used at three different stages of the audit could be extremely important. First, it would provide direct evidence of the need for a complex multistep model such as the one suggested by the authors. Further, it would ease the identification of potential biases in the process. All we need now are more specifics on how we might observe these different stages. I suggest that the authors not rely too heavily on the idea of a confirmation bias which has gained some popularity in the psychology literature. Unfortunately, at this point, it is not sufficiently well developed to provide much guidance. The principal problem lies in the fact, that, ex ante, only the choice of nondiagnostic information will assure consistency with the favored hypothesis. Some other idea will be needed to provide a framework for the differentiation of search strategies.

The authors also suggest that after the decision to audit is made, R does not change, but S does. This implies that auditors probably use different information aggregation rules at different points in the audit. Such differences could be important and may be observable.

However, other implications of the model seem less important. For example, it is suggested that gaining an understanding of the client involves "instantiation of template-schemata." All this tells me is that auditors know what they are looking for and do not gather information randomly. It is also hypothesized that auditors have models of how activities map to accounting numbers. I surely hope that this is the case as I spend many of my waking hours trying to teach this mapping to students. We are told nothing about the specifics of these models, how they develop over time, or how they follow from earlier characteristics of the model. Auditors are also suggested to use standard lists. The observation of the existence of standard audit programs supports this conclusion. However, Bouwman's [1980] innovative paper demonstrating their existence in another accounting setting is not referenced. Finally, it is indicated that how the auditor updates an opinion is an important question. It is unfortunate that concepts in the paper such as global-template-schemata do not enlighten us on this issue.

In summary, I believe that the memory model presents a number of interesting ideas, combined with a number of gratuitous comments. The primary problem lies in the fact that few of these ideas follow directly from the organizing principles of the model. It clearly lacks coherence and parsimony. Further, it does not meet the authors' own impossibly high goal for precision. It is also worth noting that the paper fails to mention existing *empirical* studies in accounting that attempt to meet Feidler's criteria, in particular, Bouwman [1980] and Weber [1980]. These papers have attempted to specify *and* demonstrate some basic organizing principles of memory.

RECOMMENDATIONS

I would like to end my discussion by making some recommendations to those who wish to investigate this important area. My first is to take a look at a small part of the problem. Even the most brilliant psychologists have not been able to develop an integrated model of these processes in a context this complex. By studying some of the unique aspects of the audit judgment process that Waller and Felix have brought to our attention, we may be able to instantiate parts of existing models or modify or extend them. Any *one* of Waller and Felix's important ideas, if properly developed, could provide an important contribution. However, the level of precision necessary to provide guidance for experimental work is impossible at this level of generality—though it is a fun exercise. Also, I suggest that the authors and others conduct experimental tests of their ideas. If you know in advance that you are going to run your ideas up against some data, it disciplines your reasoning. Finally, I suggest that we abstain from adding dramatically to our storehouse of jargon—and this applies particularly to the double-hyphenated-class.

REFERENCES

Bouwman, M.J., "The Use of Accounting Information: Expert Versus Novice Behavior," unpublished manuscript, University of Oregon (April 1980).

Ellsberg, D., " Risk, Ambiguity and the Savage Axioms," *Quarterly Journal of Economics* (1961), pp. 643-666.

Friedler, K., "Causal Schemata: Review and Criticism of a Popular Construct, *Journal of Personality and Social Psychology* (1983), pp. 1001-1013.

Roberts, H.V., " Risk, Ambiguity, and the Savage Axioms: Comment," *Quarterly Journal of Economics* (1963), pp. 327-336.

Toda, M. and E.H. Shuford, Jr., "Utility, Induced Utilities, and Small Worlds," *Behavioral Science* (1965), pp. 238-253.

Weber, R., "Some Characteristics of the Free Recall of Computer Controls by EDP Auditors," *Journal of Accounting Research* (1980), pp. 214-241.

Theodore J. Mock
University of Southern California
Miklos A. Vasarhelyi
Columbia University

Context, Findings, and Method in Cognitive Style Research: A Comparative Study

Research on human information processing in accounting has reached significant levels within the past several years. For example, the American Accounting Association [AAA, 1978] and Libby and Lewis [1977] surveyed the extant literature, and found substantial number of studies in this area. In addition, Libby [1981] links the area to the general category of behavioral decision making and quotes Slovic, Fischhoff, and Lichtenstein [1977] as having discovered more than 1,000 behavioral decision making articles which were published between 1971 and 1975.

The American Accounting Association [AAA, 1978] classified human information processing research approaches used by accountants into four major categories: (1) the Bayesian Approach, (2) the Lens Model Approach, (3) the Cognitive Complexity/Cognitive Style Approach and (4) the Process Tracing Approach.

A second set of literature surveys published in 1981 and 1982 [Ashton, 1982; Libby, 1981; Libby and Lewis, 1982] further examined this literature and also observed substantial growth. But these recent surveys tend to discount the value of cognitive style/cognitive complexity (CS) research. For example, Ashton [1982, pg. 8-9] argues that CS research "...has been criticized on several grounds, including the nature, measurement, and generality of the underlying constructs, the frequent failure to establish a link between the variables studied and measures of decision performance, and the absence of adequate criteria for evaluating decision quality." Ashton proceeds by quoting McGhee, Shields and Birnberg [1978] stating that "...personality variables do not appear to be useful in describing, understanding, or predicting human information processing."

Libby and Lewis [1982, pg. 272-273] treat the area somewhat more kindly:

> It would appear that the difficulties faced in the search for a direct link between personality or cognitive structure and decision behavior are more a reflection of the complexity of the relationships involved than a depreciation of prior research. ...recent applied research has demonstrated the need to search for more basic principles related to higher order mental processes

such as research into the role of problem representation in learning and judgment e.g. [Tversky & Kahneman, 1980 and Einhorn & Hogarth, 1981].

This shift in focus and the suggested research emphasis is questioned in this paper, which reviews several experiments conducted in the 1968-1982 period. Each study analyzed dealt, to some extent, with cognitive style and decision making within simulated decision contexts.

More specifically, this paper summarizes a series of related experimental studies into information value and cognitive style. First, some previous studies are summarized, then a model that contains several key experimental variables is briefly developed. Subsequently, some new empirical results are presented. These results reflect the more complex, cross-contextual, analytic approach of two of these experiments which deal with alternative information structures and cognitive styles. The emphasis of this discussion will be on the three points raised by Ashton [1982] and a fourth additional one: Construct, performance measurement (diagnosticity), and decision quality and context.

PREVIOUS RESEARCH

In previous studies of accounting information, many methodological approaches and problems have been delineated. Subsequent discussion will detail some of the significant studies in this area. Particularly useful criticism of the cognitive style approach is found in AAA [1978] and Libby and Lewis [1982].

Within the realm of cognitive style, overviews are found for decision style and human information processing (HIP) in Driver and Mock [1975] and Lusk [1979]; for decision approach in Mock, Estrin and Vasarhelyi [1972] and Vasarhelyi [1977]; and for judgment in Ashton [1974a, b], Magee and Dickaut [1978], and Biddle and Joyce [1978]. The experiment examined in this paper considers a number a variables that are mentioned by Birnberg [1975]. Specifically, the interpersonal differences that are related to the degree of abstraction are contained in two cognitive style classifications (decision style and decision approach). These behavioral factors are evaluated with respect to information structure variables that are experimentally controlled.

Some of the relations among these variables are presented in Figure 1, which is designed from an information systems perspective. In the figure, cues are considered to be those characteristics controllable by the accountant. Research into both cognitive models and behavioral factors is justified if it demonstrates that models of human information processing can be used to improve information system design.

Figure 1 includes a number of behavioral factors that have been shown to have a significant effect on information processing. For example, the literature in cognitive studies and artificial intelligence indicates different behavioral constraints including serial processing, limited short term memory, overload, processing constraints [i.e., Miller, 1956], and Weber's law of just noticeable differences. Research in psychology has identified a number of related behavioral factors such as anchoring, the representativeness heuristic, inconsistency and leveling [see Slovic, 1972].

FIGURE 1

Model of Information Human Information Processing and Behavioral Factors

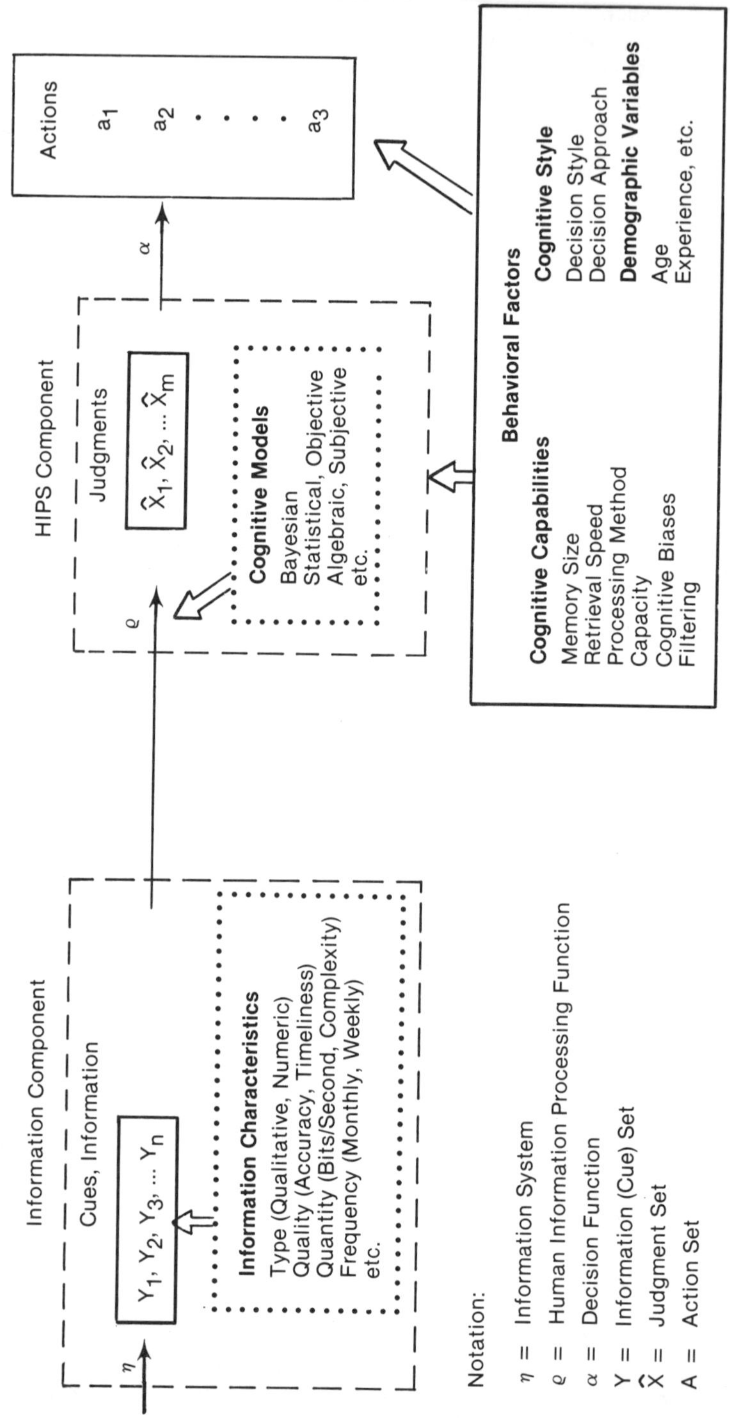

Other studies have suggested ways of dealing with some of these variables. For example, Birnberg [1975] notes that many techniques have been developed in accounting, mostly through trial and error, for coping with information overload. Among these are techniques of aggregation, precalculation, and unfolding of the data via a general description, followed by a graphic display, then aggregate financial statistics and so on [see Casey, 1981].

A number of accounting studies have experimentally investigated the relationships between information variables, behavioral factors and performance. For example, Casey [1981] examined bank loan officers' bankruptcy predictions and found no improvement in predictive ability and a substantial increase in decision time when a financial footnote was added to the available information. Chervany and Dickson [1974] tried to measure overload situations experimentally by comparing two groups of students, one given statistically summarized data and the other raw data. In addition to this overload factor, concepts such as filtering of information, quantity of information, type of information, and aggregation of information have been noted in the literature as being important HIP factors. Other variables, such as experience, time pressure, effort, and motivation are also pertinent.

Let us first address the issues raised by Ashton and an additional one (context) which is of equal importance as shown in the literature in other areas [Wright, 1975].

Construct

Ashton's first question concerns the nature, and thus the validity of the underlying constructs of CS research. This question can be examined in terms of a framework designed to aid in the prediction of a particular behavior or to segregate individuals with similar traits. If this CS construct has discriminating ability (e.g. predictive validity), it can help in the understanding of human decision processes by providing a means for clustering different decision approaches.

Diagnosticity

Ashton's second concern has been referred to in the literature as diagnosticity, which relates to the linkage of the decision variables and performance. Most decision analysis contexts should specify: (1) States of the world, (2) Information, (3) Judgments, (4) Actions, and (5) Outcomes [Mock and Vasarhelyi, 1978]. However, in the social sciences the observed relationships between information (a soft and often public good) and outcomes are often statistically weak and interdependent. For example, accounting information and bankruptcy prediction, gathered audit evidence and audit opinion, and accounting information and security prices are all linked by solid logical reasoning but weak empirical relationships. These statistical findings are further confounded by the nature of the measurement used to capture the information and the choice and quality of outcome measurement. Additionally, the linkages between judgments and actions are poorly specified and entail further study. Finally, management actions have a stochastic relationship with outcomes. The chaining of a series of stochastic relationships from the states of the world to final outcomes results in weak statistical linkages.

At this stage of basic research, the intermediate steps (1) between the states of the world (X) and the information set (Y), (2) the information set and judgments (X), (3) judgments and actions (A), as well as (4) actions to the set of multiattribute outcomes (O) are tenuous. Therefore, in testing for categories of individuals (C_1, C_2, $\in$ C) where each C_1, C_2 etc. refers to a discrete decision style that would lead to different sets of outcomes, we have a comparison:

$$o_1 = f(x, \hat{x}_1, y_1) \text{ for sub-population } c_1$$

and

$$o_2 = f(x, \hat{x}_2, y_2) \text{ for sub-population } c_2$$

where c_1 and $c_2 \in c$.

In addition to the measurement problems regarding the relationships of 0, Y, $\hat{X}$ and X, there are inherent psychometric limitations in discriminating among the measures of cognitive style.

Decision Quality

Ashton's third concern is with the difficulties inherent in the measurement of decision quality. Business decisions and outcomes are often multiple objective, multi-attribute phenomena and yet they tend to be evaluated on one dimension with a limited set of states of nature. For example, bankruptcy tends to be judged via the filing or not filing for Chapter 11 status; audit judgment by the issuance of a clean versus a qualified opinion; and, stock selection through limited period portfolio gains and losses. These simplifications lead to a substantial weakening of the relationships between 0 and the multi-attribute state-of-the-world $x_{i,j,t}$ (the states of the world for attribute i, in relation to objective j in period t).

Context

Basic research into the natural and physical sciences can take decades to be incorporated into everyday life. The questions concerning generalizability, then, are perhaps misleading, and more probably premature, as basic research into human information processing cannot be expected to immediately be applicable to a wide set of problems. Unlike the physical sciences, the social sciences are confronted with a large set of confounding variables.

There are still very complex issues concerning measurement and context validation that have not been addressed. Of particular concern is the measurement of cognitive style which has been commonly addressed by tools from psychology that were developed mostly with general human behavior predictors and classification in mind. It is likely that measurement could be substantially improved with psychometric—based, but information evaluation—oriented, classifications.

Marketing studies [Wright, 1975] have indicated that buyer behavior, for example, will be substantially affected by the marketing problem being considered. This same effect is probable in accounting settings. For example, it is likely that different information structures will prevail in stock purchase decision than in budget variance evaluation decision. Therefore, basic cross-contextual research in this area may help capture the most common effects and control for context-dependent phenomena.

In summary, the four above issues do not negate the value of cognitive style research but instead serve to attenuate researcher explanations concerning explanatory levels that can be attained. In addition, these four issues suggest a cross-contextual approach for research design and data analyses. These topics will be further discussed in the remainder of this paper vis-a-vis a series of experimental results.

The experimental research reported in the following sections is directed at the measurement and evaluation of some of these variables and the interdependence between information system design and behavioral factors. While much research has been conducted on these topics, further comments in this paper will be restricted to our own experimental studies. First, a summary of previous studies will be discussed, followed by a presentation of the results of our most recent experiments.

SELECTED STUDIES AND FINDINGS

An overview of previous studies is presented in this section to facilitate an understanding of the longitudinal aspects of the research, to help demonstrate some of the methodological difficulties and enhancements that have occurred, and most importantly, to present some new interpretations of previous results from the standpoint of human information processing. Within the span of the research, four major types of experimental settings (decision contexts) have been used. In each case, a business or economic decision model has been incorporated within a controlled experiment. Table 1 summarizes the methodological differences within each decision context.

The Experimental Settings

Four versions of the Information Structure experiments (denoted IS1, IS2,...) have previously been conducted. The IS setting is unique in its emphasis on controlled information differences and their underlying structure. Complete description and documentation for these experiments can be found in Mock [1969] and Mock and Goodfried [1975].

The second decision setting involves a more intricate forecasting problem and a more complex information and decision support system denoted as the Interactive Planning System (IPS). Rather than researching specific information differences, the IPS experiments emphasize the combined effects of cognitive style (specifically analytic versus heuristic *decision approaches*) and the type and amount of information utilized. A more complete description of IPS may be found in Vasarhelyi [1973].

The third decision context utilizes a Simulated Stock Exchange (SX) run under three specifications (SX1, SX2 and SX3). The cross-contextual research results reported in the following section involve IS4 and SX1. Like the IPS methodology, the stock market simulation emphasizes information utilization and cognitive style differences. But unlike IPS, normative decision models such as portfolio models can be referenced to evaluate performance differences.

The fourth decision context utilizes the Accounting Data Analyzer (ADA). ADA requires that an interactive portfolio choice decision be made using a three stock context. This version of a stock market setting (where a maximum exists) is highly structured and monitorable. Automatic traces of information accessed and information regarding the duration of utilization are gathered, allowing for a simplified version of process tracing. The ADA experiments, unlike their precedents, use a cognitive style and information structure matching design whereby subjects are given cognitive style tailored information systems. These "tailored" systems supply users with their "preferred" levels of data aggregation and information type. Subjects are also given, on a random basis, "counter-prescriptive" systems that are tailored to the preferences of the opposing cognitive style.

Each experiment in Table 1 has dealt in some way with cognitive style. The distinction between decision approach[1] (analytic versus heuristic) and decision style[2] (decisive, flexible, hierarchic, and integrative) lies in the complexity of the underlying behavioral models. Part of the current research involves an evaluation of various cognitive style models and measurement tools.

Summary of Previous Findings

Table 2 provides a summary of the major findings of each of the previous experiments. The results are classified according to the cognitive style variables analyzed in the study. The blanks in the table indicate that the variables in question were not evaluated in the particular experiment.

Three overall results are of interest. First, significant information structure effects have been observed in every applicable case. Of particular interest with respect to information structure effects is the interaction between information structure and decision style observed in IS3 [see Driver & Mock (1975)]. Herein lies some of the first experimental support of the impact of tailored information systems. These findings were pursued in the ADA experiments via the cognitive style tailoring of the information systems.

The second area worthy of attention concerns the results that have been obtained with respect to cognitive style. Neither the decision approach dichotomy nor the decision style model have led to consistent, unambiguous results. In many cases, the overall variance is not explained to a significant degree. However, there are some encouraging results, such as the tendency for the decision approach dichotomy to predict type of information utilized, and the general discriminatory ability of the decision approach construct with respect to decision time, learning pattern and information comfort.

The third main observation regarding HIP research concerns information processing results obtained in IS1 and IS2. In this particular decision setting, normative information-decision rules were derived and a weak, but statistically significant, relationship between decisions and available cues

TABLE 1

Classification of Experimental Settings (Decision Contexts) For the Accounting Simulation Experiments

	Methodological Differences			
Experiment Name	Decision Setting and Rule (α)	Information System (η)	Information Utilization (ρ)	Behavioral Factors (B)
Information Structure (IS) Experiments	Highly Structured Micro-economic Game, Optimizable	Controlled Differences (Timel ness, Coarse-ness, Completeness)	Specific Informa-tion Processing Rules Tested	Decision Approach, Decision Style
Interactive Planning System (IPS)	Unstructured Financial Planning Case, Not Optimizable	Single Structured Planning System	Measures of Type, Amount of Informa-tion Used	Decision Approach
Simulated Stock Exchange (SX) Experiments	Capital Stock Market, Theoretical Decision Models (i.e. Portfolio Theory)	Not Controlled	Measures of Type, Amount of Informa-tion Used	Decision Approach, Decision Style
Accounting Data Analyzer (ADA)	Structured Stock Selection Setting, Optimum Available	Prescriptive, Counter-Prescrip. or Neutral	Information Usage Training, Times and Decisions	Decision Approach

was observed. Actually, these relations are composite information processing and decision functions. The important differences between this approach and the Lens model approach [e.g., Ashton (1974c)] should be apparent. In most research utilizing the Lens model, a hypothetical or normative relation between cues and decisions or judgments is not derived. Thus ANOVA and correlational models are used to estimate, but not test, precise theoretical relations. In contrast, in more structured decision situations, such as IS and SX, normative decision theory can be used to postulate information processing and decision functions, and to test the various HIPS models.

The previous experiments have generated some evidence on the relationship between information utilization and cognitive style. For example, the IPS results indicated significant cognitive style related differences in the amount of information utilized. Also, when cognitive style was classified in terms of decision style, significant differences in decision times were observed in IS3. This was taken as being indicative of differences in the amount of information processed.

TABLE 2

Summary of Prior Research

	EXPERIMENTS			
Experimental Variables	IS1 Mock 1969	IS1a Mock et al 1972	IS2 Mock 1973	IPS Vasarhelyi 1973
Cognitive Style—Decision Approach	—	First Study Using Decision Approach	—	Significant Differences in Information Utilization (Quantity)
Cognitive Style—Decision Style	—	—	—	—
Result	Optimal Information Processing Rules Significant	Performance Learning and Decision Approach Effects	Optimal Information Processing Rules Not Significant	Miller's Hypothesis Supported
Primary Focus of Experiment and/or Analysis	Methodology, Value of Timely Information	Effect of Decision Approach	Value of Budget Information	Tailored Decision Support System, Information Utilization

TABLE 2 (continued)

	EXPERIMENTS			
Experimental Variables	IS3 Driver & Mock 1975	SX1 and IS4 1976	SX2 and SX3 1979-80	ADA 1981
Cognitive Style—Decision Approach	—	Significant (Pre-Test) Differences Information Type and Quantity Preferences	Regression Modeling of Decisions Made Across Cognitive Style	Differences in Information Preferences - Aggregation - Type Style
Cognitive Style—Decision Style	Significant Decision Speed Effects	Significant (Pre-Test) Differences Information Type and Quantity Preferences	Significant Pre-Post Attitude Change	—
Result	—	Optimal Information Processing Rules Significant but Individual Differences Dominant	Relationships Between Decision Approach and Decision Style	—
Primary Focus of Experiment and/or Analysis	Decision Style Theory Tailored Accounting Feedback	Cross-Contextual Methodology, Cognitive Style, Information Value	Cognitive Style Information Utilization	Cognitive Style Tailoring of Information Systems

Overall, the previous experiments have provided some tentative results for researchers interested in information structure and human information processing analysis. Although these results are derived from three different settings, no particular variable has been evaluated in an ex ante, multiple setting (cross-contextual) design. The results reported in the next section do take advantage of an ex ante, cross-contextual design for both cognitive style/performance and cognitive style/information perception analyses. By presenting identical subjects with different tasks, the generality of any findings should be enhanced. This type of research approach may be viewed as addressing some of the context and generalizability issues raised earlier.

A CROSS-CONTEXTUAL ANALYSIS

Experimental Setting and Method

This section describes the results of two experiments (IS4 and SX1), as analyzed under a cross-contextual framework. The two settings encompass a micro-economic and a stock market game (see Table 1). These contexts provide measures of subjects' performance and their attitudes toward the type and quantity of information available during the experiment. Two independent variables are analyzed: type of information provided (information structure) and cognitive style. The discussion begins with a description of the experiments. Specific hypotheses and their underlying justifications are incorporated within the presentation of results.

The IS4 experiments used a population of 130 graduate business students and a 2 by 2 factorial design. The IS4 setting involves a multiple-decision, multiple equation game. Subjects are asked to read a case and make decisions concerning advertising, quantity to be produced and materials input used. Additionally, subjects are asked to prepare a budget for each decision period. These decisions are then entered into the model through a computer terminal, with subjects receiving different modes of feedback for that period. Following this feedback, they make their next decision. This cycle is repeated several times before the completion of the experiment (three hours or ten decision periods). The controlled or experimental variables in this factorial design are the *coarseness* of the feedback information and the *completeness* of budget variance information.

The SX1 experiments are based on a hybrid stock market game. The simulation used current stock market prices of 50 New York Stock Exchange (NYSE) stocks that could be traded by subjects. A detailed description of the setting may be found in Vasarhelyi et al. [1981].

Ninety-seven of the 130 MBA students who had completed IS4 participated in the SX1 experiment. All transactions were monitored by means of a transaction form. Biographical data and pre-test and post-test attitudes concerning the stock market and information utilization were obtained through questionnaires. A computer system kept track of portfolio situations and issued bi-weekly reports.

For both experimental contexts, cognitive styles were measured by means of the self-evaluation questionnaire [decision approach, Vasarhelyi, 1977] and the IST test [decision style, Driver and Mock, 1975]. One of the initial concerns was whether these two tests were measuring independent or interdependent classifications of cognitive style. As the definitions of analytics and hierarchics are quite similar [see Mock et al., 1972 and Driver and Mock, 1975], a significant correlation among the classifications was hypothesized. In order to examine these effects a 2 x 5 factorial design was used for analysis. Table 3 classifies the subjects who took both the self-evaluation questionnaire and the IST test into the cognitive taxonomies. These data indicate a weak but definite relationship (α = .076) between the two taxonomies. In the analysis, hierarchics tended to be classified as analytics and integratives as heuristics. As these results are consistent with the construct definitions of each classification, a degree of construct validity was provided here.

TABLE 3

Classification of Subjects By Decision Approach and Style (Frequency and Percentage)

Decision Approach	Decision Style D	F	H	I	C
Analytic	8 8.3%	12 12.5%	10 10.4%	6 6.3%	10 10.4%
Heuristic	15 15.6%	10 10.4%	4 4.2%	14 14.6%	7 7.3%

Statistics

Chi Square = 8.46

Significance = 0.076

Uncertainty Coefficient = 0.07 (with D/A dependent)
= 0.03 (with D/S dependent)

Notation

D = Decision
F = Flexible
H = Hierarchic
I – Integrative
C = Complex
D/A = Decision Approach
D/S = Decision Style

Cognitive Style Effects

One of the three basic areas researched in these experiments concerns cognitive style effects (see Figure 1). The primary interest in these effects stems from the implication of a potential for tailoring accounting systems, and other aspects of decision making, to the cognitive style of the decision maker. Our initial analyses considered the relationship between decision style (D/S), decision approach (D/A), and the subjects' performance within each experiment. This was designed to answer questions such as: "Is cognitive style a determinant of performance?" The analysis then continued to seek information concerning the subjects' perceptions of the type and availability of information.

Table 4 summarizes some of the cognitive style analyses that were performed. Both models of cognitive style were analyzed. The *Decision Approach* partitioned subjects into analytics (A) or heuristics (H), while the *Decision Style* theory used the decisive (D), flexible (F), hierarchic (H), integrative (I), and complex (C) decision styles.

The analysis in Table 4 shows the effect of cognitive style on performance, type of information preferred, and perceptions concerning quantity of information. The measurement instruments used for decision style and decision approach, their validity and reliability have been discussed in the references cited earlier. However, the consistency and predictive ability of such instruments remains a concern. As cognitive style was determined in an ex post facto manner (subjects were placed in an experimental setting and later tested on their cognitive style), the resulting design was a factorial analysis with unequal cell frequencies (see Table 4).

TABLE 4
One Way Analysis of Cognitive Style Effects

Performance		Decision Approach A (56)	H (51)	F-Value	Decision Style D (22)	F (22)	H (16)	I (25)	C (17)	F-Value
IS4: Profits (in thousands)		102.4	109.7	n.s.	111.0	98.9	113.1	101.0	104.0	n.s.
SX1: ROI (% of Investment)		6.4	4.8	n.s.	5.5	6.9	7.4	5.9	5.6	n.s.
Information Perceptions										
Preference for Quantitative	PRE	45.7	36.3	2.8	47.9	45.7	32.7	29.2	44.4	1.86
Data 1) (SX1)	POST	44.8	38.5	n.s.	41.8	45.9	34.5	36.6	45.6	n.s.
Preference for Qualitative	PRE	37.3	46.9	3.1	40.2	24.2	45.9	50.7	46.2	2.2
Data 1) (SX1)	POST	43.8	52.7	2.4	47.9	48.2	52.7	54.6	45.3	n.s.
Information Sufficiency 2)	PRE	3.84	4.08	n.s.	4.1	4.4	3.4	3.8	3.9	n.s.
(SX1)	POST	4.43	4.23	n.s.	4.0	4.9	4.6	3.6	4.5	3.2
Information Quantity 3)	PRE	4.11	3.45	5.6	3.5	3.9	4.7	3.5	3.5	2.1
(IS4)	POST	4.33	4.00	n.s.	3.6	4.7	4.5	4.2	4.2	2.1

1) What type of information did you use in making your trading decisions (in relative percentages)?
Quantitative? Qualitative? Other (specify)?

2) Do you feel you had enough data to make your decisions? (Too little = 1, Too much = 7)

3) Please rate the absolute amount of information in the experiment. (Very little = 1, Very much = 7).

Performance Effects

Both simulations used aggregate performance measures. For the IS4 experiments, average period profit was used. In SX1, performance (ROI) was computed as a function of stock portfolio value change, dividends received and interest earned by the investment of unused cash balances in government securities.

A priori, differences in cognitive style were not expected to result in performance differences. This should hold true for either task, especially under the stock market scenario used.

> H1: Differences in cognitive style are not expected to result in significant performance differences in either decision task.

This hypothesis was tested using a one-way ANOVA for each cognitive style and decision approach. The results show that in neither case was cognitive style a discriminating factor vis-a-vis subject performance. Although the overall averages are not significant, a comparison of these results with previous versions of IS is of some interest. In fact, many of the results for both D/A and D/S are contrary to previous findings. For example, while analytics outperformed heuristics in IS1, IS4 shows the opposite tendency. Also note that the decisives performed well in IS4 whereas the overall profit performance was by far the worst in IS3.

Note also that the IS4 and SX1 contexts show similar results, giving more credibility to the experimental findings; therefore, cross-contextual designs may serve to better assess relationships that are theoretically expected to be difficult to measure.

Self Perception of Type and Quality of Information Used

> H2: There will be significant differences in the type of information being used by individuals with different cognitive styles.
>
> H3: Cognitive style differences lead to different perceptions of the need for and usage of information.

These hypotheses are based on the findings by previous studies such as Vasarhelyi [1977], and the theoretical specification used regarding the nature of individuals with different decision styles. The cognitive style framework [see Driver and Mock, 1975] uses as one dimension of its classification grid the variable quantity of information used for decisions.

Information was divided into two major types: quantitative and qualitative. Analytics are expected to focus on quantitative information while heuristics are expected to focus on qualitative. Vasarhelyi [1977], using a planning framework, tested for information type. In this paper we examine information type in both the IS and the SX settings.

Quantity of information is an extensively explored topic. It is connected to issues such as content of information and information overload [Chervany and Dickson, 1974; Dickson, et al., 1977]. The attempts to relate information quantity to cognitive style is a natural extension of these studies. Conclusive results in this area can be of major importance in the tailorization of information systems.

SX1 tested the subject's perception of his usage of quantitative and qualitative information in the simulation. One of the questions requested subjects to break down the type of information they used (or expected to use) between quantitative, qualitative and other, using a 100 point fractionation scale. Additional questions asked subjects to rate on a Likert scale (from 1 to 7) the importance of these types of information. The correlations among the fractionation measures and the corresponding Likert scale ratings were high, and all were significant at the 1 percent level. Given these high correlations, the fractionated data was used in the analysis of information type.

The results presented in Table 4 indicate some cognitive style differences in an individual's information preferences. For instance, on the pre-tests analytics showed a preference for quantitative information while heuristics emphasized qualitative data. Also, the decision styles that emphasized information (H and I) showed a preference for qualitative information. These differences were significant in only one case for the post-tests.

Both experimental contexts asked subjects (again on a pre-post basis) their perceptions regarding the quantity of information they were given. As Birnberg [1975] remarked, information need perception is an important design constraint for accounting information systems. The results indicate that there were some differences in both information need perception and the attitude toward actual information availability among the different cognitive styles. The pre-questions could be interpreted as having measured information need perception, while the post questions tended to concentrate on the degree of satisfaction with actual information available.

These conclusions reinforce the two points discussed in section on Performance Effects. There is cross-contextual agreement which increases the confidence in the statistical results, and low performance diagnosticity which supports our current but limited understanding of cognitive style-based informational differences.

INFORMATION STRUCTURE EFFECTS

The second major area of analysis facilitated by these experiments was the empirical evaluation of alternative information structures. IS4 was primarily designed for a two by two factorial study of the coarseness (aggregation) and completeness (variance feedback) of information. Four different information structures were supplied to subjects on a random basis. The four information structures were: I1 = coarse information without complete feedback I2 = coarse information with complete feedback, I3 = fine information without complete feedback, and I4 = fine information with complete variance feedback. *Fine* information entailed additional detail concerning manufacturing costs whereas *complete* variance feedback added absolute and relative accounting variance measures to the financial statements.

This particular research design was an extension of earlier studies by Mock [1973] and by Mock and Driver [1975] which analyzed the effect of complete variance information on performance. The current two-way design facilitated analysis of more comprehensive variance feedback (I2 and I4), of finer information, and interaction effects.

Although it may be argued that each information set is payoff relevant, the provision of explicit variance information and finer cost information may provide some attention-directing value to the subjects. The additional feedback eliminates some of the subjects' processing needs. Thus, improved performance may be hypothesized for subjects receiving the more complete feedback.

H4: Subjects receiving more complete feedback (I2, I3, and I4) are expected to outperform other subjects.

The results of basic profit performance analysis are presented in Table 5. A two-way analysis of variance revealed significant main (coarseness and completeness) and interaction effects. (When decision time and number of decisions were analyzed, the main effects were not significant).

It may be noted that a one-way analysis of profits in relation to information structure does not result in any significant differences (see Vasarhelyi and Mock [1976]). However, once the factorial analysis is introduced, a clear pattern of interaction and main factor influence can be observed. This pattern indicates the influence of differences in information structures on decision-maker performance. These results are consistent with the earlier ones [Mock (1973)] that attributed superior performance to explicit budget variance information. As seen in Table 5, decision-makers that were supplied with coarse information and complete budget variance information showed the highest profit performance. The finding that the finer feedback

TABLE 5

Effect of Coarseness of Information and Completeness of Feedback on Performance [IS4 Experiment]

	Average Profits Earned ($1,000)	
	Incomplete Variance Feedback n = 54	Complete Variance Feedback n = 66
Coarse Information (n = 56)	$96.10	$124.70
Fine Information (n = 64)	97.10	97.40
	F - Values	Significance Level
Coarseness	7.1	.03
Completeness	4.5	.01
Interaction	3.5	.06

information (details in the various cost components) did *not* have a positive effect on profit performance was a significant result.

The results in this section show much higher performance diagnosticity than the previous ones. This can be explained by a series of factors. First, results are not being examined vis-a-vis cognitive styles, therefore compensatory behavior in omitted variables is not involved; secondly, the IS context is more analytical in nature and has built-in relationships that determine outcome and finally, an improved statistical methodology, using the 2 x 2 design allows for further explanation of the results.

JOINT EFFECTS OF INFORMATION STRUCTURE AND COGNITIVE STYLE

The previous analyses have not considered the interactions that may take place between information and cognitive style. These effects are denoted in the preceding paragraph as compensatory behavior in omitted variables. For example, if the integrative decision style is indeed more complex and has a preference for a greater amount of environmental load (in this case feedback), integratives may be expected to perform best in I4 conditions. Obviously a number of hypotheses could be formulated for each cognitive style and information set (see, for example, Driver and Mock [1975]). As cognitive style effects were not significant, such hypotheses will not be developed.

In Table 6, the average profits and decision times are computed for each cognitive style and information structure. It can again be noted that because of the ex post facto cognitive style classifications, cell frequencies are quite uneven. This of course leads to a number of statistical problems. Nevertheless, a two way analysis of these performance variables, plus number of decisions completed, was conducted. As the results in Table 7 show, only information structure differences were significant.

SIGNIFICANCE OF FACTOR PRICE CUES

Finally, we consider the problem of determining the decision maker's information processing (ϱ) and decision (α) functions within an experimental context. As was discussed earlier (see Table 2), regression analysis was used in IS1 and IS2 to estimate the relationship between factor price cues (i.e., costs of inputs in a manufacturing setting) and actual subject decisions. This analysis is now developed in more detail.

In Figure 1, a subject's chosen action 'a' was specified as depending on a decision function α, an information processing function ϱ and an information system η, or

$$a = \alpha(\varrho(\eta(x))) \tag{1}$$

The action that will be analyzed is the material input decision M_t. In the IS experiments, all subjects received one-period-lagged cues concerning factor input prices for labor cost ($P_{L,t-1}$) and unit materials cost ($P_{M,t-1}$). Thus in this case equation (1) becomes

$$M_t = \alpha(\varrho(P_{M,t-1}, P_{L,t-1})) \tag{2}$$

TABLE 6

Supporting Data for Table 7
Average Profits (P) and Decision Times (T) Classified by Cognitive Style (C/S) and Information Structure (I/S)

Decision Style			Information Structure			
			I_1 P 95.8 T 23.7	I_2 P 111.9 T 18.8	I_3 P 107.3 T 17.9	I_4 P 96.7 T 25.6
D	P(thousands)	111.0	81.8	66.7	140.6	101.1
	T (min)	23.0	15.6	15.1	23.5	30.9
	(N)		9	2	4	10
F	P	98.9	97.5	113.6	78.9	80.2
	T	22.3	28.5	18.9	15.7	24.2
	(N)		6	7	4	6
H	P	113.1	117.8	126.8	143.2	100.9
	T	28.7	38.6	21.8	15.2	24.1
	(N)		6	2	1	7
I	P	101.0	98.7	129.9	79.5	103.8
	T	21.5	17.8	17.7	12.4	25.8
	(N)		9	1	2	13
C	P	104.0	90.4	142.3	—	90.2
	T	23.7	24.6	20.3	—	22.1
	(N)		8	1	0	16
Decision Approach			I_1 P 98.0 T 21.6	I_2 P 130.9 T 18.1	I_3 P 97.1 T 19.1	I_4 P 95.1 T 24.6
A	P	102.4	100.6	139.6	91.2	94.6
	T	21.6	24.5	18.9	17.1	24.0
	(N)		18	6	8	26
H	P	109.7	95.5	125.1	106.4	95.7
	T	21.4	18.3	17.5	22.3	25.3
	(N)		18	9	5	22

NOTATION:

Information Structure

I_1 = Coarse & Incomplete
I_2 = Coarse & Complete
I_3 = Fine & Incomplete
I_4 = Fine & Complete

Decision Style

D = Decisive
F = Flexible
H = Hierarchic
I = Integrative
C = Complex

Decision Approach

A = Analytic
H = Heuristic

MISCELLANEOUS:

P = Profits
T = Decision Time
N = Cell frequencies

Clearly various decision/information processing models could be formulated and experimental data could then be used to test these models. In

IS1, normative decision theory was used to derive an hypothesized model

$$M_t = .5(P_{L,t-1}, P_{M,t-1})^{.5} \quad (3)$$

This model was consistent with observed results, although a great amount of the explained variance was not accounted for. The normative formulation was based upon the best linear unbiased estimator (information processing function)

$$\varrho^*: P_{Mt} = P_{M,t-1} \quad (4)$$

and

$$P_{L,t} = P_{L,t-1}$$

And an optimal (maximum expected monetary payoff) decision rule

$$\alpha^*: M_t = .5(\varrho^*(P_{L,t-1}/P_{M,t-1}))^{.5} \quad (5)$$

Equation (5), then, is the hypothesized material decision and information processing rule. Based upon this formulation, regression analysis was performed for IS4, with the results as seen in Table 8. The analysis was conducted according to the four information structure treatments (I_1, I_2, I_3, and I_4). For each subject population, regressions were run for both M_t and normalized M_t decisions. The latter analysis was done in an attempt to

TABLE 7

Two-Way Anova of Information Structure and Cognitive Style [IS4] F-Values and Significance Levels

	Average Profits	Number of Decisions	Decision Time
Information Structure	3.3 (.10)	6.9 (.05)	3.1 (.10)
Decision Approach	n.s.	n.s.	n.s.
Interaction	n.s.	n.s.	n.s.
Information Structure	n.s.	7.4 (.05)	3.99 (.05)
Decision Style	n.s.	n.s.	1.57 (.20)
Interaction	n.s.	n.s.	1.95 (.10)

Note: n.s. = not significant.

TABLE 8

Regression Analysis Results for Material Decisions Related to Factor Price Cues (IS4)

Experiment and Subject Population	Dependent Variable (Material Decision)	Independent Variable (Factor Price Cues)	$\hat{\beta}$	t value (significance)	R^2
1. I_1 (n = 39)	M_t	$(P_{Lt-1}/P_{Mt-1})^{.5}$	.63	1.67 ($\alpha = 05$)	.01
2. "	M_t Normalized	"	1.65	3.33 ($\alpha .01$)	.05
3. I_2 (n = 17)	M_t	"	.49	1.6 ($\alpha = .10$)	.03
4. "	M_t Normalized	"	.98	1.94 ($\alpha = .05$)	.04
5. I_3 (n = 15)	M_t	"	.68	1.49 ($\alpha = .10$)	.03
6. "	M_t Normalized	"	1.84	3.84 ($\alpha = .01$)	.17
7. I_4 (n = 48)	M_t	"	.36	n.s.	.01
8. "	M_t Normalized	"	1.28	2.79 ($\alpha = .01$)	.03

minimize the individual differences in decision strategy which had been shown to be significant in Table 9. The normalized M_t were the actual material decisions divided by the individual's mean M decision. By removing some of the individual's differences, overall subject's reactions to cue changes could be more precisely measured. In fact, in Table 8 all IS4 subpopulations show a significant relationship (at the .05 level or better) between the factor price cues and the normalized material decisions. But again, very little of the variance is explained.

For the regressions using M_t, the theoretical value of $\hat{\beta}$ (.05) is of interest (see equation 5). The empirical results vary from that value, but it is apparent that the theoretical model does perform reasonably well.[3]

These results indicate that a number of variables other than changes in factor price cues are affecting the subjects' decisions. It is probable, for example, that some subjects "anchored" on a reasonable estimate of M^*_t, and then reacted in a heuristic, trial-and-error manner to factor price changes. The results contained in Table 8 support this scenario.

In order to evaluate the impact of individual differences and the decision period (a surrogate for period factor price changes) on a subject's performance, a one way ANOVA was applied to the IS4 material decisions (see Table 9). Consistent with the reported regression results, the period effects were more significant for the normalized M_t. As anticipated, for each set of subjects the individual differences accounted for a major proportion of the observed variance.

These results also support the importance of investigating individual models of human information processing and decision-making (such as cognitive style) if one is interested in a complete specification of the processes contained in the decision and information processing components of Figure 1. The value of a formal decision theory derivation of the possible information processing and decision functions is also apparent. Without such theoretical guidelines, any analyses of human judgment are exploratory.

TABLE 9

1-Way ANOVA of Material Input Decisions According to Period Effects and Individual Difference Effects (IS4)

Experiment and Subject Population	Variable Analyzed Classification (Treatment)	M_t Decision Period	M_t Individual Differences	M_t Normalized Decision Period
I1 (n = 39)	F	.91	2.9	2.95
	d.f.	4,38	38,156	4,38
	significance	n.s.	.01	n.s.
I2 (n = 17)	F	2.13	3.39	4.04
	d.f.	4,80	16,68	4,80
	significance	.10	.01	.01
I3 (n = 15)	F	.78	12.9	6.31
	d.f.	4,70	14,60	4,70
	significance	n.s.	.01	.01
I4 (n = 48)	F	.53	2.05	2.18
	d.f.	4,235	47,192	4,235
	significance	n.s.	.01	.10

SUMMARY

In summary, this paper has presented material in three areas of interest to researchers concerned with accounting systems vis-a-vis (1) behavioral variables, (2) human information processing rules, and (3) decision rules. The paper began with a review of the literature and a brief introduction to a model (Figure 1) that contained the variables of interest. This model can be viewed as continuing the normative perspective of information economics and the more exploratory efforts of describing important behavioral and HIP processes.

The second major segment of this paper considered the information processing evidence contained in four previous experimental studies. Next, some new experimental results derived from two decision contexts were presented. The last section of this paper examined behavioral and informational variables in two experimental settings. In terms of information-use perceptions, the results indicated consistent information structure effects with less consistent cognitive style effects.

The new results can be classified within four areas, two of which were seen to hold for both experimental contexts. In each experiment, cognitive style differences did not explain a significant amount of variation in performance but did result in significant differences in perceptions concerning the type and amount of information. In the IS experiment, information structure effects were seen to explain performance differences, but only a weak relationship was established between factor price cues and factor input decisions.

The latter result indicates that future research will have to utilize and test more complex models of individual differences (such as cognitive styles) and of human information processing. The experimental separation of both information processing and decision functions should be attempted. The ultimate goal of such research is to provide an improved model of decision-making, and thus an increased capability for accounting system design.

On a methodological level, cross-contextual analysis served to increase the confidence on results with low statistical significance. Improved laboratory and statistical techniques may be used to improve this process. Cross-contextual findings discrepancies may serve to indicate context-dependent methods and/or hypotheses.

In addition, the results indicate that the existence of low outcome diagnosticity simply points out the need for the examination of additional component variables and does not necessarily invalidate the underlying theory. Finally, many of these additional component variables should be studied to provide a fair assessment of decision quality instead of the rather simplistic examination of a single outcome (performance) in multi-attribute decision settings.

NOTES

[1]See Mock, Estrin, and Vasarhelyi [1972].

[2]See Driver and Mock [1975].

[3]One reason why the regression model does not perform as well in IS4 as in IS1 may be the fewer (5 versus 12) number of decision periods.

REFERENCES

American Accounting Association, *Report of the Committee on Human Information Processing,* Sarasota, Florida 1978-2.

Anderson, N.H., "Integration Theory and Attitude Change," *Psychological Review* (May 1971).

Ashton, R.H., "An Experimental Study of Internal Control Judgments," *Journal of Accounting Research* (Spring 1974a).

——————, "Cue Utilization and Expert Judgments: A Comparison of Independent Auditors With Other Judges," *Journal of Applied Psychology* (August 1974b).

——————, "The Predictive-Ability Criterion and User Prediction Models," *The Accounting Review* (October 1974c).

——————, "User Prediction and Models in Accounting: An Alternative Use," *The Accounting Review* (October 1975).

——————, *Human Information Processing in Accounting,* Studies in Accounting Research #17, AAA (1982).

Barriff, M.L. and E. Lusk, "Cognitive and Personality Tests for the Design of Management Information Systems," *Management Science* (April 1977, pp. 820-829).

Benbasat, I. and R.G. Schroeder, "An Experimental Investigation of Some MIS Design Variables," *Management Information Systems Quarterly* (March 1977), pp. 37-50.

Benbasat, I. and A. Dexter, "Individual Differences in the Use of Decision Support Aids," *Journal of Accounting Research* (Spring 1982), pp. 1-11.

Biddle, G.C. and E.J. Joyce, "Heuristics and Biases: Their Implications for Probabilistic Inference in Auditing," Working Paper, University of Chicago (1978).

Biggs, S.F. and T.J. Mock, "Auditor Information Search Processes in the Evaluation of Internal Controls," *Journal of Accounting Research* (forthcoming, 1983).

Birnberg, J.G., "Human Information Processing and Financial Disclosure," Working Paper presented at the Accounting Research Colloquium, Ohio State University (April 1975).

Brehmer, B. and G. Quarnstrom, "Information Integration and Research, Subjective Weights in Multiple-Cue Judgments," *Organizational Behavior and Human Performance* (October 1976), pp. 118-126.

Casey, Cornelius J., "The Effects of Disclosure of the Price Probability of Failure on Loan Judgments," Working Paper, Harvard Business School (1981).

Chervany, N.L. and G.W. Dickson, "An Experimental Evaluation of Information Overload in a Production Environment," *Management Science* (June 1974).

Collins, F., "The Interaction of Budget Characteristics and Personality Variables with Budgetary Response Attitudes," *The Accounting Review* (April 1978), pp. 324-335.

Dickson, G.W., J.A. Senn and N.L. Chervany, "Research in Management Information Systems: The Minnesota Experiments," *Management Science* (May 1977), pp. 913-923.

Driscoll, D.A. and T.J. Mock, "Models of Behavioral Factors in Human Information Processing," Working Paper, University of Southern California (November 1976).

Driver, M.J. and T.J. Mock, "Human Information Processing, Decision Style Theory, and Accounting Information Systems," *The Accounting Review* (1975).

Henderson, J.C. and P.C. Nutt, "The Influence of Decision Style on Decision Making," *Management Science* (April 1980), pp. 371-386.

Hoffman, P.J., P. Slovic and L.G. Rorer, "An Analysis of Variance Model for the Assessment of Configural Cue-Utilization in Clinical Judgment," *Psychological Bulletin* (May 1968).

Hofstedt, T.R., "A State-of-the-Art Analysis of Behavioral Accounting Reseach," *Journal of Contemporary Business* (Autumn 1975).

—————— and G.D. Hughes, "An Experimental Study of the Judgment Element in Disclosure Decisions," *The Accounting Review* (April 1977), pp. 379-395.

Howell, W.C., and S.H. Burnett, "Uncertainty Measurement: A Cognitive Taxonomy," *Organizational Behavior and Human Performance* (August 1978), pp. 45-68.

Libby, R., "The Use of Simulated Decision Makers in Information Evaluation," *The Accounting Review* (July 1975).

——————, "Man versus Model of Man: The Need for a Nonlinear Model," *Organizational Behavior and Human Performance* (June 1976), pp. 23-26.

——————, "The Impact of Uncertainty on the Loan Decision, *Journal of Accounting Research,* Supplement (1979), pp. 35-57.

______ and B.L. Lewis, "Human Information Processing Research in Accounting," *Accounting Organizations and Society* (1977), pp. 245-268.

______, *Accounting and Human Information Processing: Theory and Applications* (Prentice Hall, 1981).

______ and B.L. Lewis, "Human Information Processing Research in Accounting; The State of the Art in 1982," *Accounting, Organizations and Society* (1982), pp. 231-286,

Lusk, E.J., and M. Keisnick, "The Effect of Cognitive Style and Report Format on Task Performance: The MIS Design Consequences," *Management Science* (August 1979), pp. 787-798.

______, "A Test of Differential Performance Peaking for a Disembedding Task," *Journal of Accounting Research* (Spring 1979), pp. 286-294.

Magee, R.P. and J.W. Dickaut, "Effects of Compensation Plans on Heuristics in Cost Variance Investigations," *Journal of Accounting Research* (Autumn 1978), pp. 294-314.

McGhee, W., M.D. Shields and J.G. Birnberg, "The Effects of Personality on a Subject's Information Processing," *The Accounting Review* (July 1978), pp. 681-697.

Miller, G.A., "The Magic Number Seven Plus or Minus Two: Some Limits on Our Capacity for Processing Information," *Psychological Review* (1956), pp. 81-97.

Mock, T.J., "Comparative Values of Information Structures," *Journal of Accounting Research,* Supplement (1969).

______, "The Evolution of Alternative Information Structures," Unpublished Ph.D. Dissertation, University of California, Berkeley (1968).

______, T. Estrin and M.A. Vasarhelyi, "Learning Patterns, Decision Approach and Value of Information," *Journal of Accounting Research* (Spring 1972), pp. 129-153.

______, "The Value of Budget Information," *The Accounting Review* (July 1973) Economics and Lens Models," *Journal of Accounting Research* (Autumn 1978), pp. 414-423.

______ and M.A. Vasarhelyi, "A Crosscontextual Investigation of Information Processing Models, Cognitive Style and Accounting Information," Working Paper, University of Southern California (June 1977).

______ and L. Goodfried, "Documentation for the Information Structure Experiments," Working Paper, University of Southern California (February 1975).

Pankoff, L.D. and R.L. Virgil, "Some Preliminary Findings from a Laboratory Experiment on the Usefulness of Financial Accounting Information to Security Analysts," *Journal of Accounting Research* Supplement, (1970).

Rapoport, L. and D.A. Summers (Eds.), *Human Judgment and Social Interaction* (Holt, Rinehart and Winston, Inc., 1973).

Slovic, P., "Psychological Study of Human Judgment: Implications for Investment Decision Making," *The Journal of Finance* (September 1972).

______, D. Fleissner and W.S. Bauman, "Analyzing the Use of Information in Investment Decision Making: A Methodological Proposal," *The Journal of Business* (1972).

______, B. Fischoff and S. Lichtenstein, "Behavioral Decision Theory," *Annual Review of Psychology* (1977), pp. 1-39.

Steinman, D.O., "The Effects of Cognitive Feedback and Task Complexity in Multiple-Cue Probability Learning," *Organizational Behavior and Human Performance* (April 1976), pp. 168-179.

Taylor, R.N. and I. Benbasat, "Cognitive Styles Research and Managerial Information Use: Problems and Prospects," prepared for the ORSA/TIMS National Meeting, Colorado Springs (1980).

Tiessen, P., "An Investigation of Some Effects of Data Aggregation and Cognitive Style on Decision Making Performance," Unpublished dissertation, University of Minnesota (1976).

Vasarhelyi, M.A., "Man-Machine Planning Systems: A Cognitive Style Examination of Interactive Decision Making," *Journal of Accounting Research* (Spring 1977), pp. 138-153.

_____________, "Information Processing in a Simulated Stock Market Environment," *Proceedings of the National Meeting of the SMIS* (Boston, 1981).

_____________ and T.J. Mock, "An Information Processing Analysis of Budget Variance Information," University of Southern California (Rev. 1977).

_____________, "Cognitive Style Tailored Information Systems," Working Paper, Graduate School of Business, Columbia University (1982).

_____________, M. Kimberland and M. Tennant, "Stock Market Simulation: A Documentation," Research Working Paper, Columbia University (February 1981).

Wright, W.F., "Financial Information Processing Models: An Empirical Study," *The Accounting Review* (July 1977), pp. 676-689.

_____________, "Self-insight into the Cognitive Processing of Financial Information," *Accounting Organizations and Society* (1977), pp. 323-331.

Zmud, R.W., "Effects of 'Think-Time' and Cognitive Style on User Performance with and Appreciation of On-Line Decision/Information Systems," presented at Atlanta Joint TIMS/ORSA National Meeting (November 1977).

_____________, "On the Validity of the Analytic-Heuristic Instrument Utilized in the Minnesota Experiments," *Management Science* (June 1978), pp. 1088-1090.

_____________, "Individual Differences and MIS Success: A Review of the Empirical Literature," *Management Science* (October 1979), pp. 966-979.

Phillip D. Harsha
The University of Oklahoma

Discussant's Comments on:

"Context, Findings, and Method in Cognitive Style Research: A Comparative Study"

I commend the authors for their persistence in this area of research. It is my belief that we have a great need for a set of principles that would help guide the tailoring of decision support systems. The micro computer has made this tailoring of systems to individuals or classes of individuals practical. Furthermore, the auditing profession in particular and the rest of the accounting profession in general will be among the primary beneficiaries of this type of research.

Because of the time constraint on my presentation, I will focus my comments more on methodological issues than on other issues that probably deserve equal if not greater attention. I will begin by making some general comments about the objectives of the paper and the degree to which these objectives were achieved. Next, I will raise several issues concerning the research methodology. Finally, I will end with a few comments about the conclusions that might be drawn from this paper.

OBJECTIVES

My starting point relative to evaluating this paper was to identify the authors' objectives so that I could make some statement about the degree to which the authors did what they said they were going to do. However, it does not appear to me that the paper contains a clear statement of objectives. This made my task more difficult, and I believe, it may reduce the paper's contribution to the literature. Consequently, I was not able to tie the empirical results and conclusions back to the objectives with any level of confidence. Since any further comments about objectives would be mostly speculation, I will proceed to methodological issues.

METHODOLOGICAL ISSUES

Most of my comments about research methodology relate to more than one of the four rather distinct sets of analyses. Therefore, I will make these comments first and leave a few comments about specific analyses until near the end.

Univariate vs. Multivariate Analyses

In experiment IS4, which generated the empirical data analyzed in at least part of all four sets of analyses, there were several measurements taken on each participant. That is, there were multiple criterion variables. Yet, in none of these analyses were multivariate techniques utilized. Instead, multiple univariate analyses were performed. It seems that in the second and third sets of analyses there might have been justification for using multivariate analysis of variance.

Post-Classification vs. Preclassification of Participants by Cognitive Styles

In the first and third sets of analyses, cognitive style was one of the main factors. However, the instruments used to classify the participants according to their cognitive styles were administered after the simulation experiments were completed. It seems that it would have been more appropriate to administer these instruments and classify the participants before the simulation experiments were conducted. This would have allowed participants to be screened according to their cognitive styles so that equal cell sizes in the experimental design matrix could have been achieved. Equal cell sizes might have resulted in more powerful statistical tests. Since a large portion of the effects were not statistically significant in these analyses, preclassification and control might have been helpful.

Separate vs. Combined Analyses for the Second and Third Sets of Analyses

In the second set of analyses, a 2 X 2 full factorial analysis was utilized. The two factors were named "coarseness" of the supplied information and "completeness" of the variance feedback. In the third set of analyses, the same data were analyzed again but this time by including cognitive style as a factor. However, a three factor analysis was not subsequently performed. Instead, the two information factors, coarseness and completeness, were collapsed into a single factor called "information structure." Then, a two factor analysis was performed to test for significant effects of cognitive style and information structure as well as for their interaction.

It seems that if the two information variables had not been combined, a three factor analysis might have been possible. Such an analysis might have been a richer one. Maybe this was not possible because cognitive style was determined after the simulation experiment was completed which might have led to unmanageable empty cells in the design matrix.

Issues Relating to Specific Sets of Analyses

In the first set of analyses, it is not clear why both pretest and post-test questionnaires to determine the participants' perceived information preferences were administered. Interestingly, most of the pretest effects of cognitive style on these perceived information preferences were significant, while most of the post-test effects were not significant. The reason for this might have been revealing. For example, suppose participants did not believe the simulation was realistic and that their decisions were not adequately reflected in the performance measures. This might have resulted in a post-test perception that the type and amount of information in the simulation made little difference in the outcome. This, in turn, might have been communicated by way of no significant information preferences on the post-test. In addition, this perception by the participants might have resulted in a lack of motivation to do well in the simulation. This in turn might have been reflected in the nonsignificant performance effect.

Also in the first set of analyses, it is not clear why two decision contexts were used. The two simulations were conducted completely independently with no specifically controlled and manipulated task characteristics. Consequently, no conclusions can be drawn about the interaction between cognitive style and characteristics of the task. Based on the authors' remarks in the introduction, I thought this set of analyses was going to address the criticism that task characteristics need to be considered in cognitive style research.

I have no questions specifically about either the second or third sets of analyses. As for the fourth set, I honestly do not understand it well enough to make comments. A more complete presentation of this set of analyses might be helpful, although I suspect my own limitations are probably strong contributing factors.

CONCLUSIONS

Professors Mock and Vasarhelyi began this paper by recognizing several of the criticisms levied at cognitive style research. In response, they agreed that there were many problems to overcome. They went on, however, to say that these problems in themselves do not lead one to conclude that a complete redirecting of the research focus in this area is necessary, as suggested by some [Libby and Lewis, 1982, p. 273]. Although I agree with their statement in the literal sense, I also believe the evidence shows that a different approach might be beneficial.

This last statement is based on two things. First, in the review by Libby and Lewis [1982, pp. 271-272], the argument was made that research in psychology indicates cognitive style is directly relevant at the perceptual level rather than at the level being measured by performance variables. If this is true, the relationship between cognitive style and performance is indirect. This could explain why the results of this paper, as well as the results of prior accounting research, have typically not found a significant relationship between cognitive style and performance but have found significant relationships between cognitive style and perceptual variables.

REFERENCES

Libby, R. and B.L. Lewis, "Human Information Processing Research in Accounting: the State of Art in 1982", *Accounting, Organizations and Society* (1982), pp. 231-285.

Barry L. Lewis
University of Pittsburgh

Discussant's Comments on:

"Context, Findings, and Method in Cognitive Style Research: A Comparative Study"

Mock and Vasarhelyi [1984], hereinafter referred to as MV, have attempted to defend the value of cognitive style research in accounting by addressing specific criticisms of earlier research and by reporting the results of more recent experiments. The paper is valuable in that it reviews and summarizes the state of the art of their own focus in cognitive style research. In my opinion, however, they have not successfully defended the value of this line of research; nor have they suggested fruitful directions for future research.

My discussion of this paper is organized into three sections. In the first section, an overview of cognitive style research is presented. This overview includes the goals of the research, the necessary conditions to achieve those goals and the progress made toward those goals. The second section contains more specific criticism concerning aspects of the experiments discussed by MV. Finally, I present my idea of a more promising direction for future research.

COGNITIVE STYLE RESEARCH

My impression of the goal of cognitive style research is the design of an information system based on cognitive characteristics of the system users. That also appears to be the motivation behind the MV reference to the interdependence of information system design and behavioral factors (page 63). Although this goal is usually interpreted as providing the information in the form, quantity, etc. *desired* by the user, I assume it could also be interpreted as providing information in such a way as to compensate for weaknesses that may be associated with certain cognitive styles.

The viability of this research rests on two, not necessarily independent, conditions. First, there must be some way to categorize individuals according to a relevant cognitive characteristic. Second, there must be an interaction between levels of that characteristic and types of information presented as they affect some measure of performance or decision quality [Lusk, 1979; Benbasat and Dexter, 1972]. These necessary conditions form the basis of Ashton's criticism of cognitive style research [1982]. His focus was primarily on construct validity and measurement issues.

Where do we stand with respect to the goals outlined in this section? My interpretation of the results of the current set of experiments, as well as the earlier experiments, is that we have no reason to believe that we could or should base the design of information systems on the cognitive characteristics of the users. The overwhelming evidence to date is that information structures affect performance, that cognitive characteristics do not affect performance and that information structures and cognitive characteristics do not interact with respect to performance. Despite the authors' contention that the latest experiments serve to increase the confidence in results with low statistical significance, I maintain the opposing view. They posit an interaction of behavioral factors and information structures. They test this relationship by trying to reject the null hypothesis of no relationship. The more often they fail to reject this null hypothesis, the more confident I become that no relationship exists.

It is not even clear where the problem lies. This is due in part to the measurement problems mentioned by Ashton. It could be that decision approach/decision style are not the relevant cognitive characteristics. It could be that the relationships have not been tested in the appropriate circumstances. It could be the case that the theoretical basis of the research is incorrect.

SPECIFIC CRITICISMS

The preceding overview of cognitive style research did not address methodological problems. In other words, it pointed to problems with this line of research given adequate research design, analysis and interpretation. In this section, I discuss certain reservations with regard to the experiments reported by MV.

Cross-contextual Nature of the Research

Although the paper stressed the cross-contextual approach, I found little evidence of such an approach. Only the overall performance measures appeared in comparable form in both the IS and SX experiments. Information type, defined as preference for qualitative or quantitative data, was said to have been examined in both experiments, but Table 4 seems to indicate data for only one of the experiments. Some notion of information quantity was included in both experiments, but it was measured in extremely different ways (sufficiency versus absolute quantity), thus impairing any comparison across contexts. If the intent was to obtain cross-contextual information, the experiments should have maximized the similarity of measures across tasks.

Statistical Analysis

Intuitive analysis of individual cell means despite the absence of significant main effects or interactions is not very helpful. If there are a priori reasons to look at only a few relationships, they should be stated in advance and the experiments should be designed to test only those relationships. Failure to find a significant effect can only be interpreted as being unable to reject the hypothesis that cell means associated with a particular variable are equal.

Since the theory used by the authors implies directions of effects, the hypotheses should be stated in those terms rather than in terms of mere differences. In particular, H2 and H3 should specify who is believed to use more or less of which types of information. Reporting of the results should then be related to the more specific hypotheses.

In reporting the results of the effects of coarseness of information and completeness of feedback, the authors failed to provide statistical support to back up their intuitive analysis. In the presence of an interaction, they should have tested for simple main effects to describe the levels at which the main effects hold [Kirk, 1968].

DIRECTIONS FOR FUTURE RESEARCH

It is not very difficult to believe that human information processing, a cognitive activity, is affected in some way by the cognitive characteristics of an individual. For that reason alone, I believe there is merit in continuing this line of research. I do not feel, however, that the MV approach is the best approach. Perhaps their approach is simply premature. We do not yet know enough about the cognitive aspects of information processing to know which characteristics are important or how they might affect behavior.

I believe that we must place more of an emphasis on process. Although MV's Figure 1 purports to be a model of information processing, it is really a table of presumably important factors that might be in a model of information processing. The impetus behind the Lens model research and other modeling efforts was to attempt to describe a process so that the effect of these presumably important factors could be studied. I am not suggesting that statistical models of process are good enough; I am suggesting that cognitive style research similarly concern itself with basic cognitive processes. In this regard I can only repeat the comment made in Libby and Lewis [1982] which MV seem to have rejected at the outset of their paper.

A human decision model can be viewed as a decision maker's internal representation of the task environment [Einhorn and Hogarth, 1981; Newell and Simon, 1972]. This representation incorporates a goal structure and an evaluation function involving cue selection and the weighting and combining of those cues. In complex decision situations, the internal representation is often viewed as being driven by schema, scripts or frames [Abelson, 1981; Fiske and Linville, 1980]. It seems reasonable to pursue the notion that different cognitive characteristics would be associated with different schema which would drive different processing models. Such a direction for research would initially stress the need to describe cognitive processes, memory structures and schema through verbal protocols and other process tracing methods. Descriptions of the cognitive processes could form the basis for deciding which cognitive characteristics to study and could also form the theoretical basis for generating hypothesized effects.

REFERENCES

Abelson, R.P., "Psychological Status of the Script Concept," *American Psychologist* (1981), pp. 715-729.

Ashton, R.H., *Human Information Processing in Accounting,* Studies in Accounting Research #17, AAA, (1982).

Benbasat, I. and A. Dexter, "Value and Events Approaches to Accounting: An Experimental Evaluation," *The Accounting Review* (October 1979), pp. 735-749.

Einhorn, H.J. and R.M. Hogarth, "Behavioral Decision Theory: Processes of Judgment and Choice," *Journal of Accounting Research* (Spring 1981), pp. 1-41.

Fiske, S.T. and P.W. Linville, "What Does the Schema Concept Buy Us?" *Personality and Social Psychology Bulletin* (1980), pp. 543-557.

Kirk, R.E., *Experimental Design: Procedures for the Behavioral Sciences* (Brooks/Cole, 1968).

Libby, R. and B. Lewis, "Human Information Processing Research in Accounting: The State of the Art in 1982," *Accounting, Organizations and Society* (1982), pp. 231-285.

Lusk, E.J., "A Test of Differential Performance Peaking for a Disembedding Task," *Journal of Accounting Research* (Spring 1979), pp. 286-294.

Mock, T.J. and M.A. Vasarhelyi, "Context, Findings and Method in Cognitive Style Research: A Comparative Study," in S. Moriarity and E. Joyce (Eds.), *Decision Making and Accounting: Current Research,* (University of Oklahoma, Center for Economic and Management Research, 1984), pp. 58-82

Newell, A. and H. Simon, *Human Problem Solving* (Prentice-Hall, 1972).

D. Paul Newman
Lawrence A. Tomassini
University of Texas

Calibration of Subjective Probability Assessments: A Methodological Perspective

1.0 Introduction

Since the development of the expected utility theorem, allowing separation of beliefs and preferences in decision making under uncertainty, the assessment of subjective probabilities has been widely studied. Recently, a significant amount of research has focused upon the "quality" of such assessments, using the *calibration* of probabilistic judgments as a criterion. As Lichtenstein, Fischhoff, and Phillips [1982, p. 306] state:

> ...a judge is well-calibrated if, over the long run, for all propositions assigned a given probability, the proportion that is true equals the probability assigned. Judges' calibration can be empirically evaluated by observing their probability assessments, verifying the associated propositions, and then observing the proportion true in each response category.

Thus, the calibration criterion is based upon a comparison of observed frequencies with assessed subjective probabilities. In an ideal setting, the perfectly-calibrated individual has a probability distribution which matches the underlying distribution of the relevant population.[1] Given the constraints of settings in which such probabilistic judgments are made, surrogate indices are typically used to measure calibration.

During the past decade, several researchers have taken a Bayesian approach to studying the audit decision-making process [Kinney, 1975]. This approach has largely been aimed at the assessment of subjective probabilities [Corless, 1972; Felix, 1976; and Solomon, Krogstad, Romney, and Tomassini, 1982]. Only recently, the importance of calibration in audit risk assessments has been studied analytically [Beck, Solomon, and Tomassini, 1983] and some preliminary empirical evidence about auditor miscalibration has been reported [Tomassini, Solomon, Romney, and Krogstad, 1982]. The latter two papers examine calibration in a continuous variables context—auditors' prior probability distributions regarding the accuracy of client account balances.

1.1 Purpose and Outline of the Paper

The purpose of this paper is to raise and discuss some methodological issues which are inherent in such calibration studies in auditing and other contexts. In particular, we discuss the sensitivity of calibration findings to the typical surrogate indices used and to the number of sampling observations on which these indices are based. Our analysis highlights some potential problems in interpreting the empirical results of these calibration measures, leading us to suggest an alternative methodology for examining the calibration of probabilistic judgments in audit and similar settings.

In the next section, a typical methodology for testing calibration with continuous probability assessments is described. The third section includes some examples which indicate some of the potential problems associated with the methodology. Section 4.0 discusses an alternative methodology. Comments and conclusions are presented in the final section.

2.0 Calibration Methodology

The methods used to measure calibration of probabilistic judgments depend upon the task under study. In discrete probability contexts (e.g., estimating the probability that a particular hypothesis is true), calibration is (as stated above) a function of relative frequencies. If, for example, a meteorologist assesses the probability of rain to be 80 percent on certain days of the year, (s)he is considered well calibrated if the observed frequency of rainy days among this population is not significantly different from 80 percent. The meteorologist is said to be *overconfident (underconfident)* if the observed frequency of rainy days is less (more) than 80 percent. Calibration curves are used to depict these relative frequencies over the entire probability scale [see Lichtenstein et al., 1982].

In continuous probability contexts (e.g., the audit account balance setting), the calibration construct relates to the population density function. Figure 1 illustrates the matter of confidence in such judgments. If a perfectly-calibrated (or one essentially so) auditor, for example, assesses a "true" account balance with density function B, normally distributed around a mean value (M), an overconfident (underconfident) auditor's distribution is too tight (diffuse). These miscalibrated judgments are depicted by density functions A and C, respectively.

The most popular method for assessing continuous subjective probability distributions is the CDF-fractiles technique. With this technique, the subjects are asked to specify outcome values (e.g., account balances) for various fractiles (.50, .25, .75, .10, .90, .01, .99, etc.) in order to approximate the probability distribution which reflects their confidence about the outcome being judged or predicted.

Once the fractiles have been elicited and the subjects' distributions formed, comparisons are made with observed outcomes (e.g., audited account balances). Two types of indices are then computed to evaluate the calibration of the probabilistic judgments. The *interquartile index* represents the percentage of assessed distributions for which the observed outcome value falls within the interquartile range (between the values assigned to the .25 and .75 fractiles). The *surprise index* represents the percentage of observed outcomes falling outside the extreme fractiles. For example, the 2 percent (20 percent) surprise index is computed with observations falling outside the .01 and .99 (.10 and .90) fractiles. Perfect calibration is represented by an interquartile index of 50, a 2 percent surprise index of 2, and a 20 percent surprise index of 20.

FIGURE 1

Illustration of Judgment Confidence

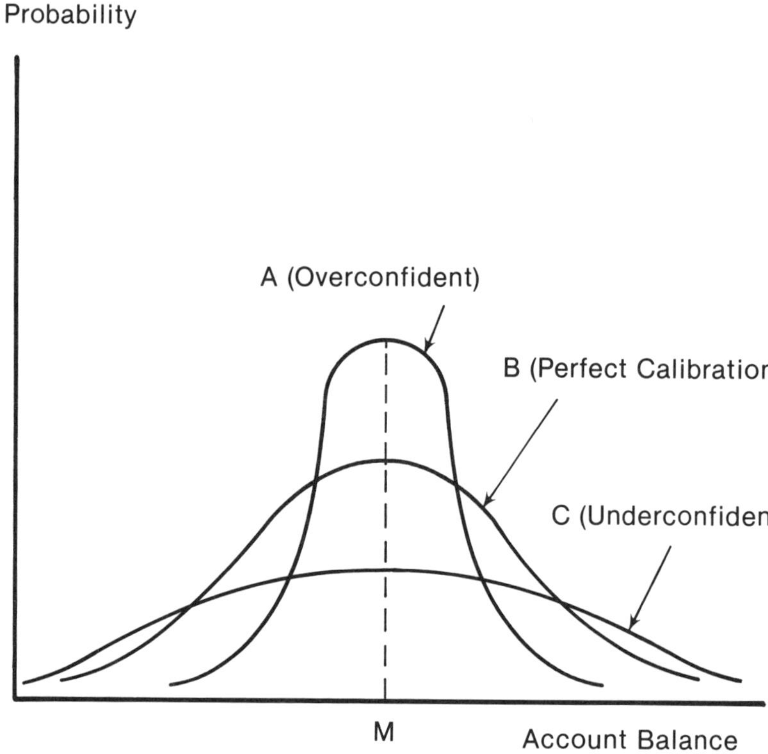

Lichtenstein et al. [1982] provide a thorough summary of results regarding calibration which we will not replicate here. Virtually all reported studies (both with expert and novice/student subjects) indicate significant degrees of miscalibration, most of which appear to represent *overconfidence.* Hence, in studies of continuous distributions, subjects tend to indicate beliefs which, *ex post,* appear to be too tight (surprise indices which are exceedingly large and interquartile indices significantly less than 50).

Tomassini et al. [1982], on the other hand, reported findings which indicated relatively less miscalibration among auditors and a slight tendency toward *underconfidence.*

3.0 Potential Methodological Problems

As noted earlier, an ideal measure of calibration would be based upon a direct comparison of assessed and observed distributions for each individual. This would permit unequivocal statements about the nature of miscalibration for particular individuals and the implications for risk assessments and decision making. The practical constraints of most experimental studies, particularly those with experts (e.g., practicing auditors) in realistic tasks, cause at least two types of concessions to this ideal: (1) use of aggregated calibration measures (a between-subjects, rather than within-subjects, design),[2] and (2) use of a limited number of cases for which observed criterion values are known.

The first concession, due to the limited availability of expert subjects' time and the desire to use realistic task scenarios, limits the calibration conclusions to those representing a set of auditors who are, by implication, essentially homogeneous.[3] The second concession, upon which we primarily focus here, ignores the inherent uncertainty of the phenomenon being assessed.[4] We examine here the implications of this methodological choice for answering the following question: What is the probability that the experimenter will incorrectly identify a subject as miscalibrated when the standard calibration indices are used? In other words, what is the Type 1 error in such studies where the null hypothesis maintained is that of perfect calibration? We attempt to examine this question below by positing the ideal—a subject who is perfectly calibrated over all assessed distributions.

3.1 Analysis of Calibration Indices: Type 1 Errors

In the typical calibration experiment, subjects are provided with a number of independent cases for which their probability distributions are elicited. For this analysis, we assume that each case used is inherently random (for convenience) and may be characterized by different parameters (mean, variance, skewness, etc.).[5] The outcome observed by the experimenter may be viewed as a draw from a distribution of potential results from a particular generating process.[6] For example, an audited account balance is one of many possible results from the theoretical distribution formed by the contextual circumstances (i.e., the client size, industry, strength of internal controls, etc.). In this view, the assessments of subjects are compared to single draws from each theoretical distribution in formulating calibration indices.

To pose the potential inferential problem, consider first the computation of an interquartile index for our hypothetical, perfectly-calibrated subject. Given perfect calibration, the probability of any draw from a particular distribution falling between the .25 and .75 fractiles is .5. The probability of two draws from two distributions both falling in the interquartile range (IR) is .25 (.5 × .5). If, for example, six experimental cases are used in developing the index (i.e., six draws are taken from the theoretical distribution), we can compute the following:

P(n observations ϵ IR) (rounded)	**Observed Interquartile Index**
$P(0 \epsilon IR) = \binom{6}{0} (.5)^6 (.5)^0 = .0156$	0.0
$P(1 \epsilon IR) = \binom{6}{1} (.5)^5 (.5)^1 = .0938$	16.7
$P(2 \epsilon IR) = \binom{6}{2} (.5)^4 (.5)^2 = .2344$	33.3
$P(3 \epsilon IR) = \binom{6}{3} (.5)^3 (.5)^3 = .3125$	50.0
$P(4 \epsilon IR) = \binom{6}{4} (.5)^2 (.5)^4 = .2344$	66.7
$P(5 \epsilon IR) = \binom{6}{5} (.5)^1 (.5)^5 = .0938$	83.3
$P(6 \epsilon IR) = \binom{6}{6} (.5)^0 (.5)^6 = .0156$	100.0

Notice that the *expected* interquartile index is 50. If the experimenter sets an α (probability of Type 1 error) level of .05, the null hypothesis (i.e., perfect calibration) can be rejected only if the observed index is 0 or 100. In other words, indices ranging from 16.7 to 83.3 are *consistent* with perfect calibration given the underlying noise in the data (the exact α level is .0312). Table 1 summarizes confidence intervals of the interquartile index (I) for various sample sizes. (Recall that the ideal interquartile index is 50 in each case.)

TABLE 1

Confidence Intervals of the Interquartile Index

Sample Size	Confidence Interval ($\alpha = .05$)
1	Never reject H
6	$0 < I < 100$
10	$10 < I < 90$
20	$25 < I < 75$
100	$40.2 < I < 59.8$[a]
1000	$46.9 < I < 53.1$[a]

[a]Using the normal approximation to the binomial distribution.

Not surprisingly, the confidence interval shrinks as the sample size increases. However, to achieve a large number of observations, rather than provide each subject with additional cases, experimenters typically pool (aggregate) subject responses. Thus, 10 case responses from each of 10 subjects are treated as 100 data items (observations). Unfortunately, if the cases are identical and the subjects are all perfectly calibrated (and, hence, no between-subject variability exists), this pooling will result in an understatement of the Type 1 risk.

To illustrate, suppose that the mean interquartile index of the 10 subjects is 40. If the sample size is assumed to be 100, this mean index would result in a rejection of the null hypothesis. However, since the cases presented to the subjects are identical, the actual sample size is only 10, and the null should not be rejected. To make this point more evident, consider 1000 cases provided to a single subject versus a single (identical) case presented to 1000 subjects. With the single case (and α equal to .05), the null hypothesis could never be rejected, whereas with 1000 cases, the confidence interval becomes rather tight.

Now consider the 20 percent surprise index (SI). The probability that a particular observation will fall in the upper or lower 10 percent tails of the distribution is .20. The same procedure is used to evaluate the probability of inferential error for the hypothetical, perfectly-calibrated subject. In the six case experiment, the results are as follows:

P(n observations ϵ 10 percent tails) (rounded)	Observed 20 percent SI
P(0 ϵ 10% tails) = $\binom{6}{0}(.2)^6(.8)^0$ = .2621	0.0
P(1 ϵ 10% tails) = $\binom{6}{1}(.2)^5(.8)^1$ = .3932	16.7
P(2 ϵ 10% tails) = $\binom{6}{2}(.2)^4(.8)^2$ = .2458	33.3
P(3 ϵ 10% tails) = $\binom{6}{3}(.2)^3(.8)^3$ = .0819	50.0
P(4 ϵ 10% tails) = $\binom{6}{4}(.2)^2(.8)^4$ = .0154	66.7
P(5 ϵ 10% tails) = $\binom{6}{5}(.2)^1(.8)^5$ = .0015	83.3
P(6 ϵ 10% tails) = $\binom{6}{6}(.2)^0(.8)^6$ = .0001	100.0

In this setting, the *expected* 20 percent SI is 20. If α is set at .05, the null hypothesis can be rejected if a 20 percent SI of 66.7, 83.3, or 100 is observed. Thus a 20 percent SI of up to 50 is still consistent with perfect calibration for a sample size of 6 and an α level of .05. Table 2 provides confidence intervals of 20 percent and 5 percent surprise indices for various sample sizes.

Again, the possibility of inferential error is evident if cases are treated as independent over subjects. Of course, if each case is independent, then pooling across subjects may not yield such inferential error.

3.2 Analysis of Calibration Indices: Type 2 Errors

To this point, we have assumed perfectly-calibrated subjects and examined the potential Type 1 error (false rejection of the subjects' perfectly-calibrated state) inherent in the use of typical experimental methods and related calibration indices. To consider the issue of identifying miscalibrated individuals (the Type 2 error problem) with such indices requires additional assumptions, particularly the parameters of the subjects' probability distributions and of the theoretical distributions of the underlying generating process.

TABLE 2

Confidence Intervals of the 20 Percent and 5 Percent Surprise Indices

Sample Size	Confidence Interval ($\alpha = .05$) 20 Percent SI	5 Percent SI
1	Never reject H	Never reject H
6	SI < 66.7	SI < 33.3
10	SI < 50	SI < 30
20	0 < SI < 40	SI < 20
100[a]	12.2 < SI < 27.8	.7 < SI < 9.3
1000[a]	17.5 < SI < 22.5	3.7 < SI < 6.4

[a]Using the normal approximation to the binomial distribution.

To illustrate some of the possibilities, assume a theoretical distribution that is normal with a mean of 0 and a variance of 1. The subjective distributions of four hypothetical individuals are described in Table 3, along with expected interquartile indices (I) and 20 percent surprise indices (SI).

TABLE 3

Some Hypothetical Distributions and Related Indices

Individual	Distribution	Expected I	Expected 20% SI
A	N(0,.5)	65.8	7.0
B	N(0, 2)	36.2	32.7
C	N(1, 1)	32.3	40.1
D	N(− 1,1)	32.3	40.1
True	N(0, 1)	50.0	20.0

The individuals in Table 3 have the following characteristics:
A: unbiased, distribution too tight (overconfident)
B: unbiased, distribution too diffuse (underconfident)

C: upward bias, dispersion correct
D: downward bias, dispersion correct

A variety of issues are raised by this characterization. It is apparent that pooling subjects' responses may have significant implications in terms of our ability: (1) to detect miscalibration, and (2) to identify the nature of miscalibration.[7] For example, if the responses (distributions) of subjects A and B are pooled, the expected interquartile index and 20 percent surprise index are 51 and 19.85, very nearly that of perfect calibration. Thus, pooling may obscure certain subject specific data that are of concern to the experimenter. Similarly, combining the responses of subjects A and C yields an expected interquartile index and 20 percent surprise index of 49.05 and 23.55, respectively.

In addition, a great deal of information is ignored by the conventional indices. For example, comparing subjects B and C, the indices do not identify the nature of the miscalibration. Similarly, for subjects C and D, bias in opposite directions results in identical indices. In real settings, the nature of miscalibration may be important, depending upon the loss function of the subject. These issues are reconsidered, using alternative methodologies, in section 4.0.

4.0 An Alternative Calibration Methodology for Auditing

The analysis in sections 3.1 and 3.2 illustrates a severe problem with usual calibration studies, especially those in which subjects are practicing auditors with limited available time to participate. We have shown that the number of cases used must be large to reduce the probability of Type 1 errors. Either the subject must evaluate many similar, but distinct, cases (in studies of individual subjects), or the experimenter must prepare a large number of independent cases, a few of which are given to each subject (in studies with pooled subject responses). Neither of these alternatives appears too attractive.

In addition, typical calibration studies ignore a great deal of information by focusing on rather simple indices (interquartile and surprise indices). For example, it is impossible to distinguish between a biased subjective distribution (i.e., mean is "incorrect") and one which is too tight or diffuse (i.e., variance is "incorrect"). Each may lead to conclusions of overconfidence or underconfidence, but they have different implications for practicing auditors. Similarly, skewness is overlooked. Of course, these indices were developed under rather restrictive conditions, where no frequency distributions were available. In an audit setting, however, it may be possible to simulate account balance distributions to achieve a frequency distribution. Such a possibility should be fully exploited.

Suppose, for example, the experimenter can construct a realistic audit scenario in which the dollar balance in a particular account is the variable of interest. The determining factors for this balance may be a combination of a series of random events whose probabilities can be manipulated by the experimenter (and disclosed to the subject). The experimenter should be able to construct a simulation model using various input parameters for each of the factors in the determination of the account balance, thereby generating an objective frequency distribution of balances to compare to the elicited subjective distribution. The sample size (number of points in the frequency distribution) can then be easily manipulated by the experimenter.

There are a variety of ways in which the elicited and observed distributions can be compared. For example, the Pearson Goodness-of-Fit Test determines how well an observed frequency distribution agrees with a theoretical (subjective) probability distribution defined by I mutually exclusive categories.[8] The test statistic is defined as:

$$\chi^2 = \sum_{i=1}^{I} \frac{[x_i - E(x_i)]^2}{E(x_i)}$$

$$= \sum_{i=1}^{I} \frac{[x_i - np_i]^2}{np_i}$$

where n = number of points in the frequency distribution

p_i = the theoretical (subjective) probability of category i

x_i = the observed frequency of category i

If $\chi^2 > \chi^2_{S:\,1-\alpha}$, where S = I-1 degrees of freedom, then the null hypothesis (no difference in subjective and observed distributions) is rejected.

The Kolmogorov Goodness-of-Fit Test represents another technique for comparing distributions.[9] With this test, the subjective cumulative probability ($P(x < x_i)$) is determined for each category i. These probabilities are compared to the corresponding relative frequencies ($\hat{P}(x < x_i)$). The test statistic, $K = \max |P(x < x_i) - \hat{P}(x < x_i)|$, is compared to $K_{I:1-\alpha}$. If $K > K_{I:1-\alpha}$, the null hypothesis of no difference is rejected.

Of course, there are other tests of goodness of fit that can be applied to continuous distributions. Note that these tests do not distinguish between overconfidence and underconfidence. However, if the distributions are concluded to be different, the investigator can easily compute mean, variance, and skewness statistics to identify the sources of differences. By doing so, overconfidence and underconfidence measures can be subdivided into a variety of miscalibration types.

There are several advantages of this methodology for evaluating calibration. First, it exploits more of the available information in audit and similar settings (i.e., continuous random variables). Second, the sample size can be arbitrarily selected by the experimenter. The subject does not need to evaluate a large number of cases. The tests of goodness of fit require several categories of data. However, typical elicitation methods generate these subjective intervals (e.g., the CDF-fractiles method). Third, various scenarios can be constructed by varying parameters within the simulation model, allowing sensitivity analysis on calibration. Thus, for example, auditors may be miscalibrated in some settings and not in others. Fourth, various parameters of observed and elicited distributions can be compared, expanding the characterization of miscalibration.

Of course, there are also disadvantages of the methodology. It cannot be directly applied to groups of subjects. In addition, many types of data cannot easily be treated as continuous random variables; thus, observed frequency distributions may be unavailable. This does not seem to be an overwhelming problem in audit settings.

5.0 Comments and A Concluding Note

The immediate implications of the above analysis can be briefly summarized. Since there is some underlying randomness (noise) in the outcomes (values) assessed by subjects in calibration studies, a perfectly-calibrated individual may easily be misclassified as overconfident or underconfident. Pooling of subjects does not appear to mitigate the problem, unless each subject is given independent cases.

The study of calibration is intuitively important to accounting and auditing research. As Tomassini et al. [1982] point out, an underconfident auditor may do more substantive testing (e.g., sampling) than that required to achieve an acceptable risk level. Beck et al. [1983] analytically identify both effectiveness and efficiency errors which can result from miscalibration. While this suggests it may be costly to identify miscalibrated individuals, further research is needed to provide an economic rationale for the persistence, if any, of significant miscalibration in practice.

Finally, the notion and implications of group calibration are not well defined in the literature. It may be useful to analyze and investigate the effects of aggregating individual probabilistic judgments in calibration studies. Since, as this paper suggests, calibration is ideally measured by comparing an individual's personal probability distribution with the underlying frequency distribution, additional measures (e.g., bias) should be incorporated into future research. In many situations, such a "true" distribution may not be observable. However, for purposes such as auditing research, it may be instructive to develop simulations of an assumed generating process for which such calibration comparisons could be made.

NOTES

[1]We recognize that there are a variety of definitions of calibration. The simplest possible setting is one in which there exists a single random variable with an underlying "true" distribution and a subjective distribution, that must be compared along all dimensions (moments). Thus, for *every* interval in the distribution, the observed frequency of outcomes corresponds to the number expected for that interval. Ferrell and McGoey [1980, p. 32] state "...there is wide agreement that such (subjective) probabilities ought to be consistent with relative frequencies in the sense that the proportion of actual occurrences of events which were assigned a given probability number should, in the long run, approach that number." If the frequency distribution and the subjective distribution agree along all moments, then *any* definition of calibration will be satisfied (the converse is *not* true). In addition, using all moments to define calibration unambiguously permits us to conclude that a well-calibrated assessor is always preferable to one who is miscalibrated.

[2]As Lichtenstein et al. [1982] point out, most studies in the literature group probabilities across assessors in order to secure sufficiently large samples of data needed for stable calibration estimates.

[3]The necessity of this assumption and the interpretations of aggregate (group) probability assessments are debatable issues which are beyond the intended scope of this paper. See Solomon [1982] for a discussion of such issues.

[4]For example, in substantive testing phase of an audit, we might view the phenomenon of interest (the account balance) as a random variable with uncertain parameters (mean, variance, etc.). If a calibration study uses observed audit values as criteria, the account balance parameters are not incorporated into the analysis.

[5]For mathematical convenience, most of the Bayesian auditing literature considers the account balance as normally-distributed with an unknown mean, but a known (or predictable) variance [e.g., Kinney, 1975]. Hence, the subjective distribution assessed within the context is viewed as an expression of one's uncertainty about the process mean. We allow for uncertainty of the process (any parameters) in characterizing subjective distributions and in our construct of calibration. This is consistent with Kinney's own admission (p. 131) that the known variance assumption may be unwarranted and may require that the variance be represented by a density function in the decision model.

[6]The empirical existence or the observability of such underlying distributions (sometimes referred to as "super populations") is a debatable matter. We limit our discussion of this issue to the methodological suggestion made in section 4.0.

[7]We are ignoring the probability of detecting miscalibration for a single individual because, as the analysis in section 3.1 shows, that analysis depends upon sample size. In addition, most studies reject perfect calibration, so the issue does not seem as significant as the probability of a Type 1 error. Finally, subjects are usually not exposed to issues drawn from the same underlying distribution (as is assumed above). This fact makes computation of Type 2 error probabilities tedious even under convenient assumptions.

[8]See, for example, Marascuilo and McSweeney [1977, p. 247].

[9]See, for example, Marascuilo and McSweeney [1977, pp. 248-9].

REFERENCES

Beck, P.J., I. Solomon, and L.A. Tomassini, "Subjective Probability Assessments and Audit Risk," unpublished working paper, University of California, Los Angeles, August 1983.

Corless, J. C., "Assessing Prior Distributions for Applying Bayesian Statistics in Auditing," *The Accounting Review* (July 1972), pp. 556-566.

Farrell, W.R. and P.J. McGoey, "A Model of Calibration for Subjective Probabilities," *Organizational Behavior and Human Performance* (August 1980), pp. 32-53.

Felix, W.L., "Evidence on Alternative Means of Assessing Prior Probability Distributions for Audit Decision Making," *The Accounting Review* (October 1976), pp. 800-807.

Kinney, W.R., "A Decision Theory Approach to the Sampling Problem in Auditing," *Journal of Accounting Research* (Spring 1975), pp. 117-132.

Lichtenstein, S., B. Fischhoff, and L.D. Phillips, "Calibration of Probabilities: State of the Art to 1980," in D. Kahneman, P. Slovic, and A. Tversky, (eds.), *Judgement Under Uncertainty: Heuristics and Biases* (Cambridge University Press, 1982), pp. 306-334.

Marascuilo, L.A. and M. McSweeney, *Nonparametric and Distribution-Free Methods for the Social Sciences* (Brooks/Cole Publishing Company, 1977).

Solomon, I., "Probability Assessment by Individual Auditors and Audit Teams: An Empirical Investigation," *Journal of Accounting Research* (Autumn 1982), Part II, pp. 689-710.

Solomon, I., J.L. Krogstad, M.B. Romney, and L.A. Tomassini, "Auditors' Prior Probability Distributions for Account Balances," *Accounting, Organizations and Society,* Vol. 7, No. 1 (1982), pp. 27-41.

Tomassini, L.A., I. Solomon, M.B. Romney, and J.L. Krogstad, "Calibration of Auditors' Probabilistic Judgments: Some Empirical Evidence," *Organizational Behavior and Human Performance* (December 1982), pp. 391-406.

G.R. Chesley
Dalhousie University

Discussant's Comments on:

"Calibration of Subjective Probability Assessments: A Methodological Perspective"

Professors Newman and Tomassini present a thought provoking analysis of some of the limitations of an increasingly popular methodology for studying and training auditors to better express themselves in terms of subjective or personal probabilities. While as a reviewer, I should express my views as to the shortcomings of the paper, I am in basic sympathy with the objectives behind its presentation. Except for the detailed editorial comments that I will briefly mention, my criticisms of the study are expressions of my values and preferences and, therefore, represent suggestions for future studies in this area.

The paper presents some of the methodological issues inherent in calibration. After cleverly describing a basic and well known problem of calibration, namely the problem of obtaining a sufficient sample size to permit a stable calibration estimate [see Lichtenstein et al, 1977] the discussion turns to how the peculiarities of the audit environment can be exploited to improve the ease with which calibration can be applied. Goodness-of-fit testing and simulation of audit populations are suggested as ways of improving current methodology.

Lichtenstein et al [1977, p. 280-284] present a rather comprehensive review of the history and difficulties of calibration. As early as 1906, a Western Australian Astronomer named W. Ernest Cooke, calibrated 1,951 predictions in terms of actual results. In the year 1951, calibrations of 1,095 twelve-hour precipitation forecasts were presented. In fact, the U.S. Weather Bureau forecasts have been the subject of numerous calibration studies because of the abundance of actual data with which to test forecasts. The Weather Bureau has been able to train and evaluate personnel using various forms of calibration for many years.

Comparison of subjective probability assessments with actual results or distributions represents an interesting issue. A subjective probability is a degree of belief in a proposition whose truth has not been ascertained. As such, so long as it obeys the usual axioms of probability (and even this is debatable), it cannot be "right" or "correct" or be compared to a "true" probability which unfortunately does not exist [Lichtenstein et al 1977, p.

275]. Calibration recognizes this and attempts to avoid the issue by suggesting that subjective probabilities are reflections of how much one knows. As such, "...there should be a systematic relationship between probability and truth." [Lichtenstein and Fischhoff, 1980, p. 149] Thus, over the "long run" a well calibrated individual assigns probabilities equal to the "true" probability. If a person is not well calibrated, he or she should be trained or debiased. One fundamental question relevant to calibration is obvious from this brief description. If a known empirical distribution exists, why use the subjective results? If it does not exist, why debias an assessor using an incorrect distribution? How such training on known distributions might generalize to subjective environments still appears to be an open question [Lichtenstein and Fischhoff, 1980, p. 170].

The paper points out that most experimental studies use between subjects designs and a limited number of cases from which to observe criterion values. Using Type I and Type II error characteristics, the analysis in the Newman and Tomassini paper proceeds to show the percentage of errors possible for a perfectly calibrated model and how confidence intervals vary depending on sample sizes. Only when $n = 1000$ do reasonably tight Type I confidence intervals arise for the interquartile range. Obviously, auditors are unlikely to make 1000 plus assessments. If multiple subjects are used then the paper suggests perfect dependence between subjects would reduce the effective sample size. Therefore, different cases should be presented to each subject. While it is true that ten identical subjects become one if they are all perfectly dependent, what is necessary here is the study of the effect of varying degrees of dependence in varying circumstances and its implication for Type I errors. Also whether or not assumed independent questions are in fact independent needs careful review [see Harrison, 1977]. The existence of heuristics and artifacts are well known in typical questioning situations.

Type II errors occur when miscalibrated persons are identified as being well calibrated. The paper shows the effect of aggregating different distributions representing poorly calibrated persons and how this potentially hides specific problems. The suggestion is also made that the standard measures of calibration such as interquartile range and surprise indexes are not very sensitive measures. Also mentioned is the fact that the importance of miscalibration depends on the loss function of the subject. These well known problems lead naturally to the solutions proposed in the paper.

First and foremost is the suggestion that a realistic audit scenario could be constructed which would permit the use of simulation to manipulate parameters to provide calibration standards against which to test subject assessments. Second, more sensitive tests of calibration are possible which would help reduce the required number of responses and improve the diagnosis of calibration problems. As the paper suggests, the tests and the model have numerous diagnostic advantages such as sensitivity and experimenter control but still cannot cope with noncontinuous data, groups of subjects and the distinction between under and over confidence. Of course, more direct tests of means, medians, variances and other moments are possible. The proposal to use simulation and goodness-of-fit tests is an interesting reversal of the usual approach to such comparisons. The proposal here is to use the simulation to generate the observed frequencies in sufficient numbers to fit the simulation to the subjective distribution rather than the other way one usually thinks of doing the fit. This would enable the researcher to generate a sample of sufficient size from the simulation to permit the cell sizes of the Chi square test or the nonparametric equivalent to be satisfied. Thus a single subjective distribution could be tested to the simulation. Interestingly, if a known distribution were substituted for the simulation, the goodness-of-fit test could not be conducted because no frequencies would be available. Also, if the simulation were run long enough, a small difference between the simulation and the subjective distribution would be significant at some reasonable Type I error level. For example, a subjective distribution of N(0,1) is not significantly different from a simulated one N(0,1.1) at a sample size of 800. It is, however, significantly different using a Chi square test at 10 percent using a sample size of 4000 and at .5 percent in 8000 iterations. Care will be necessary to assure a significant difference is a "real" difference.

FURTHER SUGGESTIONS

To close this review, a number of suggestions for future study will be outlined. One area that can serve as an adjunct to the general calibration methodology is a review of how reconciliation of multiple probability assessments can or should be undertaken. Freeling [1981] provides a preliminary analysis of how the question of reconciling the different subjective probabilities for the same event might be undertaken to obtain one probability (or distribution). The fact that a number of the elicitation techniques provide discrete approximations to continuous distributions suggests a second line of research. Obviously, if as suggested by Miller and Rice [1983] that discrete approximations systematically underestimate the moments of the original distribution, research extending the proposed gaussian quadrature would improve the calibration of subjective distributions. Savage [1972] suggested that probabilities of probabilities would lead to an infinite regress of accuracy expressions. Yet a theory of subject errors is a necessary extension of calibration beyond the general heuristics statements made by researchers such as Kahneman and Tversky [1972] and others. At present, Lichtenstein et al [1977, p. 316] characterize the area as "dust-bowl empiricism" that needs considerable fine-tuned studies of a variety of areas concerned with the specific patterns of auditor responses. In such a study, care is needed to avoid some of the pitfalls of the early conservatism studies where Bayes revision difficulties were found to result from experimental artifacts rather than real problems [see Chesley, 1975]. As Lichtenstein et al [1977, p. 293] point out, calibration of very difficult tasks tends to be very poor and the degree of calibration varies with the task difficulty. Care will also be needed to avoid using cases prepared from Neter and Loebbecke [1975] material as was done by Tomassini, et al [1982] if we are to avoid testing the auditor's knowledge of such a study rather than the more general experience of the auditor. [See Cohen, 1981 for a more general discussion of the questions concerned with comparing subjective responses to standard probability distributions and the implications of such comparisons). One last suggestion comes from the flat maximum problem found with scoring rules [Lichtenstein et al, 1977, p. 314]. Audit decision problems need to be studied to ascertain the extent to which they are insensitive to calibration problems. Without such an analysis the importance of calibration to auditing in unknown.

I would like to conclude by congratulating the authors for an interesting paper and expressing my wish that they continue their analysis of the calibration issue in the field of auditing.

APPENDIX

Editorial Comments

1. The first sentence on page 90 is somewhat misleading because the subjective concept of probability can be traced as far back as probability itself (see Cohen, L.J., "Some Historical Remarks on the Baconian Conception of Probability," *Journal of the History of Ideas* (1980), pp. 219-231).
2. The last sentence of footnote 1 is misleading because the study of rationality and the benefits of perfect calibration are far from complete at the present time (see Cohen, 1981, in references).
3. The reference to the popularity of the CDF technique on page 91 seems to be too strong from my unofficial view of the literature. I certainty would not say it was "the most popular method."
4. Page 97 contains no reference to the idea of pooling subjects. Since pooling is a very general term, I assume from the illustration that aggregation (addition) is implied.
5. An illustration of the type of simulation of account balance distributions referred to on page 97 would provide help in interpreting the suggestions because the empirical frequency of errors is not generally known because auditors observe only those errors they discover. The distribution of sample means is, of course, easy if that is what is meant.

REFERENCES

Chesley, G.R. "Elicitation of Subjective Probabilities: A Review," *The Accounting Review* (1975), pp. 325-337.

Cohen, L.J., "Can Human Irrationality be Experimentally Demonstrated," *The Behavioral and Brain Sciences* (1981), pp. 317-370.

Freeling, A.N.S., "Reconciliation of Multiple Probability Assessments," *Organizational Behavior and Human Performance* (1981), pp. 395-414.

Harrison, J. M., "Independence and Calibration in Decision Analysis," *Management Science* (1977), pp. 320-328.

Kahneman, D. and A. Tversky, "Subjective Probability: A Judgement of Representativeness," *Cognitive Psychology* (1972), pp. 149-171.

Lichtenstein, S. and B. Fischhoff, "Training for Calibration," *Organizational Behavior and Human Performance* (1980), pp. 149-171.

Lichtenstein, S., B. Fischhoff, and L.D. Phillips, "Calibration of Probabilities: The State of the Art," in *Decision Making and Change in Human Affairs,* ed., by H. Jungermann and G. DeZeeuw (D. Reidel, 1977), pp. 275-324.

Miller, A.C. and T.R. Rice, "Discrete Approximation of Probability Distributions," *Management Science* (1983), pp. 352-362.

Neter, J. and J.K. Loebbecke, *Auditing Research Monograph No. 2: Behavior of Major Statistical Estimations in Sampling Accounting Populations* (AICPA, 1975).

Newman, D.P. and L.A. Tomassini, "Calibration of Subjective Probability Assessments: A Methodological Perspective," in S. Moriarity and E. Joyce (Eds.) *Decision Making and Accounting: Current Research,* (University of Oklahoma, Center for Economic and Management Research, 1984), pp. 90-100.

Savage, L.J., *The Foundations of Statistics,* 2nd ed., (Dover Publications, 1972).

Tomassini, L.A., I. Solomon, M.B., Romney, and J.L. Krogstad, "Calibration of Auditors' Probabilistic Judgments: Some Empirical Evidence," *Organizational Behavior and Human Performance* (1982), pp. 391-406.

Ira Solomon
University of Illinois

Discussant's Comments on:

"Calibration of Subjective Probability Assessments: A Methodological Perspective"

INTRODUCTION

Professors Newman and Tomassini (N&T) have raised some interesting methodological issues relevant to the study of probability calibration. Their paper briefly reviews how calibration typically has been measured in probabilistic judgment studies, describes some apparent problems with such practices (particularly as they relate to the control of inferential errors) and concludes with a suggestion for an alternative approach to testing for proper calibration. My comments on the N&T paper are organized as follows. First, I provide preliminary observations related primarily to the calibration concept employed in the paper. In particular, I explain that the N&T concept of calibration is different from that found in the subjective probability and behavioral (probability elicitation) literatures and actually is one of a class of composite measures of assessor skills. Next, I discuss N&T's analysis of the risk of inferential errors in calibration studies. Here I explain that, although N&T raise some interesting issues, there actually is little support for a conclusion that the methodology of calibration studies adversely affects the probability of such errors. My comments conclude with a brief examination of the alternative methodology presented by N&T and suggestions for future probability calibration research.

Preliminary Observations

Over 30 years ago, noted philosopher Bertrand Russell [1948, p. 397] identified what he considered to be perfect rationality which "... consists not in believing what is true but in attaching to every proposition a degree of belief corresponding to its credibility." This perfect rationality is the calibration concept found in the subjective probability literature [e.g., de Finetti 1937, 1962, Savage 1972 and Kyburg 1974] and, hereafter, is referred to as the "traditional calibration concept." It typically has been evaluated in empirical studies, as N&T describe, by measuring the correspondence between the fractiles of a PPD ensemble and relative outcome frequencies.[1] Such correspondence, as noted by Hogarth [1980, p. 215] depends primarily upon the PPD's dispersion (variance) and, therefore is concerned less with whether the assessor knows than whether the assessor knows how much he/she knows [see Lichtenstein and Fischhoff 1977].[2]

The calibration concept discussed in the N&T paper is, however, somewhat different from the traditional concept. N&T state on page 90 that a perfectly calibrated assessor would specify a PPD that matches the underlying process distribution. However, one must examine their footnote 1 to identify what actually meant by the term "match"—coincidence between all moments of the PPD and the process (theoretical) distribution. Focussing on the PPD presently (see below for a discussion of the "theoretical" distribution), notice that N&T's calibration concept requires both that the PPD dispersion be "appropriate" and the PPD center be at the process mode while the traditional concept of calibration requires only the former. Hence, if one were to assess a PPD whose mean is displaced from the process mode, one would be considered miscalibrated by N&T even if the PPD fractiles were spread so that the relative frequency of outcomes which fall above and below each fractile are consistent with the fractile definitions (e.g., the interquartile range (IQR) contains 50 percent of the outcomes, etc.).

There is, of course, nothing inherently wrong with N&T's measure of assessor skill. However, four observations are in order. First, as noted above, the N&T calibration concept is not the traditional calibration concept and, therefore, the use of the term calibration in the N&T paper is potentially misleading.[3] Second, the N&T calibration concept actually measures a composite of assessor skills. The probability elicitation literature distinguishes between calibration and another aspect of PPD conformance—extremeness [see Seaver, von Winterfeldt and Edwards 1978]. PPD extremeness is directly concerned with the assessor's substantive knowledge of the uncertain process. It, therefore, focuses on the assessor's ability to assign high probabilities to events which obtain and low probabilities elsewhere and, typically, has been evaluated by measuring the conformance between outcomes and the central tendency of the PPD. N&T's calibration concept effectively incorporates both extremeness and calibration.

Third, there are many such composite measures of assessor skills which have been discussed in the probability elicitation literature [see Stael von Holstein 1970]. These composite measures typically are called scoring rules and there are a host of problems associated with their usage including the unavoidable arbitrary weighting of each of the components.[4] Because of such problems, recent research studies have employed the more fundamental assessor skill measures (extremeness and the traditional calibration concept) which always could be used to compute composites. Moreover, the fundamental skill measures highlight assessor deficiencies which could be obscured if a scoring rule were employed.

My final preliminary observation is that Russell's perfect rationality notion (see above), which is consistent with the traditional calibration concept, is likely to be more palatable to subjectivists than N&T's calibration concept [see Kyburg 1974] since it can be shown to be an implication of coherence (i.e., conformance with the probability axioms, [see Kadane and Lichtenstein 1982]). Hence, although subjectivists might cringe at the general idea of comparing PPDs with outcomes, since under their view of probability all beliefs are equally valid, even they would likely find something to be amiss if an assessor's beliefs could place him/her in a situation in which a series of wagers (i.e., a "dutch book") could be constructed which guarantees a loss.[5]

The Type I Error Analysis

N&T's analysis of the risk that a researcher will commit a Type I error in evaluating an assessor's calibration is conducted by positing a perfectly calibrated assessor and identifying the probability that the researcher will incorrectly conclude that he/she is miscalibrated. For example, they observe that a perfectly calibrated assessor's PPD would capture a known percentage (50 percent) of the draws from the uncertain process (i.e., outcomes) in the IQR and thus, the family of binomial distributions can be used to compute the probabilities of obtaining any of the possible number of outcomes (e.g., one to six) in the IQR. Subsequently N&T note, based upon such computed probabilities, that for a small number of cases, it is very difficult to reject a null hypothesis of perfect calibration irrespective of the number of outcomes which actually are observed in the IQR. They illustrated this problem by showing that if six cases were to be employed, either zero out of the six or six out of the six outcomes would have to fall in the IQR for the researcher to be able to reject the null hypothesis of perfect calibration at usual levels of statistical significance.

The issue I should like to raise about this "problem" is fairly simple—what is the problem? Recall that the Type I error analysis was begun by postulating a hypothetical assessor who was *perfectly calibrated.* Thus, I fail to see how it can be viewed as problematic that a researcher would have difficulty rejecting a null hypothesis of perfect calibration in the case of an assessor who is perfectly calibrated.

Next the authors examine the role of sample size in the above "problem." As one might expect, N&T show that a larger sample size increases the researcher's statistical power to reject the null hypothesis. Notice, however, that since their analysis assumes a perfectly calibrated assessor, only one inferential error (Type I) can be made. Consequently, the increased ability to reject the null hypothesis actually inflates the researcher's Type I error probability since any rejection of the null hypothesis is incorrect. This leads one to the interesting conclusion that, *ceteris paribus,* a smaller sample size is preferable to a larger sample size and, therefore, such methods as pooling PPDs to increase sample size must be detrimental. While I do believe that there are other important issues surrounding such pooling (see below), I do not believe that N&T identified one in their Type I error analysis. Rather, their conclusion seems to flow directly from the assumption of perfect calibration which results only in Type I errors being possible. I am confident that a joint analysis of Type I and Type II errors would lead to a more intuitive conclusion regarding sample size and reveal that pooling of PPDs has only limited implications for controlling inferential risks in calibration studies (see below).

One final point about the Type I error analysis is noteworthy. On page 97, N&T state, "We have shown that the number of cases used must be large to reduce the probability of Type I errors." This conclusion suggests that N&T have shown that larger sample sizes permit control of the risk of inferential errors in calibration studies. However, while it is an appealing conclusion, it does not follow from their analysis. Rather, to repeat my earlier point, N&T's analysis, by ignoring Type II errors, actually shows that smaller sample sizes are preferable since they typically will result in an inability to reject the null hypothesis of perfect calibration and, thus, inferential errors (Type I) will be minimized.

The Type II Error Analysis

N&T's main arguments in this section are that pooling PPDs across assessors can cause the researcher to fail to identify miscalibration when it exists (i.e., commit a Type II error) and that pooling can obscure the type of miscalibration (i.e., overconfidence vs. underconfidence). These are potentially important points which depend upon the assumption that the subject-assessor population is heterogeneous with respect to the skill measured by calibration. Hence, if assessors tend to be consistently overconfident in a given situation [as often is the case, see Lichtenstein et al 1982], pooling across subjects is not likely to change the risk of Type II error. It seems appropriate, therefore, to call for empirical research at the individual subject-assessor level to determine if auditors are relatively homogeneous (or heterogeneous) with respect to calibration deficiencies.

An additional point, related to the Type II error analysis concerns N&T's observation that calibration studies ignore part of the uncertainty inherent in the uncertain process for which the PPD is assessed, by constructing calibration indices based upon only one outcome from a "super population" (e.g., the actual quantity of precipitation or the actual value of the accounting population). While viewing the experimentor-observed outcome as a draw from a super population as N&T suggest, is intuitively appealing, three observations are in order. First, irrespective of the context and type of study being conducted in practice, one can observe only a single draw (the event which obtained) from any super population. Hence, if calibration research studies have not recognized part of the uncertainty which the subject faces (i.e., the variability in possible outcome values), such nonrecognition is not unique to calibration studies. Indeed this "criticism" is applicable in varying degrees to any study in which the accuracy of judgments, predictions or decisions was investigated including bankruptcy-prediction studies [e.g., Libby 1975, Casey 1980], stock-price prediction studies [e.g., Wright 1977] and bond-rating prediction studies [e.g., Kessler and Ashton 1980].

Second, their point, in and of itself, does not suggest that the traditional calibration methodologies should be scrapped but instead that further empirical research is required to determine how sensitive calibration findings are to possible outcome variability. Hence, using the traditional framework one could simulate calibration curves and indices using several outcome values. I suspect, however, that this suggestion and the suggestions made by N&T in their Section 3 (see p. 97) would be difficult to implement at this time since we know very little about the variability of actual super-populations. Hence, once again empirical research would appear fruitful.

Finally, consider what the actual consequences of understating the uncertainty facing the assessor (by ignoring potential variability in outcomes) are likely to be. For example, an assessor, who the researcher classifies as miscalibrated (overconfident), based on a traditional calibration analysis, may be seen to be even more overconfident if additional uncertainty (due to outcome variability) is taken into account. But such an assessor is not likely to be misclassified as well calibrated since non-recognition of the superpopulation uncertainty only could have made the overconfident assessor appear more sensitive to the limitations of his/her subjective knowledge than actually is warranted. Similarly, consider an assessor who is classified as miscalibrated (underconfident) by a researcher using the traditional calibration analysis. This assessor actually may be considered well calibrated when the additional uncertainty due to outcome variability is accounted for. However, such an error is of Type I, not as suggested by N&T, a Type II error. Moreover, its consequences are likely to be minimal and, in the Bayesian audit context, relate only to the efficiency of the audit [see Beck, Solomon and Tomassini 1983]. Finally, consider an assessor who is classified by the researcher as well-calibrated based upon a traditional calibration analysis, but actually would have been seen to be miscalibrated (overconfident) if the additional uncertainty due to outcome variability were taken into account. While the consequence of such a Type II error could be more serious than that above, the probability of its occurrence seems relatively remote since it requires that *both* the outcome from the super population and the auditor-assessor's PPD mean are biased in the same direction and by the same amount.

The Alternative Calibration Methodology

Based upon the assertion that perfect calibration requires conformance between the process distribution and the assessed PPD, N&T present a methodology to test for such conformance and concurrently recognize the potential for outcome variability. In particular, they suggest that repeated draws be taken from a simulated super population so that a theoretical distribution can be estimated. Subsequently, the PPD is compared with the theoretical distribution using one of the many goodness-of-fit tests [e.g., Pearson, Kolmogorov-Smirnov].

Recall, however, that the proposed methodology is not so much an alternative methodology as it is a methodology for a different concept of calibration (see above). The authors could have recognized this distinction to avoid further clouding of the already muddy waters. Also noteworthy is that the proposal that a statistical goodness-of-fit test be employed is not new. Rather such tests, within the framework of the traditional concept of calibration, first appeared over a decade ago in the probability calibration literature [see Stael von Holster 1970, Moore and Thomas 1975 and Solomon 1979].

Third, what N&T are proposing is more a scoring rule than it is an alternative calibration methodology since, as noted above, their test would effectively combine the traditional concepts of calibration and extremeness. As I noted earlier, several such scoring rules exist and the literature contains many examples of the problems with these composite measures of assessor skills. Furthermore, these problems are not avoided by the goodness-of-fit tests suggested by N&T. Rather, each test imposes an implicit (arbitrary) weighting which may or may not be consistent with a decision makers preferences.[6] Finally, notice that the goodness-of-fit tests actually involve a more stringent test of conformance than N&T's calibration concept requires. In particular, a point-by-point coincidence between the PPD and theoretical distribution is implicit in the Pearson goodness-of-fit test while the N&T calibration concept (see their footnote one) requires coincidence of the moments of the PPD and theoretical distribution.

Concluding Remarks

In closing I should like to reiterate that the N&T paper raised some interesting issues relevant to the methodology of probability calibration studies. I also should like to take this opportunity to provide a brief "laundry list" of related issues which are worthy of future research. These include the issues I raised earlier concerning: (1) the relative homogeneity (or heterogeneity) of auditors with respect to calibration deficiencies and (2) the sensitivity of calibration indices to realistic levels of super-population variability, (although I am not sure how to determine how much variability is realistic). Other interesting issues include: (3) Should materiality be incorporated directly in auditing calibration studies and, if so, how?; (4) What impact does the auditing context (type of account, internal control environment) have on auditors' calibration?; (5) How much of a departure from perfect calibration (which is, of course, inevitable) is meaningful in the audit context?; (6) How is assessor calibration affected by the framing of the elicitation task?; and (7) what role does confounding of assessor beliefs and preferences play in the auditing calibration results which have been reported?

NOTES

[1]Correspondence between PPD fractiles and outcome frequencies is a measure of calibration in the continuous case which is discussed by N&T. In the discrete case, a comparison of the assessed probability and the proportion of times the event is true, typically has been employed to measure calibration (see Lichtenstein, et. al. [1982]).

[2]It is noteworthy that Hogarth [1980] identified the traditional calibration concept as another form of coherence (see related discussion below).

[3]I disagree with the implication in their footnote one that probability elicitation researchers have not reached a consensus on the concept of calibration. Indeed, I am unaware of any study which has departed from what I have identified as the traditional calibration concept. Accordingly, rather than simply imposing their concept of calibration, N&T should have provided some justification for it.

[4]Scoring rules are mathematical functions which assign a score to a PPD based upon both the event which obtains and the probability associated with that event and others considered feasible. Examples of commonly employed scoring rules are the quadratic, spherical and logarithmic (see Winkler [1967a], Stael von Holstein [1970] and Slovic, Fischhoff and Lichtenstein [1977]).

[5]For example, suppose an assessor believes that P(A) = .75 and P(Not − A) = .80. Then it is possible to form two bets that individually seem fair but together put the assessor in a no-win situation:

Bet 1 – If A occurs, the assessor wins $1.
If Not − A occurs, the assessor loses $3.

Bet 2: If A occurs, the assessor loses $4.
If Not − A occurs, the assessor wins $1.

Bet 1 is based on the assessor's belief that A is three times as likely as Not − A while, bet 2 is based on the assessor's second belief that Not − A is four times as likely to occur as A. Notice, however, that together, the two bets guarantee the loss of money since if A occurs the assessor wins $1 and loses $4 (net loss of $3) while if Not − A occurs, the assessor loses $3 and wins $1 (net loss of $2).

[6]For example, my personal experience with the Pearson goodness-of-fit test, suggested by N&T, is that it assigns a great deal of weight to the tails of a PPD (e.g., .01, .99 fractiles) vis-a-vis more central fractiles (e.g., .50), thus, almost always resulting in rejection of a null hypothesis of proper calibration. The same problem exists with the Kolmogorov test but to a lesser degree due to the use of an absolute value rather than squared terms in computing the statistic.

REFERENCES

Beck, P.J., I. Solomon and L.A. Tomassini, "Subjective Prior Probability Distributions and Audit Risk," unpublished working paper, The University of Illinois (September 1983).

Casey, C.J., "Variation in Accounting Information Load: The Effect on Loan Officers' Prediction of Bankruptcy," *The Accounting Review* (January 1980), pp. 36-49.

de Finetti, B., "Foresight: Its Logical Laws, Its Subjective Sources," *Annales de l'Institut,* Henri Poincare 1 (1937), reprinted in English: *Studies in Subjective Probability.* Edited by H.E. Kyburg, Jr. and H.E. Smokler (Wiley, 1964).

de Finetti, B., "Does it Make Sense to Speak of 'Good Probability Appraisers'?" *The Scientist Speculates: An Anthology of Partially Baked Ideas* (Basic Books, 1962).

Hogarth, R.M., *Judgement and Choice* (John Wiley & Sons, 1980).

Kadane, J.B. and S. Lichtenstein, "A Subjectivist View of Calibration," unpublished Decision Research Report 82-6 (Decision Research, 1982).

Kessler, L. and R.H. Ashton, "Feedback and Prediction Achievement in Financial Analysis," *Journal of Accounting Research* (Spring 1981), pp. 146-162.

Kyburg, H.E., Jr., *The Logical Foundations of Statistical Inference* (D. Reidel Publishing Co., 1974).

Libby, R., "Accounting Ratios and the Prediction of Failure: Some Behavioral Evidence," *Journal of Accounting Research* (Spring 1975), pp. 150-161.

Lichtenstein, S. and B. Fischhoff, "Do Those Who Know More Also Know More About How Much They Know," *Organizational Behavior and Human Performance* (December 1977), pp. 159-183.

Lichtenstein, S., B. Fischhoff, and L.D. Phillips, "Calibration of Probabilities: State of the Art to 1980," in D. Kahneman, P. Slovic, and A. Tversky, eds., *Judgment Under Uncertainty: Heuristics and Biases* (Cambridge University Press, 1982).

Moore, P.G. and H. Thomas, "Measuring Uncertainty," *Omega* (December 1975), pp. 657-672.

Newman, D.P. and L.A. Tomassini, "Calibration of Subjective Probability Assessments: A Methodological Perspective," in S. Moriarity and E. Joyce (Eds.) *Decision Making and Accounting: Current Research,* (University of Oklahoma, Center for Economic and Management Research, 1984), pp. 90-100.

Russell, B., *Human Knowledge: Its Scope and Limits* (Simon and Schuster, 1948).

Savage, L.J., *The Foundations of Statistics,* 2nd Edition, (Dover Publications, 1972).

Seaver, D.A., D. von Winterfeldt and W. Edwards, "Eliciting Subjective Probability Distributions on Continuous Variables," *Organizational Behavior and Human Performance* (1978), pp. 379-391.

Slovic, P., B. Fischhoff and S. Lichtenstein, "Behavioral Decision Theory," *Annual Review of Psychology (1977), pp. 1-39.*

Solomon, I., "Aggregating Prior Probability Distributions for Audit Decision Making," Unpublished Ph.D. dissertation, University of Texas at Austin (1979).

Stael, von Holstein, C-A. S., *Assessment and Evaluation of Subjective Probability Distribution,* The Economic Research Institute at the Stockholm School of Economics (1970).

Winkler, R.L., "The Assessment of Prior Probability Distributions in Bayesian Analysis," *Journal of the American Statistical Association* (1967a), pp. 776-800.

Winkler, R.L., "The Quantification of Judgment: Some Experimental Isssues," *Proceedings of the American Statistical Association* (1967b), pp. 386-395.

Wright, W.F., "Financial Information Processing Models: An Empirical Study," *The Accounting Review* (July 1977), pp. 676-689.

Stanley F. Biggs
Bashir A. Biuk
Amal A.W. Mahmoud
University of Wisconsin-Madison

Experimental Evidence on Conformance With the Independence Axiom of Normative Decision Theory

This study investigated the effect of two variables on conformance with the independence axiom: (1) the level of knowledge of Expected Value technique, and (2) the probability of a bad outcome. The results indicate that conformity among non-knowledge subjects and some of the conformity among the knowledge subjects was due to decision strategies such as avoiding high probability of a bad outcome, high payoff, etc. Also, it was found that the conformity among knowledge subjects was higher than the conformity among non-knowledge subjects. This can be attributed to the knowledge of Expected Value technique. Thus, it can be concluded that training in the Expected Value technique may result in decisions that show greater conformance with normative decision theory.

INTRODUCTION AND BACKGROUND

Decision (or choice) behavior forms the basis for much of the theoretical and empirical research in accounting. It is fair to say that over the past three decades one model of choice behavior, the expected utility model, has dominated the literature in accounting,[1] as well as other fields (e.g., economics, psychology and finance). The model is concerned with choices among risky prospects, and implies that the individual multiplies probabilities and utilities of each prospect's outcomes, sums these products and chooses the prospect that has the greatest sum. A relatively simple axiomatic structure underlies the expected utility theory [Savage, 1954] and gives it a mathematical tractability that has made it a very attractive model for various theoretical works in accounting.

The purpose of this paper is to report the results of several experiments involving the independence axiom of the expected utility model. Before describing this axiom and the related experiments, a brief discussion of where this research fits with other research on the expected utility model is presented.

Schoemaker [1982] suggests that expected utility theory can serve four purposes. First, expected utility theory can be used to *descriptively* model decision processes underlying risky choice. If expected utility theory is to be thought of as a descriptive model, it is relevant to examine the validity of the underlying axioms and to determine if individuals process information in ways that are consistent with the theory. In reviewing the evidence, Schoemaker [1982, p. 552] concludes the following:

> As a descriptive model, seeking insight into how decisions are made, EU theory fails on at least three counts. First, people do not structure problems as holistically and as comprehensively as EU theory suggests. Second, they do not process information, especially probabilities, according to the EU rule. Finally, EU theory, as an "as if" model, poorly predicts choice behavior in laboratory situations. Hence, it is doubtful that the EU theory should or could serve as a general descriptive model. However, there may be exceptions. For well-structured repetitive tasks, with important stakes, and well-trained decision makers, EU maximization may well describe the actual decision processes...

The above quote indicates that further research involving the descriptive validity of the expected utility model may be pointless. However, some accounting research [R. Ashton, 1979; and A. Ashton, 1982], which was not reviewed by Schoemaker, has found greater descriptive validity for expected utility theory. Both of these studies found fewer violations of the independence axiom than prior research. A. Ashton suggested that having experienced auditors make familiar judgments contributed to her subjects' greater conformance, and R. Ashton suggested that his subjects' training in the expected value technique resulted in greater conformance. Note, that both of these conclusions are consistent with the "exceptions" Schoemaker discusses above. That is, training and experience may be relevant variables in explaining the descriptive validity of the expected utility model.

The second purpose of the expected utility model is to use it in a *predictive or positivistic* way. In this view, the realism of the axioms are not important. The important factor is to determine if the model offers higher predictive accuracy than competing models of similar complexity.

The third usage of the expected utility model Schoemaker [1982, p. 539] refers to as *postdictive*. In this view, all observed behavior is consistent with the expected utility theory provided it can be modeled through ex post consideration of additional factors such as costs.

The final use of the expected utility model is the *prescriptive* or *normative* view. The goal of this approach is to improve decision making by using the expected utility model as the criterion for determining how decisions should be made.

All four uses of expected utility theory have generated considerable research, and each have proponents and detractors. Some of the views, for example predictive and postdictive, have been criticized for being nonfalsifiable [Schoemaker, 1982]. Since the purpose of this brief discussion has been to provide perspective for the experimental research, the reader is referred to Schoemaker [1982] for detailed discussion of the issues related to the various approaches.

The research reported here is concerned with the *descriptive* use of the expected utility model, and attempts to identify the reasons underlying choices that conform with the independence axiom. As discussed earlier, accounting-related research on the descriptive validity of the independence axiom has achieved greater conformance than research in other fields. Therefore, research that identifies reasons for conformance may provide important insights about the descriptive validity of the expected utility model.

Prior descriptive research has indicated that of all the axioms of rational choice, the independence axiom is the one most often violated by decision makers, e.g., [MacCrimmon, 1968; MacCrimmon and Larsson, 1975]. The independence axiom maintains that if alternatives have identical outcomes under a particular state of nature, then the ordering of those alternatives should be independent of the value of that common outcome. In other words, "identical outcomes of alternative decisions should be made utilizing only the remaining information" [Slovic and Tversky 1974].

Studies of the independence axiom typically are based on a decision problem originally suggested by Allais [1953]. The problem presents an individual with two decision situations, each involving a pair of gambles (as shown in Table 1). An individual who chooses gamble 1 over gamble 2 in situation A must choose gamble 3 over gamble 4 in situation B in order to conform to the axiom. That is, the axiom prescribes that the identical outcomes in gambles 1 and 2 (0.89 probability of receiving $1,000,000) and the identical outcomes in gambles 3 and 4 (0.89 probability of receiving $0) should be disregarded. Once the common outcomes have been eliminated, gambles 1 and 3 are identical (as are gambles 2 and 4) and thus the choice of gamble 1 (2) should be accompanied by the choice of gamble 3 (4). The choice of gamble 1 (2) in situation A and gamble 4 (3) in situation B violates the axiom and hence violates the Expected Utility theory.

Several studies have reported tests of the independence axiom [see MacCrimmon 1968; Slovic and Tversky 1974; Moskowitz 1974; and MacCrimmon and Larsson 1975]. One common characteristic of these studies, is that they all used the Allais problem setting and they all reported a substantial degree of violation of the independence axiom (the rate of violation ranged from 30 percent to about 60 percent) even under experimental conditions design to ensure that subjects understood the axiom's implications.

In contrast to the above studies, Ashton [1979] found that only 14 percent of his subjects made initial choices that violated the axiom. He explained his result by the fact that his subjects made decisions in accordance with the expected value (EV) technique and this led to a higher degree of conformity with the axiom than previous studies.

The discrepancy between Ashton's study and prior research motivated the present study. One possible explanation for this discrepancy is that Ashton's subjects were business students who may have had knowledge of the EV technique while subjects in most of the other studies may not have had such knowledge. In this study, Ashton's research was extended by controlling for the subject's knowledge of the EV technique. Controlling for this variable was expected to provide additional insight about the extent to which conformance rates may be due to the use of the EV technique.

Secondly, an alternative explanation of Ashton's results is examined. It was suggested by Lichtenstein [1979] that the characteristics of the task may have caused Ashton's subjects to avoid situations where there was a high probability of a bad outcome. This study tests whether another decision strategy, avoidance of bad outcome, provides an equally plausible, if not better, explanation of Ashton's results than the EV technique. Finally, a within-subject design is provided, which provides insight into individual subject's choices across different decision settings.

TABLE 1

Allais Paradox

Decision Situations	Probability of Winning	Amount to Win
Situation A		
Gamble 1	1.00	$1,000,000
Gamble 2	0.10	$5,000,000
	0.89	$1,000,000
	0.01	$ 0
Situation B		
Gamble 3	0.11	$1,000,000
	0.89	$ 0
Gamble 4	0.10	$5,000,000
	0.90	$ 0

OVERVIEW OF THE RESEARCH

In order to achieve the above objectives, four experiments were conducted. Experiments I and II were replications of Ashton's experiments I and II, respectively, with a slight change in Ashton's experiment I.[2] The third experiment was conducted to develop an alternative explanation to Ashton's results. In this experiment the probability of a bad outcome was experimentally manipulated to investigate Lichtenstein's explanation of Ashton's results. Finally, in experiment IV, a within-subject design was utilized. In this experiment, we examined subject's choices across different decision settings. Subjects' knowledge of the EV technique was controlled for in all four experiments.

Subjects

The subjects consisted of two groups. One group, the non-knowledge group (NK), was composed of 181 freshmen and sophomore level students enrolled in an introductory accounting course in the Business School at the University of Wisconsin-Madison. Ordinarily these students would not have been exposed to the EV technique. However, to determine if any subject possessed knowledge of the EV concept, they were asked to indicate if they had taken any of the courses which would have exposed them to the concept of the EV. The NK subjects who had been exposed to the EV concept were eliminated from the study.

The second group, the knowledge group (K), was composed of 183 senior students enrolled in a corporate finance course in the Business School at the University of Wisconsin-Madison. This group had been taught utility theory and expected value concepts in several courses.

Procedures

Subjects in experiments I, II and III were given a booklet which contained instructions and three independent sets (each set represented one of the first three experiments where the order was randomized across subjects). The instructions were as follows:

> You are a divisional manager in a firm and you are expected to make investment decisions. Your performance is evaluated according to the amount of return achieved in your division. In this type of business the minimum desired amount of return is 8 percent. In the following pages you will be given various independent sets. Each set will include two decision situations and each situation has two investment alternatives. For each investment alternative, you are given a probability which represents the likelihood of achieving the given amount of return.

In addition, in each set the subjects were given the following instructions:

> Consider the following two decision situations—each involving a pair of investment alternatives. Indicate which alternative you prefer in each situation by circling either investment 1 *or* 2 in situation A, and either investment 3 *or* 4 in situation B.

The choices were presented as in Ashton's study. The following hypothetical decision situation is used as an illustration:

	Probability of Return	*Amount of Return*
Situation A		
Investment 1	1.00	28%
Investment 2	0.20	115%
	0.50	28%
	0.30	1%

	Probability of Return	*Amount of Return*
Situation B		
Investment 3	0.50	28%
	0.50	1%
Investment 4	0.20	115%
	0.80	1%

After choosing between the alternative investments in the two situations, the subjects were asked to explain, in their own words, how they arrived at their decisions.

After making decisions in the first three experimental settings, the subjects were given the two arguments (Savage and Allais' arguments, see Appendix A) as in Ashton [1979] and asked to rate each argument on a scale from 1 (not compelling at all) to 11 (very compelling). Then they were given the opportunity to reconsider their initial choices for the set representing experiment I and they were told:

> You have now had a chance to study the arguments of person X and person Y. Please respond to set (set number depended order for particular subjects) again by indicating below your choices if they are different from your original choices. If you do not wish to change your original choices leave this part unanswered.

Following this statement they were given the hypothetical decision situation again.

For experiment IV, one group of knowledge subjects made five decisions. This group was given five decision sets (the order was randomized) which were of the same general type as given in experiments I, II, and III, but the probability and outcome values were different. In addition, the subjects were not given the Savage and Allais' arguments.

EXPERIMENT I

Objective:

The purpose of this experiment was to extend Ashton's results by controlling for the level of knowledge of the EV technique. Thus, differences in conformance rates between K and NK subjects can be attributed to the knowledge of the EV technique.

Design:

This experiment was a replication of Ashton's experiment I (with a slight change, see footnote 1). As in Ashton [1979], the probabilities were varied across two levels: extreme as in the Allais problem (.1, .89, .01) and less extreme (.35, .64, .01). Also, as in Ashton [1979], the payoffs were varied across two levels, 450 percent and 45 percent. In this experiment we considered both subjects who have knowledge of the EV technique and those who do not have knowledge of the EV technique. The basic design for experiment I is given in Table 2.

Results:

Analysis of the data of the first experiment for both K and NK subjects revealed a high degree of conformity to the independence axiom (see Table 3). For the 106 NK subjects, 88 (about 83 percent) made choices which conformed to those prescribed by the axiom. As for the K subjects, the degree of conformity was even higher with 147 of 154 K subjects (96 percent) making conforming choices. The difference in conformance between K and NK subjects was statistically significant (χ^2, $p<0.01$).

As expected, the degree of violation, for both K and NK subjects, was greater for groups receiving the more extreme probability distribution (groups 1 and 2), see Table 4. However, the degree of violation was lower for NK groups receiving the more extreme payoff (groups 1 and 3) than of those who received less extreme payoff (groups 2 and 4). This difference was statistically significant (χ^2, $p<0.01$). The degree of violation for K subjects was slightly lower for groups receiving less extreme payoff (groups 2 and 4) than of those who received more extreme payoff (groups 1 and 3) but it was not statistically significant (χ^2, $p>0.9$).

For the NK subjects, four of the 18 subjects (22 percent) who initially violated the axiom, changed their choices to conform with the axiom after reading the two opposing arguments (Savage and Allais' arguments). Of the 88 subjects who initially conformed to the axiom, seventeen subjects (19 percent) changed their choices to violate the axiom after reading the two arguments.

For the K subjects, none of those who initially violated the axiom changed their choices to conform to the axiom after reading the two arguments. Of the 147 subjects who initially conformed to the axiom, eight (5 percent) changed their choices to violate the axiom.

The overall rate of violation of the axiom, for the NK subjects, was about 17 percent for the initial choices and 29 percent for choices made after reading the two arguments. For the K subjects, the rate of violation was 4 percent for the initial choices and 10 percent for the second choices.

Discussion:

The results of Experiment I support, to a great extent, the findings of Ashton [1979]. The level of conformity with the axiom was found to be very high for both K and NK groups under study (note Ashton did not distinguish between K and NK subjects in his first experiment).

Consistent with Ashton's results, it was found that most of the conformers, in both K and NK groups, chose the investments with the higher expected value (i.e., investments 2 and 4). For group 1 in Table 5, for example, the percentage of K and NK subjects who chose investments 2 and 4 was 87 percent and 75 percent respectively (see Table 5).

The response to the ratings of the two arguments (Savage and Allais' arguments) was very weak. For this reason it was decided to eliminate it from the analysis. Also, the difference between the initial and second choices was found to be non-significant for both K and NK subjects. This result reinforces our decision to ignore the two arguments and their ratings in the following sections.

TABLE 2

Basic Design for Experiment (I)

Decision Situations	Probabilities	Returns for Group (percentage) 1	2	Probabilities	Returns for Group (percentage) 3	4
Situation A						
Investment 1	1.00	9	9	1.00	9	9
Investment 2	0.10	450	45	0.35	450	45
	0.89	9	9	0.64	9	9
	0.01	1	1	0.01	1	1
Situation B						
Investment 3	0.11	9	9	0.36	9	9
	0.89	1	1	0.64	1	1
Investment 4	0.10	450	45	0.35	450	45
	0.90	1	1	0.65	1	1

TABLE 3

Subjects' Choices for Experiment (I)

Investment Choices		Group 1		Group 2		Group 3		Group 4		Total	
		n	percent	n	percent	n	percent	n	percent	n	percent
Conformers:											
1, 3	K	1	3	2	4	1	3	0	0	4	3
	NK	3	13	0	0	2	8	0	0	5	5
2, 4	K	27	87	42	88	33	97	41	100	143	93
	NK	18	75	21	75	20	83	24	80	83	78
Subtotal	K	28	90	44	92	34	100	41	100	147	96
	NK	21	88	21	75	22	92	24	80	88	83
Violators:											
1, 4	K	2	7	4	8	0	0	0	0	6	4
	NK	2	8	6	21	1	4	6	20	15	14
2, 3	K	1	3	0	0	0	0	0	0	1	0
	NK	1	4	1	4	1	4	0	0	3	3
Subtotal	K	3	10	4	8	0	0	0	0	7	4
	NK	3	12	7	25	2	8	6	20	18	17
Overall	K	31	100	48	100	34	100	41	100	154	100
Total	NK	24	100	28	100	24	100	30	100	106	100

Note: All percentages are rounded to the nearest whole number.

TABLE 4

Degree of Violation for Subjects (percentage)

Group		n	Initial Choices Conforming	Initial Choices Violating	Changes in Second Choices From Conforming To Violating	Changes in Second Choices From Violating To Conforming	Second Choices Choices After Reading The Two Arguments Conforming	Second Choices Choices After Reading The Two Arguments Violating
1	K	31	90	10	7	0	84	16
	NK	24	88	12	29	0	65	35
2	K	48	92	8	2	0	90	10
	NK	28	75	25	5	29	70	30
3	K	34	100	0	12	0	88	12
	NK	24	92	8	32	0	65	35
4	K	41	100	0	3	0	97	3
	NK	30	80	20	13	33	79	21
Groups 1 and 2 Extreme	K	79	91	9	4	0	87	13
Probabilities	NK	52	81	19	17	20	68	32
Groups 3 and 4 Less Extreme	K	75	100	0	7	0	93	7
Probabilities	NK	54	83	17	15	25	73	27
Groups 1 and 3	K	65	95	5	10	0	86	14
Extreme Payoff	NK	48	90	10	30	0	65	35
Groups 2 and 4 Less Extreme	K	89	96	4	2	0	93	7
Payoff	NK	58	75	25	9	31	75	25
All	K	154	96	4	5	0	90	10
Subjects	NK	106	83	17	19	22	71	29

TABLE 5

Expected Values and Conformity to the Axiom for Experiment (I) (percentage)

Group	EV_1	EV_2	EV_3	EV_4	$EV_2 - EV_1$; $EV_4 - EV_3$	Percentage of Subjects Choosing 2 & 4	
1	9.00	53.02	1.88	45.90	44.02	K	87
						NK	75
2	9.00	12.52	1.88	5.40	3.52	K	88
						NK	75
3	9.00	163.27	3.88	158.15	154.27	K	97
						NK	83
4	9.00	21.52	3.88	16.40	12.52	K	100
						NK	80

EXPERIMENT II

Objective:

The purpose of this experiment was to extend Ashton's Experiment II results by controlling for the level of knowledge of the EV technique. This, as in Experiment I, was expected to provide some insight concerning the extent to which the conformance rate differences between K and NK subjects were attributable to the use of the EV technique.

Design:

In designing Experiment I, Ashton confounded two elements, expected values and maximum payoffs. For this reason it was difficult to conclude from the subjects' choices, whether they relied exclusively on the EV technique or used some other decision rules. So, in designing Experiment II (see Table 6), Ashton concentrated on two factors. The first factor is based on prior research which had shown that the frequency of using the EV strategy increases with increases in the expected value differences, [e.g., Miller and Lanzetta, 1962]. As a result, the second experiment had smaller expected value differences than the first experiment. The other factor that affected the design of Experiment II is the possibility of a dislike for "conservative" choice (i.e., Investment 1). This conclusion was drawn from the fact that in Ashton's Experiment I, all conformers except one, chose investments 2 and 4. To deal with this problem, Ashton designed Experiment II so that in groups A and B investments 1 and 3 will have higher expected value while in groups C and D investments 2 and 4 will have higher expected value. Expected values and expected value differences, as in Ashton, are given in Table 7.

TABLE 6

Basic Design for Experiment (II)

Decision Situation	Probabilities	Returns for Group (percentage)			
		A	B	C	D
Situation A					
Investment 1	1.00	28	18	8	18
Investment 2	0.07	115	115	180	180
	0.40	28	18	8	18
	0.53	1	1	1	1
Situation B					
Investment 3	0.60	28	18	8	18
	0.40	1	1	1	1
Investment 4	0.07	115	115	180	180
	0.93	1	1	1	1

TABLE 7

Expected Values for Experiment (II) (percentage)

Group	EV_1	EV_2	EV_3	EV_4	$EV_1 - EV_2$; $EV_3 - EV_4$
A	28.00	19.78	17.20	8.98	8.22
B	18.00	15.78	11.20	8.98	2.22
C	8.00	16.33	5.20	13.53	(8.33)
D	18.00	20.33	11.20	13.53	(2.33)

Results:

Analysis of the second experiment's data for both K and NK subjects, yielded results slightly different from those found by Ashton. The overall conformity rate was 78 percent for NK subjects and 87 percent for the K subjects (see Table 8). The difference was not statistically significant (at χ^2, $p > .95$). Comparable rates of conformity in Ashton's second experiment were 84 percent and 71 percent for first-year MBA subjects and second-year MBA subjects respectively.[3]

For K subjects, 9 of the 20 subjects (45 percent) who made violating choices chose investments 1 and 4. Of the 138 K subjects who made conforming choices, 118 subjects (86 percent) chose investments 1 and 3. As for the NK subjects, 12 of the 23 subjects (52 percent) who made violating choices chose investments 1 and 4. Of the 83 NK subjects who made conforming choices, 65 subjects (78 percent) chose investments 1 and 3.

Discussion:

The results of Ashton's study were unexpected. That is, except for one subject, all subjects who conformed with the axiom, in the four groups A, B, C and D, chose investments 1 and 3. Two related reasons could be offered as an explanation for these results. First, subjects might have considered the difference in the expected values to be very small and hence decided not to be consistent in using the EV technique. Secondly, the structure of the stimuli might have suggested an alternative decision rule to the subjects. That is, subjects may have simply avoided alternatives where there was a high probability of a bad outcome and thus chose investments 1 and 3.

In our experiment (Experiment II), consistent with Ashton's results, the majority of the K and NK conformers, in the four groups, selected investments 1 and 3. To explain this result the subjects written comments were

TABLE 8

Subjects' Choices for Experiment (II)

Investment Choices		Group (A)		Group (B)		Group (C)		Group (D)		Total	
		n	percent	n	percent	n	percent	n	percent	n	percent
Conformers:											
1, 3	K	46	90	28	80	14	47	30	71	118	74
	NK	20	72	14	61	12	50	19	61	65	61
2, 4	K	1	2	2	6	8	26	9	22	20	13
	NK	4	14	2	9	6	25	6	19	18	17
Subtotal	K	47	92	30	86	22	73	39	93	138	87
	NK	24	86	16	70	18	75	25	80	83	78
Violators:											
1, 4	K	2	4	4	11	1	3	2	5	9	6
	NK	2	7	2	9	4	17	4	13	12	11
2, 3	K	2	4	1	3	7	24	1	2	11	17
	NK	2	7	5	21	2	8	2	6	11	11
Subtotal	K	4	8	5	14	8	27	3	7	20	13
	NK	4	14	7	30	6	25	6	19	23	22
Overall	K	51	100	35	100	30	100	42	100	158	100
Total	NK	28	100	23	100	24	100	31	100	106	100

analyzed. Several decision rules were given as a rationale for the choices made by conformers (choosing investments 1 and 3). Among the decision rules used, both expected values and risk averseness (i.e., avoidance of a bad outcome) were most often mentioned in the subjects' written comments. In group A, 43 percent of the K subjects who chose investments 1 and 3 used EV technique and 39 percent explicitly stated that they were risk averse. For the NK subjects who chose investments 1 and 3, 43 percent explicitly stated that they were risk averse.

In group B, both K and NK subjects who chose investments 1 and 3 wrote that they based their decisions on risk averseness strategy with percentages of 41 percent and 33 percent respectively. In group C, it was found that 23 percent of the K subjects who chose investments 1 and 3 used the risk averseness strategy and 20 percent of the K subjects who chose investments 2 and 4 followed the EV technique. While 42 percent of the NK subjects stated that they were risk averse and selected investments 1 and 3. Finally, for group D, the highest percentage of risk averseness was found for both K and NK subjects (i.e., 60 percent of the K subjects and 48 percent of the NK were risk averters).

From the above analysis, it seems that the K subjects who conformed with the axiom did not always make choices using the EV technique. Other decision strategies such as risk averseness were often mentioned as bases for their choices. Most of the time these alternative decision strategies led to choices which were in conformance with the axiom. Similar responses were found among the NK subjects.

EXPERIMENT III

Objective:

The purpose of this experiment was to develop an alternative explanation to Ashton's results. It was suggested by Lichtenstein [1979] that the characteristics of the task may have caused Ashton's subjects to avoid situations where there was high probability of a bad outcome. In this experiment, the probability of a bad outcome was experimentally manipulated to investigate Lichtenstein's explanation of Ashton's results.

Design:

In this experiment, the probability of a bad outcome was varied from 47 percent to 1 percent (group 1 through group 5, see Table 9). As a consequence of varying the probability of a bad outcome, the EV difference ranged from 3.99 percent to 28.44 percent (group 1 through group 5, see Table 10).

Following the EV technique, subjects in group 1 should choose investments 1 and 3 which gives a higher EV and avoids the bad outcome in investment 2. In all other groups, investments 2 and 4 will have higher EV. In groups 2 through 5, the EV difference was systematically increased. This was expected to cause the percentage of subjects choosing investments 2 and 4 to increase as the EV difference increases from group 2 to group 5. For the NK subjects, assuming they are risk averse (as found in Experiment 2), it is expected that their decisions will be governed by the probability of a bad outcome. In particular, as the probability of a bad outcome decreases from

0.47 to 0.01 (group 1 through group 5) it is expected that fewer subjects will choose the alternative with the certain payoff (investment 1).

Results:

Overall, 121 of the 157 K subjects (77 percent) chose the investments which conformed with the axiom. The NK subjects had a lower degree of conformity of 57 percent (see Table 11).

By considering the choices made by the K subjects, it was found that in group 1, 73 percent of the subjects chose investments 1 and 3 which corresponded to the investments with higher EV. In groups 2 through 5 the percentage of subjects who chose investments 2 and 4 were 43 percent, 51 percent, 74 percent and 94 percent respectively. This result was consistent with our expectations. For group 2 where the EV difference was relatively low, the K subjects made decisions that were consistent with both the EV technique (43 percent chose 2 and 4) and the strategy of avoiding a bad outcome (36 percent chose 1 and 3). However, as the EV difference increased across groups 3 through 5, the percentage of K subjects making choices consistent with the EV technique (investments 2 and 4) steadily increased.

As for the NK group, the results show that in groups 1 and 2 a higher percentage of subjects chose investments 1 and 3 (32 percent and 36 percent respectively). In group 3 the conformers' choices were almost equally divided between investments 1 and 3 and investments 2 and 4. In groups 4 and 5 the percentage of conformers who chose investments 1 and 3 dropped to zero.

The written comments of the subjects shed some light on the above results.[4] The responses were classified into seven categories. These were: Expected Value (EV), Satisficing (S), Risk Averse (RA), Risk Taking (RT), High Payoff (HP), Guess (G), and No Response (NR). These categories are defined in Table 12. Each of the authors independently classified the subjects' responses into the above categories. Agreement between the authors was high.

The decision-rules used by the subjects in their decision-making are shown in Table 13.

It was found that among the subjects in group 1 who chose investments 1 and 3, about 33 percent wrote that they were risk averse and only 21 percent stated that they used the EV technique to choose. Obviously, the percentage of subjects who did not choose according to EV strategy represented a large majority of the total conformers who chose investments 1 and 3.

In group 2, out of the 43 percent who chose investments 2 and 4, about 35 percent based their decisions on EV technique. Contrary to group 1, the RA strategy and EV technique did not lead to the same investments choice. The conformers who based their decision on RA strategy (20 percent) continued to choose 1 and 3. In group 3, it seems that the probability of a bad outcome had less of an effect on the choices made by the subjects than in groups 1 and 2. Only 11 percent stated that they were RA and chose investments 1 and 3 while a larger percentage followed EV technique and chose investments 2 and 4 (43 percent). In groups 4 and 5 no RA strategies were found. This might indicate that the subjects considered the probability of a bad outcome to be low. In group 4, about 52 percent calculated EV and chose investments 2 and 4, but in group 5 only 25 percent chose according to EV decision rule and 59 percent based their decisions on the Satisficing strategy.

In general, it seems that the K subjects were affected by the probability of a bad outcome and those who made choices consistent with EV technique did not always use the technique. For example, among the five levels of probability of a bad outcome that were considered in this experiment, it has been shown that when the probability of a bad outcome was high (.47 in group 1) more subjects chose according to RA strategy (33 percent). Similarly, when the probability of a bad outcome was low (.01 in group 5) no risk averters were found and more subjects chose according to Satisficing strategy (59 percent). It is important to note that both strategies—RA and Satisficing—led to the same investments choice as EV strategy (i.e., investments 1 and 3 and investments 2 and 4 respectively).

With respect to NK subjects, the results in Table 11 indicate that in groups 1 and 2 a higher percentage of conformers chose investments 1 and 3. However, in groups 3 through 5 most of the conformers chose investments 2 and 4 (35 percent, 43 percent and 58 percent respectively). This is consistent with our expectations because as the probability of a bad outcome decreased from .47 in group 1 to 0.01 in group 5, the percentage of NK conformers who chose investments 1 and 3 decreased from 32 percent to 0 percent (except for group 2 where there was a slight increase).

According to Table 13, most of the NK subjects who chose investments 1 and 3 in groups 1 and 2 followed a RA strategy. In groups 3 and 4 most of the conformers who chose investments 2 and 4 based their decisions on HP decision rule. Finally, in group 5 most of the NK conformers used the same strategy as K subjects (i.e., the Satisficing strategy). In this group, 50 percent of the conformers followed this strategy and chose investments 2 and 4.

Discussion:

The above results have several implications. First, the findings of this experiment give some support to the results of Experiment II. In particular, it was shown that the probability of a bad outcome was an important factor governing the choices made by both K and NK subjects. Secondly, a striking feature of the above results is that although the NK subjects had a lower level of conformity due to the use of more diversified decision rules, some of these decision rules led them to the same choices as the EV technique (e.g., RA strategy in group 1 and Satisficing strategy in group 5). Finally, the fact that some K subjects used decision rules other than EV technique offers some support to previous research where it has been shown that EV is not the only criterion that govern choice between risky investments. For example, Lichtenstein, Slovic and Zink [1969] found that EV was used sparingly by their subjects, even when the concept was carefully explained and clearly displayed. Edwards [1956], Lee [1971], Suydam [1965] and Taub and Myers [1961] found that expected regret ratio was often a more important choice criterion than was expected value difference.

TABLE 9

Basic Design for Experiment (III)

Decision Situation	Probability of Return for Group					Amount of Return (percentage)
	1	2	3	4	5	
Situation A						
Investment 1	1.00	1.00	1.00	1.00	1.00	28
Investment 2	0.10	0.20	0.25	0.30	0.33	115
	0.43	0.50	0.55	0.60	0.66	28
	0.47	0.30	0.20	0.10	0.01	1
Situation B						
Investment 3	0.57	0.50	0.45	0.40	0.34	28
	0.43	0.50	0.55	0.60	0.66	1
Investment 4	0.10	0.20	0.25	0.30	0.33	115
	0.90	0.80	0.75	0.70	0.67	1

TABLE 10

Expected Values for Experiment (III)
(percentage)

Group	Probabilities	EV_1	EV_2	EV_3	EV_4	$EV_1 - EV_2$; $EV_3 - EV_4$
1	(.10 .43 .47)	28.00	24.01	16.39	12.40	3.99
2	(.20 .50 .30)	28.00	37.30	14.50	23.80	(9.30)
3	(.25 .55 .20)	28.00	44.35	13.15	29.50	(16.35)
4	(.30 .60 .10)	28.00	51.40	11.80	35.20	(23.40)
5	(.33 .66 .01)	28.00	56.44	10.18	38.62	(28.44)

TABLE 11

Subjects' Choices for Experiment (III)

Investment Choices		Group 1		Group 2		Group 3		Group 4		Group 5		Total	
		n	percent	n	percent	n	percent	n	percent	n	percent	n	percent
Conformers:													
1, 3	K	19	73	11	27	5	14	0	0	0	0	35	22
	NK	6	32	8	36	6	30	0	0	1	4	21	20
2, 4	K	4	15	17	43	19	51	17	74	29	94	86	55
	NK	4	21	5	23	7	35	9	43	14	58	39	37
Subtotal	K	23	88	30	70	24	65	17	74	29	94	121	77
	NK	10	53	13	59	13	65	9	43	15	62	60	57
Violators:													
1, 4	K	1	4	6	15	4	11	4	17	2	6	17	11
	NK	4	21	4	18	6	30	11	52	9	38	34	32
2, 3	K	2	8	6	15	9	24	2	9	0	0	19	12
	NK	5	26	5	23	1	8	1	5	0	0	12	11
Subtotal	K	3	12	12	30	13	35	6	26	2	6	36	23
	NK	9	47	9	41	7	35	12	57	9	38	46	43
Overall	K	26	100	40	100	37	100	23	100	31	100	157	100
Total	NK	19	100	22	100	20	100	21	100	24	100	106	100

TABLE 12

Categories of Subjects' Responses

Decision Rule	Definition
(1) Expected Value	For each investment, multiply probability by amount of return, and sum the products. Choose the investment with the highest expected value (sum).
(2) Satisficing	The subject explicitly stated that she/he considered both probability and payoff, but did not calculate an expected value.
(3) No Response	No explanation was given by the subject.
(4) Risk Averse	The subject explicitly stated that she/he based her/his decision on a sure thing, or avoidance of a bad outcome or risk averseness.
(5) Risk-Taking	The subject indicated that she/he deliberately took a chance on a risky but high outcome investment.
(6) High Payoff	The subject explicitly stated that she/he based her/his decision on payoff without considering its associated probability.
(7) Guess	The subject stated that she/he was guessing.

TABLE 13

Decision Rules Used By Subjects (percentages)[a]

Investment Choices	EV		S		NR		RA		RT		HP		G	
	K	NK	K	NK	K	NK	K	NK	K	NK	K	NK	K	NK
Group 1														
1,3	21.2	—	7.7	—	11.5	5.0	32.7	26.0	—	—	—	—	—	—
2,4	3.8	—	3.8	—	7.7	5.0	—	—	—	—	—	10.0	—	5.0
1,4	—	—	—	—	—	10.0	1.9	3.0	1.9	—	—	3.0	—	5.0
2,3	3.8	—	1.9	—	—	8.0	1.9	3.0	—	—	—	16.0	—	—
Group 2														
1,3	7.5[b]	—	—	4.5	—	9.0	20.0	23.0	—	—	—	—	—	—
2,4	35[b]	—	2.5	—	5.0	14.0	—	—	—	4.5	—	—	—	4.5
1,4	3.8[b]	—	—	2.0	2.5	2.0	5.0	4.5	—	—	3.8	—	—	9.0
2,3	2.5[b]	—	5.0	2.0	—	9.0	7.5	7.0	—	2.0	—	2.0	—	—
Group 3														
1,3	—	—	—	5.0	2.7	5.0	10.8	20.0	—	—	—	—	—	—
2,4	43.2	—	2.7	5.0	—	10.0	—	—	2.7	—	2.7	20.0	—	—
1,4	—	—	2.7	—	—	5.0	8.1	15.0	—	—	—	5.0	—	5.0
2,3	9.5	—	—	—	2.7	—	6.8	—	—	—	5.4	—	—	5.0
Group 4														
1,3	—	—	—	—	—	—	—	—	—	—	—	—	—	—
2,4	52.2	—	8.7	5.0	4.3	—	—	—	4.3	5.0	—	28.0[a]	4.3	5.0
1,4	2.2	—	2.2	7.0	4.3	21.0	6.5	14.0	—	—	—	10.0[a]	2.2	—
2,3	8.7	—	—	—	—	—	—	2.0	—	—	—	2.0	—	—
Group 5														
1,3	—	—	—	—	—	—	—	4.0	—	—	—	—	—	—
2,4	25.0	—	59.4	50.0	3.1	—	—	—	—	—	—	8.0	3.1	—
1,4	—	—	3.1	13.0	—	4.0	3.1	15.0	—	2.0	—	4.0	—	—
2,3	—	—	—	—	—	—	—	—	—	—	—	—	—	—

[a]Percentages sum to percentages shown in Table 11.

[b]Any inconsistencies are due to subjects making calculation errors (i.e. miscalculated EV) or indicating a decision rule for only one investment.

EXPERIMENT IV

Objective:

The purpose of this experiment was to provide insight into a K subject's choices across different decision settings. This was of particular interest since it made it possible to determine the extent to which the individual subject was consistent in using EV across the various settings.

Design:

In this experiment one group of K subjects made five decisions. The decision settings varied by probability of a bad outcome (range from .40 to .01) and consequently led to expected value differences (range from 1.5 to 31.21). Following the concept of EV, the investments chosen should always be investments 2 and 4 (see tables 14 and 15). Although the payoffs were considered to be held constant, they were slightly varied in each set so as to discourage the subjects from making any comparison between the sets. In addition, any order effect was eliminated by randomizing the order of decision settings.

The design of this experiment was based upon the expectation that if violations of the EV strategy were to occur, they would most likely occur in decision settings where the probability of a bad outcome was high. Thus, it was expected that some subjects would switch from (to) the EV technique as the probability of a bad outcome became higher (lower).

Results:

The results of Experiment IV are summarized in Figures 1 and 2. The first figure represents the percentage of subjects who were consistent in choosing investments 2 and 4 across the decision settings. For example, the first 41 percent represents the percentage of subjects who chose Investments 2 and 4 in all five decision settings. The second 41 percent represents the percentage of subjects who chose investments 2 and 4 in sets 2 to 5. Next, 52 percent of the subjects chose investments 2 and 4 in sets 3 to 5. This analysis is continued until set 5 where all the subjects chose Investments 2 and 4.

The same procedure is followed for the conformers who chose investments 1 and 3. Figure 2 indicates that none of the subjects chose 1 and 3 throughout all five decision settings. About 3 percent chose investments 1 and 3 in sets 1 to 4. Next, 10 percent of the subjects were consistent in choosing investments 1 and 3 in sets 1 to 3. Finally, it is shown that 31 percent of the subjects chose investments 1 and 3 in set 1.

Discussion:

By considering both Figure 1 and Figure 2, it seems that as the probability of a bad outcome decreased from 40 percent in set 1 to 1 percent in set 5 (or equivalently as the EV difference increased from 1.5 to 31.21), the percentage of subjects who were persistent in choosing investments 1 and 3, decreased gradually from 31 percent in set 1 to 0 percent in set 5. At the same time, Figure 1 shows that the percentage of subjects choosing investments 2 and 4 is increasing from 41 percent in set 1 to 100 percent in set 5.

The written comments of the subjects did not offer much help in explaining this result, because most of the subjects did not write how they reached their decisions. However, the Figures indicate that a higher percentage of conformers were consistent in choosing investments 2 and 4 which correspond to choices based on EV technique. This does not offer conclusive evidence that the subjects were persistent in following EV decision rule. The possibility still exists that they might have used other decision rules (similar to those in Experiment III) which sometimes lead to the same choices as EV technique.

SUMMARY AND CONCLUSION

The results of the experiments conducted in this study, support some of those reported in Ashton's study but disagree with prior studies. The results concur with Ashton, in that, fewer subjects (in both K and NK groups) than in previous studies violated the independence axiom. An attempt was made to determine the reasons, in terms of decision strategies for conformity or violation.

Conformity among NK subjects and *some* of the conformity among the K subjects was due to decision strategies such as RA, HP etc. This supports Lichtenstein's claim that conforming K subjects did not always choose according to EV rule. However, the *incremental* conformity among the K subjects over the NK subjects was due to knowledge of EV technique. Thus, it can be concluded that training in the EV technique may result in decisions that show greater conformance with normative decision theory. Also, it was noted that none of the conforming subjects mentioned anything which could be construed as recognition of the "irrelevance of identical outcomes."

Given the simplistic nature of the task, the generalizability of the results is limited. However, the results of this study offer support to the descriptive validity of one of the axioms of normative decision theory. In that sense, this study may be of value to some accounting research areas such as the prescriptive research that attempts to model choice problems in terms of maximization of an expected utility function.

TABLE 14
Basic Design for Experiment (IV)

Decision Situation	Probability of Return for Decision Set 1	2	3	4	5	Percent of Return for Decision Set 1	2	3	4	5
Situation A										
Investment 1	1.00	1.00	1.00	1.00	1.00	28	30	26	20	30
Investment 2	0.15	0.20	0.20	0.25	0.35	110	110	100	100	120
	0.45	0.45	0.50	0.55	0.64	28	30	26	20	30
	0.40	0.35	0.30	0.20	0.01	1	1	1	1	1
Situation B										
Investment 3	0.55	0.55	0.50	0.45	0.36	28	30	26	20	30
	0.45	0.45	0.50	0.55	0.64	1	1	1	1	1
Investment 4	0.15	0.20	0.20	0.25	0.35	110	110	100	100	120
	0.85	0.80	0.80	0.75	0.65	1	1	1	1	1

TABLE 15
Expected Values for Experiment (IV)

Decision Set	Probability of Bad Outcome	EV_1 (percent)	EV_2 (percent)	EV_3 (percent)	EV_4 (percent)	EV_2-EV_1 ; EV_4-EV_3 (percent)
1	.40	28.00	29.50	15.85	17.35	1.50
2	.35	30.00	35.85	16.95	22.80	5.85
3	.30	26.00	33.30	13.50	20.80	7.30
4	.20	20.00	36.20	9.55	25.75	16.20
5	.01	30.00	61.21	11.44	42.65	31.21

FIGURE 1

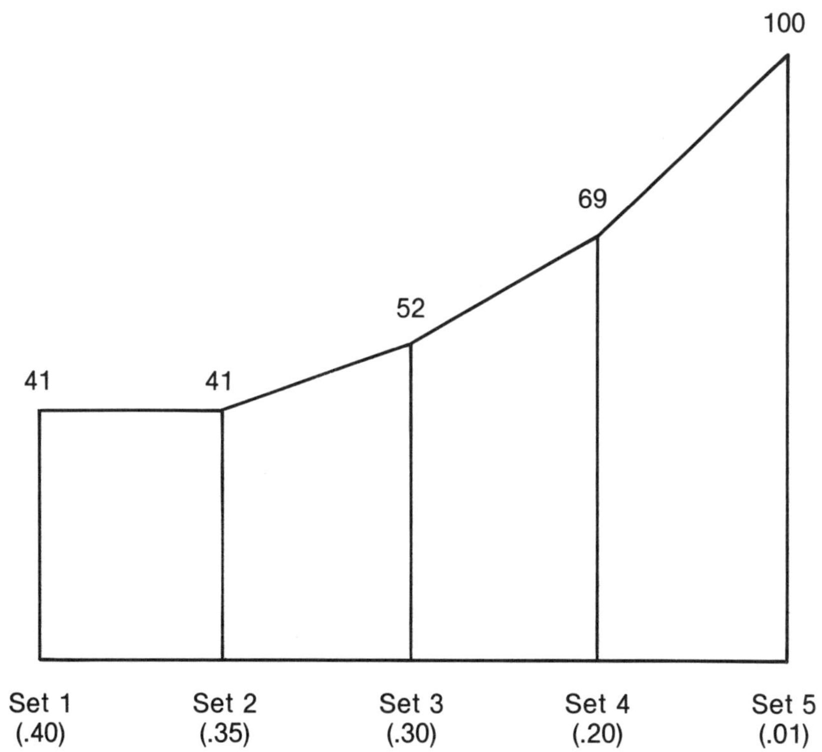

% of subjects who chose Investments 2 and 4 and kept their choices thereafter. The probability of a bad outcome is shown in parentheses.

FIGURE 2

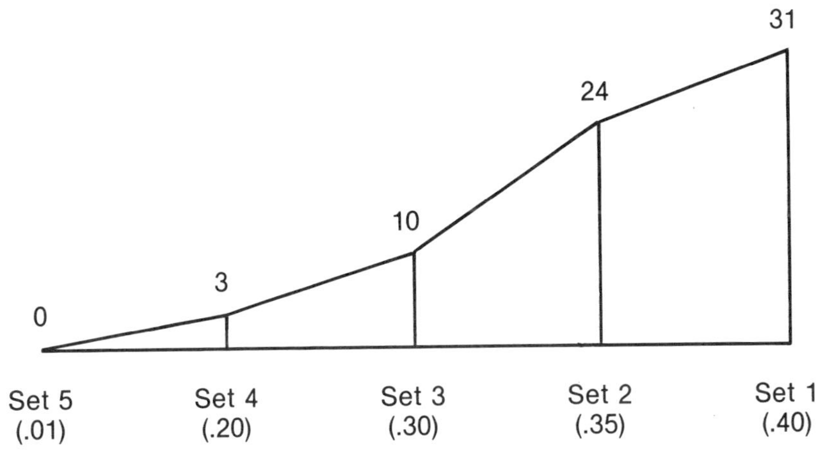

% of subjects who chose Investments 1 and 3 and kept their choices thereafter. The probability of a bad outcome is shown in parentheses.

NOTES

[1]For some examples, see Bierman and Dyckman [1971] who suggest the use of Expected Utility in managerial accounting contexts, Foster [1978] who suggests its use in financial accounting contexts, and Demski and Swieringa [1974] who suggest its use in auditing contexts.

[2]In Ashton's first experiment bankruptcy was a possible outcome. In this study the "bankruptcy" outcome is excluded because the word "bankruptcy" may bias the results. It is believed that the subjects would consider the "bankruptcy" as an unwanted outcome and would lead them to choose the alternative which guarantees no bankruptcy.

[3]Although Ashton had two groups, first-year and second-year MBA students, he did not specifically divide the groups according to their knowledge of EV.

[4]The written comments represent retrospective verbal reports obtained immediately after the subjects made their investment choices. See Ericsson and Simon [1980] for a theoretical framework and evidence concerning the validity of retrospective verbal reports.

REFERENCES

Allais, M., "LeComportement de L'Homme Rationnel devant LeRisque, Critique des postulats et Axiomes de L'Ecole Americaine." *Econometrica* (1953), pp. 503-546.

Ashton, A., "Descriptive Validity of Normative Decision Theory in Auditing Contexts," *Journal of Accounting Research* (Autumn, 1982, Part 1), pp. 415-428.

Ashton, R.H., "Behavioral Assumptions of Normative Decision Theory: An Experimental Test of the Independence Axiom in an Accounting Context," in T.J. Burns (ed.). *Behavioral Experiments in Accounting II,* (Ohio State University 1979).

Bierman, H. and T. Dyckman, *Managerial Cost Accounting* (Macmillan, 1971).

Demski, Joel S. and Robert J. Swieringa, "The Audit Choice Problem." *Accounting Review* (July 1974), pp. 506-513.

Edwards, W., "Reward Probability, Amount and Information as Determiners of Sequential Two-Alternative Decision." *Journal of Experimental Psychology* (September 1956), pp. 177-188.

Ericsson, K.A. and H. Simon, "Verbal Reports as Data," *Psychological Review* (May 1980), pp. 215-251.

Foster, G., *Financial Statement Analysis* (Prentice-Hall 1978).

Kahneman, D. and A. Tversky, "Prospect Theory: An Analysis of Decision Under Risk." *Econometrica* (1979), pp. 263-291.

Lee, W., "The Effects of Expected Value Difference and Expected Regret Ratio on Preference Strength." *American Journal of Psychology* (June 1971), pp. 194-204.

Lichtenstein, S., "Critique of Ashton's Behavioral Assumptions of Normative Decision Theory: An Experimental Test of the Independence Axiom in an Accounting Context," in T.J. Burns (ed.). *Behavioral Experiments in Accounting II,* Columbus Ohio: Ohio State University, (1979).

__________, P. Slovic, and D. Zink, "Effect of Instruction in Expected Value on Optimality of Gambling Decisions," *Journal of Experimental Psychology* (February 1969), pp. 236-240.

MacCrimmon, K.R., "Descriptive and Normative Implications of the Decision-Theory Postulates," in K. Borch and J. Mossin (eds.), *Risk and Uncertainty* (MacMillan 1968), pp. 3-23.

MacCrimmon, K.R. and S. Larsson, "Utility Theory: Axioms Versus 'Paradoxes,'" University of British Columbia Working Paper No. 311 (May 1975).

Miller, L. and J.T. Lanzetta, "Choices Among Four-Alternative Gambles as a Function of Monetary Level of Play." *Psychological Reports* (December 1962), pp. 869-894.

Moskowitz, H., "Effects of Problem Representation and Feedback on Rational Behavior in Allais and Morlat-Type Problems." *Behavioral Sciences* (April 1974), pp. 225-242.

Schoemaker, P., "The Expected Utility Model: Its Variants, Purposes, Evidence and Limitations," *Journal of Economic Literature* (June 1982), pp. 529-563.

Slovic, P. and A. Tversky, "Who Accepts Savage's Axiom?" *Behavioral Science* (November 1974), pp. 368-373.

Suydam, M.M., "Effects of Cost and Gain Ratios, and Probability of Outcome on Ratings of Alternative Choices." *Journal of Mathematical Psychology* (February 1965), pp. 171-179.

Taub, H.A. and J.L. Myers, "Differential Monetary Gains in a Two-Choice Situation." *Journal of Experimental Psychology* (February 1961), pp. 157-162.

APPENDIX A

Statement of Person X (Savage's Argument):

One way in which investments 1, 2, 3 and 4 could be chosen is by a lottery with 100 numbered tickets and with prizes (rates of return) as shown in the following table:

		Ticket Number		
		1	2-11	12-100
Situation A		(percent)	(percent)	(percent)
	Investment 1	9	9	9
	Investment 2	1	450	9
Situation B				
	Investment 3	9	9	1
	Investment 4	1	450	1

Now, if the one of the tickets numbered 12 through 100 is drawn, it will not matter, for either situation, which investment I choose. I, therefore, focus on the possibility that one of the tickets numbered 1 through 11 will be drawn, in which case my choices in situations A and B are exactly parallel. My choice in both situations depends on whether I prefer to take a sure 9 percent return or to gamble for a 450 percent return. If I prefer the sure 9 percent return, I should choose investment 1 in situation A and investment 3 in situation B. If I prefer to gamble for the 450 percent return, I should choose investment 2 in situation A and investment 4 in situation B. I imagine that I would actually choose investment 1 and investment 3.

Statement of Person Y (Allais' Argument):

I would choose investment 1 in situation A and investment 4 in situation B. In situation A, I have a choice between a 9 percent return for certain and a gamble where I might end with only 1 percent return. Why gamble? The small probability of ending up with only 1 percent return seems very unattractive to me, so I will choose investment 1. In situation B, there is a good chance that I will end up with only 1 percent return no matter what I do. The chance of getting of 450 percent return is almost as good as the chance of getting a 9 percent return, so I might as well go for the 450 percent return and choose investment 4.

Alison Hubbard Ashton
New York University

Discussant's Comments on:

"Experimental Evidence on Conformance With the Independence Axiom of Normative Decision Theory"

The Allais problem was introduced in Paris in 1952, at a colloquium entitled "Foundations and Applications of the Theory of Risk in Economics." In a paper published soon after the conference, Samuelson wrote [1952, p. 678]:

> My closing admission reverses the story of the farmer who regarded everyone in the world as crazy but himself and his wife, and who sometimes wasn't sure about her. I sometimes feel that Savage and I are the only ones in the world who will give a consistent Bernoulli answer to questionnaires of the type that Professor Allais has been circulating—but I am often not too sure about my own consistency.

The Biggs, Biuk and Mahmoud paper is based on the Allais [1954] problem. In discussing the paper, I think it is important to first consider the "so what" question: Why do accounting researchers care whether college sophomores fall for a tricky decision problem that has stumped the likes of Paul Samuelson and Leonard Savage? After addressing this issue, I will make some specific comments on the four experiments and the paper. Finally, I will conclude with some of my own preferences for directions for further research.

The descriptive validity of normative decision theory is important in at least two areas of contemporary accounting research: audit decision making and information economics. First, the theory has been prescribed as a process model for use in auditing. Kinney [1975] has proposed a decision theoretic model of audit decision making which he claims "may be sufficient for practical application" [p. 129]. Such a prescription raises an implementation issue: Are decision makers willing and/or able to make choices as the theory prescribes? If not, they will require training in order to apply decision theory in auditing.

Information economics analyses in accounting *assume* that an individual's decisions can be represented by an expected utility model. These analyses do not assume that an individual does (or can) employ the decision process implied by the model. They require only that decision makers behave "as if" they maximize expected utility. If such conformity with the theory exists in actual behavior, then the individual's demand for information can be predicted [see, e.g., Demski 1972]. Newman [1980] has discussed the implications for information economics applications when a different model, i.e., prospect theory [Kahneman and Tversky, 1979] is assumed.

To summarize, decision theory has been suggested as a process model which may be prescribed to improve decision making, and it has been used as an "as if" model to predict decision behavior which has implications for the demand for information. So why study the theory at the level of the axioms?

The expected utility model has been refined by the development of axioms that are equivalent to, but behaviorally more appealing than, the assumption that a decision maker computes and compares the expected utilities associated with decision alternatives [see Marschak 1974, pp. 81-82 for discussion]. Behavior in accordance with an axiom system guarantees the existence of a probability distribution over states or events, and a utility function over outcomes, such that one action is preferred to another if, and only if, it has greater expected utility. If the decision maker fails to conform to any axiom, then utility maximization is not guaranteed. Because of these characteristics, the axioms are a useful perspective from which to investigate the descriptive validity of decision theory relative to the accounting applications I mentioned earlier.

In research on audit decision making, the elementary nature of the axioms is of interest, because studying behavior at this level may enable identification of the source(s) of failure to conform to the theory's prescriptions. In addition, if the axioms are accepted, their compelling logic may cause a decision maker to accept the logic of the prescription—even when the global notion of utility maximization is not appealing. Understanding the nature of nonconformity with the axioms may allow specification of the decision contexts in which violations will occur, and it may allow the *ex ante* identification of violators.

For purposes of information economics, however, Friedman's [1953] positive economics argument would seem to rule out axiom studies as a means of validating normative decision theory: A theory may be a useful predictor even if its axioms (which are necessarily abstractions from reality) are descriptively false. However, axiom studies can still be useful. If one (or more) of the axioms is (are) not descriptively valid, the theory may nevertheless yield useful predictions. But if all the axioms are descriptively valid in some set of circumstances, then predictive ability is assured in those circumstances. Thus, it is important to accounting research that we understand the extent to which normative decision theory is descriptively valid, and tests of the axioms can be a useful approach to take.

But Biggs, Biuk and Mahmoud were not directly interested in either audit decision making or information economics. They were concerned with the more basic issue of decision processes that result in conformity with a particular axiom. They were using normative decision theory as a benchmark against which to compare actual behavior. Psychologists [e.g., Barclay, Beach and Braithwaite 1971] have suggested that such an approach can lead to modifications in the form and/or content of a normative model, so that a more satisfactory descriptive (process) model of decision making can be developed. The work being done by Kahneman and Tversky [1979] in developing prospect theory is an example. This is the sense in which most of us will find the Biggs, Biuk and Mahmoud study interesting.

As for the study itself, I think that Stan, Bashir and Amal should be commended for replicating and extending Ashton [1979]. Several people in this room will appreciate the difficulty and frustration experienced by mere mortals who attempt to extract further insights from Allais' [1954] marvelously insightful problem. And I think we will all agree that the replication and extension of results play a crucial role in the effort to improve decision making by better understanding human information processing.

The four experiments examined differences in responses to Allais-type problems both across and within subjects. The within-subjects design of Experiment IV is particularly appealing, since this is the preferable approach to take, if it can be accomplished. The first three experiments compared "knowledgable" subjects, i.e., those who had been taught to calculate expected value, to subjects with "no knowledge" of expected value techniques. These experiments demonstrate that a larger proportion of the knowledge group conformed to the axiom than did the group with no knowledge of expected value.

Based on several tables in the paper, I have summarized the results. The differences in the overall conformance rates of the knowledge versus no knowledge groups in the first three experiments were 13, 9 and 20 percent, respectively, or an overall difference of 14 percent between the knowledge and no knowledge groups. The violation rates for the knowledgable subjects were 4, 13 and 23 percent over the three experiments. These are low violation rates, which *may* be explained by the parameters substituted for those in the original Allais problem, as I will discuss later. It is somewhat curious that these low violation rates, similar to those found in Ashton [1979] and Ashton [1982], have been found only in studies by accountants, and in all studies by accountants, of Allais-type problems. There may be some leads here for those of us who are interested in defining the essence of accountants' "expertise".

In Experiment III, the authors' discussion must be read very carefully, because the decision strategies that can explain the results are sometimes confounded. For example, the authors suggest (p. 129) that "knowledge" subjects "chose the investments which corresponded with EV technique and the percentage of conformers increased steadily as the EV difference increased." However, increasing expected value differences are confounded with decreasing differences between the probabilities in investments 3 and 4, which makes investment 4 more attractive because of its substantially higher payoff. For example, I would not expect any subjects in Group 5 of Experiment III to even bother to calculate expected value in Choice 2, thus making the expected value *difference* irrelevant.

The conclusions drawn by the authors are appropriately modest—that is, there are more strategies to potentially explain conformity than the "irrelevance of identical outcomes" (which even gave Savage a tough time) or expected value calculation. It would have been a good idea for the authors to have designed experiments III and IV to avoid the confounding problem. In this way, the paper would add something more specific to what we already know about the effects on choices of the relative sizes of payoffs, probabilities and expected value differences.

The authors try to deal with this problem by analyzing the subjects' written comments, which purport to describe their decision strategies/processes. Table 13 presents the results of a rather sophisticated analysis, which is an example of shooting flies with elephant guns. It would have been more informative for the authors to simply have said that some subjects' comments supported the authors' hypotheses and some did not. If you are still trying to figure out Table 13, the problem is that the basis for the percentages is not disclosed in the paper. I will leave it to Stan to explain Table 13, but there is an important problem revealed by this table. Many subjects in the study described decision strategies inconsistent with their choices. This result renders the data suspect, and makes me uncomfortable about any conclusions regarding decision processes based on the subjects' comments.

Table 13 also led me to wonder if a nonknowledge subject could ever be expected to use an expected value strategy, given the authors' definitions. The authors apparently do not see this as a possibility, and, if this is actually the case, then there was really no uncertainty about some of the results. It is true that not one nonknowledge subject articulated an expected value strategy. However, nonknowledge subjects did sometimes use what the authors called a satisficing strategy, which means they considered both probability and payoff. I should also note that what is defined here as satisficing would have been called by Ashton [1979] an expected value strategy.

For anyone contemplating further research of this type, I would recommend MacCrimmon's [1979] enlightening comments on Ashton [1979], in which he deals with 15 important research issues. In view of the conclusion of Biggs, Biuk and Mahmoud that conformity with normative decision theory may be improved by teaching the expected value technique, I would point out that MacCrimmon characterized Ashton's expected-value-maximizing subjects as "pseudo-analytical types who need to be taught that expected value calculations should not be made routinely—especially in situations in which they probably would not be risk neutral." [p. 211]. MacCrimmon also comments [p. 213]:

> It is ironic that in a study based on a theory proposed 250 years ago by Bernoulli to overcome people's inappropriate use of expected value calculations, we find a majority of subjects continuing to use such calculations.

I would also reiterate a point made in Lichtenstein's [1979] critique of Ashton. To study the Allais paradox, she argued, it is appropriate to use cases that maintain the essential features of the original Allais problem. Many of the problems developed by Ashton and by the present authors do not make it attractive to violate the axiom in many cases.

This paper and future studies would be stronger if the original Allais parameters were included for at least one problem, particularly the very favorable outcome that can be received with certainty. The original parameters can then be manipulated in a systematic manner to see the point at which violation rates will change. Neither Ashton nor the present authors provided a satisfactory rationale for the parameters they chose.

Finally, I recommend research in realistic contexts involving expert subjects. The results I found with audit partners and managers [Ashton, 1982] cause me to suspect that in the real world, when subjects are experts in a familiar and meaningful decision context, the Allais problem may not be troublesome at all.

REFERENCES

Allais, M., "Fondements d'une Theorie Positive des Choix Comportant un Risque et Critique des Postulats et Axiomes de l'Ecole Americaine," *Econometrie* (1953). Cited by K.R. MacCrimmon, "An Experimental Study of the Decision Making Behavior of Business Executives," unpublished Ph.D. dissertation, University of California at Los Angeles (1965).

Ashton, A., "The Descriptive Validity of Normative Decision Theory in Auditing Contexts," *Journal of Accounting Research* (Autumn 1982), Part 1, pp. 415-428.

Ashton, R., "Behavioral Assumptions of Normative Decision Theory: An Experimental Test of the Independence Axiom in an Accounting/Business Context," in T.H. Burns, ed., *Behavioral Experiments in Accounting II* (Ohio State University, 1979).

Barclay, S., L. Beach, and W. Braithwaite, "Normative Models in the Study of Cognition, *Organizational Behavior and Human Performance* (July 1971), pp. 389-413.

Demski, J., *Information Analysis* (Addison-Wesley, 1972).

Friedman, M., "The Methodology of Positive Economics," in M. Friedman, ed., *Essays in Positive Economics* (University of Chicago, 1953), pp. 3-43.

Kahneman, D. and A. Tversky, "Prospect Theory: An Analysis of Decision Under Risk," *Econometrica* (March 1979), pp. 263-291.

Kinney, W., "Decision Theory Aspects of Internal Control System Design/Compliance and Substantive Tests," *Studies on Statistical Methodology in Auditing,* Supplement to Vol. 13 of *Journal of Accounting Research* (1975), pp. 14-29.

Lichtenstein, S., "Critique," in T.J. Burns ed., *Behavioral Experiments in Accounting II* (Ohio State University, 1979).

MacCrimmon, K., "Critique," T.J. Burns ed., *Behavioral Experiments in Accounting II* (Ohio State University, 1979).

Marschak, J., *Economic Information, Decision, and Prediction* (D. Reidel, 1974).

Newman, D.P., "Prospect Theory: Implications for Information Evaluation," *Accounting, Organizations and Society* (1980), pp. 217-230.

Samuelson, P., "Probability, Utility, and the Independence Axiom," *Econometrica* (October 1952), pp. 670-678.

Michael Gibbins
University of British Columbia

Discussant's Comments on:

"Experimental Evidence on Conformance With the Independence Axiom of Normative Decision Theory"

Do people's responses to risky situations appear to follow axioms of theories about how such responses ought reasonably to be chosen? This interesting study illustrates how this question might be studied, and in the process also raises a variety of issues surrounding such a study. The authors (I'll call them BBM, after their initials) have provided a clearly explained and analyzed paper, so rather than focus on the paper itself I will emphasize some important issues I think it raises and will refer to the paper mostly in order to elaborate on those issues. My comments fall into five groups:

1. Making descriptive use of expected utility theory/axioms;
2. Drawing accounting connections from such a study;
3. Relying on the Allais paradox as a springboard to research;
4. Further comments on the study's research design;
5. Further comments on the data analysis.

These remarks are intended to be supportive in the main, and given the constraints of my discussant role, I will undoubtedly do a better job of pointing out issues than of resolving them. The BBM study, and the Ashton [1979] study on which it is based, are commendable both for tackling the basic question above and for providing a way to think about some interesting associated issues. Many of my criticisms are directed at the value of the "paradox-based" research approach on which these and other studies are based, rather than at BBM's own efforts.

MAKING DESCRIPTIVE USE OF EXPECTED UTILITY THEORY/AXIOMS

The BBM study is concerned with the Allais paradox, related to the expected utility theoretical framework for choice under uncertainty. Though it seems reasonable that, when choice alternatives share an outcome-probability combination, then the common combination should not affect the choice, alternatives can be framed so that people's responses appear to be affected [see e.g. Schoemaker 1982, p. 532, 538, 543]. Because it is only one paradox about one axiom of one formulation of one theoretical framework, BBM quite properly are not attempting to test expected utility theory itself but rather claim to be using the theory (the axiom) descriptively. There is much debate about the validity of doing this, as BBM, Ashton and Schoemaker note, but two points about the particular BBM study strike me as important.

First, BBM give the word "descriptive" a rather normative flavor: "... identify the reasons underlying choices that conform with the independence axiom" [p. 116]. It seems to me that descriptive (empirical) science should attempt to understand how people make choices, not focus on circumstances in which people do it "right" for a change. I would like to have seen the study try to understand the motivational dynamics of the research setting, because surely that is where the explanation for the unusual conformance with the axiom lies. Since it seems well established that, in general, the expected utility framework is not descriptively valid, the reader must wonder how the researchers managed to get the results. Thus rather than extend Ashton's results by study of the Allais paradox itself, the authors might have studied Ashton's experimental context to determine why Ashton got those results. What were the subjects trying to do, how were they motivated to perform better or worse, what did they think the research was about? I suppose I am suggesting that defining the "framing" of the Allais alternatives and the experimental context in the subjects' minds [Tversky and Kahneman 1981] would help in establishing the study's contribution beyond Ashton's work.

My second point comes out of part of BBM's answer to my first one: the paper's suggestion that training in expected value techniques may be an explanation for Ashton's results. Even though EV is not the same thing as EU, I think that is very plausible. But I fear the training issue twists the matter away from the fundamental human choice questions that EU and Allais raised and turns it into an educational question: can we train students to respond using some decision technique? I have no doubt that we can, especially if we use as a measure a simple decision problem administered in a classroom setting. In fact, I hope we can, or we should put away our teaching tools! Here is the twist I worry about: we are no longer evaluating EU, or even Allais, but rather the educational effectiveness of the Wisconsin undergraduate business program.

In making these points, I mean to suggest only that an examination of the contextual dynamics of the study could improve its contribution greatly by broadening its base beyond the narrow confines of an odd case of conformance with a descriptively discredited framework.

DRAWING ACCOUNTING CONNECTIONS FROM SUCH A STUDY

Only in their first and last sentences do BBM make any connection between their study and decision making in accounting. Their reticience is proper, but perhaps as a discussant I may be less modest on their behalf. It seems to me that empirical work on the expected utility model has several important connections to accounting. The first, which BBM imply, is that the model is a fundamental part of the teaching and (economic) analysis in our business schools and accounting programs, largely because it is also fundamental to much of the theory on which we have relied, as teachers and researchers, in recent years. Serious testing of the empirical validity of the model, in business and accounting contexts, is long past due. There is evidence from other fields [see e.g. Schoemaker 1982] that the model has major shortcomings, but, to be credible and to alter ours and our colleagues' attitudes to the model, those shortcomings require demonstration in the contexts we are familiar with.

Even if we step back from testing the validity of the model, there are some cases where specific descriptive study of various axioms and implications would be useful. One is in the agency theory area, in its development of monitoring rules, sharing rules and other consequences of particular assumed decision models. A second is in the use of analytical review in auditing: many of the review techniques are directed at assessing risks and at interfacing with such classical statistical tools as statistical sampling and multiple regression.

RELYING ON THE ALLAIS PARADOX AS A SPRINGBOARD TO RESEARCH

In order to examine this issue (and the BBM paper's contribution to it) I have developed a general version of the Allais format. (For a different generalized version, which makes largely different points, see Lichtenstein's [1979] critique of the Ashton [1979] study.) Allais set up two choices, each between two lotteries. The two lotteries in each choice involved three possible outcomes and three probabilities, combined in particular ways. I will begin with the following notation:

Choice A: outcomes 01A, 02A, 03A;
probabilities P1A, P2A, (1 P1A + P2A);

Choice B: outcomes 01B, 02B, 03B;
probabilities P1B, P2B, (1 – P1B – P2B).

Using this notation, the Allais paradox (see BBM's Table 1) can be represented as in Panel I of my Table 1. Allais presented the gambles as on the left of the panel; using elementary probability notions they can be disassembled as shown on the right of the panel and the two lotteries in each choice may be compared as shown. The first term in each disassembled lottery is the same within each choice and therefore, by the axiom of independence, the choice ought to be made on the basis of the non-common terms, which are shown in the lottery comparisons. At this point, there is no paradox, because choice A involves different outcomes and probabilities than choice B and each choice would be made on the merits of the lotteries available for that choice. The claim is only that the common terms should not affect each choice.

Allais created the paradox by tying the two choices' outcomes and probabilities together (his numbers are shown in square brackets):

Set outcomes 01A and 01B equal (call this "0x": [$1,000,000]);
Set outcomes 02A and 03B equal (call this "0w": [$5,000,000]);
Set outcomes 03A and 02B equal (call this "0z": [$0]);

TABLE 1

General Formulation of Allais Paradox (millions of dollars)

	Allais' Presentation	Disassembled Presentation
Panel I		
A (1)	01A	P1A × 01A + (1-P1A) × 01A
	[1]	[.89 × 1 + .11 × 1]
(2)	P2A × 02A + P1A × 01A + (1 – P2A – P1A) × 03A	P1A × 01A + P2A × 01A + (1 – P2A – P1A) × 03A
	[.10 × 5 + .89 × 1 + .01 × 0]	[.89 × 1 + .10 × 5 + .01 × 0]
	Lottery (1) versus Lottery (2):	(1 – P1A) × (01A – 03A) vs. P2A(02A – 03A)
		[.11 × 1 vs. .10 × 5]
B (3)	P1B × 01B + (1 – P1B) × 02B	(1 – P1B) × 02B + P1B × 01B
	[.11 × 1 + .89 × 0]	[.89 × 0 + .11 × 1]
(4)	P2B × 03B + (1 – P2B) × 02B	(1 – P1B) × 02B + P2B × 03B + (PIB – P2B) × 02B
	[.10 × 5 + .90 × 0]	[.89 × 0 + .10 × 5 + .01 × 0]
	Lottery (3) versus Lottery (4):	P1B(01B – 02B) vs. P2B (03B – 02B)
		[.11 × 1 vs. .10 × 5]

Note: for reference, Allais' numbers are shown in square brackets.

TABLE 1 (continued)

General Formulation of Allais Paradox
(millions of dollars)

	Allais' Presentation	Disassembled Presentation
Panel II		
A (1)	Ox	Pu × Ox − (1 − Pu) × Ox
(2)	Pt × Ow + Pu × Ox + (1 − Pt − Pu) × Oz	Pu × Ox + Pt × Ow + (1 − Pt − Pu) × Oz
	Lottery (1) versus Lottery (2)	(1 − Pu) × (Ox − Oz) vs. Pt × (Ow − Oz)
B (3)	(1 − Pu)Ox + PuOz	Pu × Oz + (1 − Pu) × Ox
(4)	Pt × Ow + (1 − Pt) × Oz	Pu × Oz + Pt × Ow + (1 − Pt − Pu) × Oz
	Lottery (3) versus Lottery (4)	(1 − Pu) × (Ox-Oz) vs. Pt × (Ow-Oz)

Set probabilities P2A and P2B equal (call this "Pt": [.10];
Set probabilities P1A and (1-P1B) equal (call this "Pu": [.89]).

Panel II uses the new outcome and probability notation to restate the Allais and disassembled presentations. Now the paradox is apparent from the lottery comparisons: if the common terms are removed, the two choices are identical, so a person choosing lottery (1) in choice A should choose lottery (3) in choice B, and choosing (2) should go with choosing (4). Combining choice (1) with (4) or (2) with (3) is evidence of violation of the independence axiom, because the common term must have affected the choice in one or the other case.

But is that true? Panels I and II point out some of the problems in using the Allais format to investigate independence:

1. The disassembling operation is necessary in order to prove the paradox. Though that operation involves only elementary probability theory, using the paradox empirically nevertheless implies a joint (and confounded) test of the probability theory as well as the axiom. (Since expected utility theory does include probability concepts in its axioms, this jointness may not matter very much to the objective of testing the theory in total, but it does matter to using individual axioms as descriptive guidelines, if it is desired to be able to reject those guidelines.) Schoemaker [1982] is one of the many writers to point out that probability is not a simple construct nor an empirically sound one [see also Cohen 1977, 1981].
2. The Allais format is "tricky" and requires real thought to sort out what is the "correct" comparison (at least it does for me). As an empiricist, I have to question what the psychological meaning of this sort of situation is for subjects. They are led down the garden path, in a sense, and often fail to "see the point" even when it is carefully explained, as noted by Slovic and Tversky [1974], Ashton [1979], BBM and others. Look at choice A, for example: what appears to be a choice between a certain and an uncertain return turns out to be interpretable as a choice between two uncertain returns: are we really making descriptive use of an expected utility axiom here, or are we testing subjects for puzzle-solving ability? Schoemaker [1982, p. 548] points out that whether subjects' sensitivity to effects of the research context is a violation of expected utility theory is a complex question.
3. Subjects who have had some training in expected value, however, are likely to recognize the Allais format (a neat table with probabilities and outcomes matched) as just what they have been taught to handle. Their courses have shown them pathological examples of overlooking the probability calculus and if they wish to do a conscientious job of being a subject, it is fairly clear what is required. As I suggested earlier, it is not obvious that, in such a circumstance, the test of training effects has much to do with the axiom. However, if such a test does show training effects, it supports the possibility that the "paradox" results are an experimental artifact (a function of trickiness and format). BBM do find such effects.
4. Panel II shows another awkward characteristic of the paradox as

Allais designed it: though each choice has an "irrelevant" common outcome, it is not the same outcome in each (choice A has outcome "Ox" while choice B has "Oz"). By the theory, it shouldn't matter: each outcome should be "equally ignored." But empirically it is untidy because the experimenter has to be sure that the psychological meaning of ignoring (in choice A) a $1,000,000 common outcome is the same as that of ignoring (in choice B) a $0 common outcome. BBM were sensitive to this, in revising the Ashton scheme to remove bankruptcy as one of the common outcomes, but a stronger test of the axiom would involve choices both having the *same* common outcome.

5. Removing the empirical difficulty of my point 4 proves quite difficult to do. For example, if say choice B is changed to make the common outcome $1,000,000 as it is in choice A, then choice B turns out to be absolutely identical to A. The empirical operation of the paradox depends on the common outcomes being different from choice to choice, and that has caused researchers to suggest, as factors driving the paradox, other things that relate to those differences, such as the "certainty effect" of the certain outcome present in choice A but not choice B, or the high probability of a "bad" outcome (present in choice B but not choice A). The latter was of course examined specifically by BBM in their Experiment III. If the paradox depends on such differences, it is not clear to me that we are still talking about expected utility theory, even descriptively. Are we using the theory descriptively, or are we using the paradox descriptively? The second seems to be putting the cart before the horse!
6. Point 5 leads to a question that is important to evaluating the contribution of the BBM study's Experiments III and IV, which try to clarify the role of an expected value decision strategy as distinct from other ways of using the data. Can the format of the paradox accommodate a clear test among strategies that produce conformance to the axiom's apparent dictates? The format is so constrained, partly by its simplicity, that some strategies are confounded. For example, as BBM point out, varying the probability of a bad outcome in Experiments III and IV led to an inverse varying of the expected value, thereby confounding the two strategies [see also Lichtenstein 1979, p. 218]. BBM cleverly used the training variable to partially unconfound the results and showed that the less knowledgeable subjects were not sensitive to expected value but were somewhat sensitive to avoidance of a bad outcome. It is nevertheless unfortunate that the confounding results from using the Allais format.

The formulation I have used incidentally, indicates that the level of the probabilities should not be relevant to the result: any use of the common term is a violation of independence. Lichtenstein [1979], in criticizing Ashton [1979], made the point that the empirical likelihood of finding violations depends on the level of the probabilities. BBM took advantage of that in their design. But surely if the empirical likelihood is sensitive to factors the theory holds irrelevant, the format is imperfect for utilizing the theory empirically.

FURTHER COMMENTS ON THE STUDY'S RESEARCH DESIGN

I have been critical above of the Allais paradox as a way of using the independence axiom descriptively. BBM were clearly concerned with many of the same issues, and designed the research to tackle them directly. The explicit measurement of knowledge/training effects is a strength of the work and a major contribution. But I do have a worry here: by measuring, rather than manipulating experimentally, expected value knowledge, BBM have confounded that knowledge with all the other things that may distinguish sophomores and freshmen from seniors (age, general business knowledge, familiarity with questionnaires, ability to understand the research instructions' references to divisional manager and divisional return, etc.). I would like to see the paper provide more evidence that expected value knowledge was in fact the principal driving force behind the results.

The training effect is also confounded by the administration of the material. Apparently the same groups of subjects were used in all the cross-subjects experiments (I, II and III) and the experiments seem to have been administered in that order. Therefore, by Experiment III, when the knowledge/no-knowledge difference is particularly of interest, both K and NK subjects had been through a couple of rounds with the format. This might tend to weaken the effects Experiment III was trying to find and to strengthen the likelihood of artifactual format effects in the results. Perhaps precautions were taken about these matters, but the paper is silent about them.

A stronger investigation of the "avoidance of bad results" strategy might also have been mounted. All rates of return were positive, none even zero as Allais had: presumably the definition of the 1 percent return case as being "bad" is relative to the other returns, or perhaps to some opportunity cost return. I have some difficulty with this and wonder why negative returns were not used (though I appreciate that such might have caused their own problems, e.g. if the argument by Kahneman and Tversky [1979] is accepted, losses are evaluated psychologically quite differently than gains).

FURTHER COMMENTS ON THE DATA ANALYSIS

In general, BBM make good use of the data, particularly in Experiments III and IV. Two further analyses, however, might have strengthened the results.

First, we are told that the knowledge group has 183 students in it and the non-knowledge group had 181. The results tables indicate a large fall-off in both groups: Table 3 shows results for 154 and 106 subjects, Table 8 shows 158 and 106, Table 11 shows 157 and 106. As I understand it, the missing subjects in the NK group were largely freshmen and sophomores who had some exposure to expected value. Why not analyze the responses of those subjects? They would provide a nice control to strengthen the training/knowledge with the K group but share all the other confounding characteristics with the NK group. I would hope that their responses would be like those of the K group—if so, that would be strong evidence that, at least as far as this study is concerned, the knowledge was not seriously confounded.

Second, the results for the various experiments might be compared for their contribution to the "relative expected value" investigation of Experiment III. Table 5, for example, seems to indicate that subjects were not sensitive to differences in expected value (though the percentages of conformance were so high there is not much room for any sensitivity).

REFERENCES

Ashton, R.H., "Behavioral Assumptions of Normative Decision Theory: An Experimental Test of the Independence Axiom in an Accounting Context," in T.J. Burns (ed.), *Behavioral Experiments in Accounting* (The Ohio State University, 1979), pp. 175-204.

Biggs, S.F., B.A. Biuk and A.A.W. Mahmoud, "Experimental Evidence on Conformance with the Independence Axiom of Normative Decision Theory," in S. Moriarity and E. Joyce (Eds.), *Decision Making and Accounting: Current Research,* (University of Oklahoma, Center for Economic and Management Research, 1984), pp. 114-143.

________, "Can Human Irrationality be Experimentally Observed?" *The Behavioral and Brain Sciences* (1981), pp. 317-370 including comments by a large number of researchers on Cohen's ideas.

Cohen, L.J., *The Probable and the Provable,* Oxford: Clarendon Press, (1977).

Kahneman, D. and A. Tversky, "Prospect Theory: An Analysis of Decisions Under Risk," *Econometrica* (1979), pp. 263-291.

Lichtenstein, S. "Critique" (of the Ashton paper above), in T.J. Burns (ed.), *Behavioral Experiments in Accounting II* (The Ohio State University, 1979), pp. 215-220.

Schoemaker, P., "The Expected Utility Model: Its Variants, Purposes, Evidence and Limitations," *Journal of Economic Literature* (June 1982), pp. 529-563.

Slovic, P. and A. Tversky, "Who Accepts Savage's Axiom?" *Behavioral Science* (November 1974), pp. 368-373.

Tversky, A. and D. Kahneman, "The Framing of Decisions and the Psychology of Choice," *Science* (January 30, 1981), pp. 453-458.

Matthew J. Anderson
University of Minnesota

The Process Tracing Paridigm: A General View

INTRODUCTION

Recent research in human judgment and decision making has been increasingly focused on the pre-decision behavior of decision makers [Payne, Braunstein, and Carroll, 1978]. Concurrent with this development has been a move toward representative design of experiments [Ebbesen and Konećni, 1980; Payne 1980]. Both of these developments stem from a concern that the external validity of previous experimental research may be less than desirable.

One of the principal criticisms directed at earlier decision-making research was the contention that the experimental laboratory setting generally employed was too far removed from the real-life decision-making environment. It was suggested that much of real-life decision making occurred in ill-structured settings, where as most of the experimental research involved well-structured settings [Ungson, Braunstein, and Hall, 1981].[1] This argument was supported by two related findings of ongoing research. First, decision makers in the workplace failed to adopt many of the decision aids developed from the research results of laboratory experiments [Slovic, Fischhoff, and Lichtenstein, 1977]. Second, it was demonstrated that small changes in the task environment often lead to major changes in observed behavior [Simon and Hayes, 1979, Tversky and Kahneman, 1981].

This paper addresses some of the issues associated with the analysis of ill-structured problems. The principal objective of the paper is to consider the methodology of process tracing. The paper proceeds as follows. First, the process tracing paradigm is described. The coding and modelling processes are then reviewed. Problems associated with the methodology are discussed. Finally, a proposed measure of information importance for the process tracing paradigm is described in an appendix.

THE PROCESS TRACING PARADIGM

Process tracing models represent efforts to capture the process that a problem solver goes through during solution attempts. The technique involves either having the subject verbalize or 'think aloud' while processing some task, or the monitoring of eye movements during the solution process. As suggested by several researchers [Mandler, 1975; Wood, 1978], what is observed is the output of the mental processes, since the mental processes themselves are not available for observation. This paper is primarily concerned with verbal protocols.

Process tracing models are principally attractive to cognitive scientists because they may yield insights into how human decision makers solve problems (pre-decision behavior). To the extent that they represent a veridical reflection of ongoing problem solving activity, they yield at least as much information (and generally more) as that required for other analytical techniques applied to particular decision problems. Additionally, they do not suffer from the requirements of most quantitative models for parsimony. As a result, much more realistic problems may be addressed.

The process tracing paradigm is based on the theory outlined by Newell and Simon [1972]. Newell and Simon proposed that all problem solving takes place in a problem space. The problem space is an internal structure—the problem solvers internal representation of the task. It consists of all information pertinent to problem solution that is available to the processor, as well as processes for transforming and storing information. The transformation processes, or operators, are used to derive new knowledge from existing knowledge. The inputs and outputs of operators are denoted knowledge elements.

Problem solving activity is viewed as a journey through the problem space—a series of interconnected knowledge states. The task itself is viewed as the major determinant of observed behavior [Newell and Simon, 1972]. Newell and Simon state that few variations of problem representations tend to be observed for particular task settings.

The examples used in this paper are drawn from an exploratory study of information used in the investment domain. The experimental task was the examination of a prospectus from an initial offering of equity securities. Four professional and four nonprofessional analysts were instructed to analyze the stock as a potential investment vehicle, and to 'think aloud' during the entire process. They were informed that there was no right or wrong answer to the problem. However, there was a general presumption that subjects would adopt the fundamental approach to security valuation [Reilly, 1979]. The research was essentially a one-shot case study. The case study approach was suggested by Payne [1980] as a way to achieve increased external validity.

As stated above, process tracing involves having the subjects "think aloud" as they perform a task. Based on the model proposed by Ericcson and Simon [1980], the verbalizations should reflect the ongoing thought processes as long as verbalizations are collected concurrently and subjects are not required to "search" for specific knowledge or "explain" what they are doing. The general effect of the verbalizations is a slowing down of the thought processes, with no change in the processes themselves. The model is robust over assumptions concerning memory organization and other physiologic constraints.

The verbalizations, or protocols, of the problem solver are recorded and used to build models of the subject in the particular task domain. Based on a task analysis, which outlines the general requirements for successful completion of the task (and therefore becomes a theory of the task[2]), the models and underlying behavior are assessed. The derived models are also viewed as theories of the task [Newell, 1973].

The model-building processes involve several stages, each of which embodies a different representation of the processing behavior of subjects. Each stage consists of applying certain criteria to the collected subject verbalizations. The approach adopted in this study followed that used by Bouwman [1978, 1980]. Bouwman's work includes the following set of representations (not all of which need be utilized in a particular study), after the procedure outlined by Waterman and Newell [1971, 1976]: 1) the audio tape representation, 2) the lexical representation, 3) the topic representation, 4) the element representation, 5) the group representation, 6) the problem behavior graph and 7) the trace.

The tape representation is simply the audio tape itself. The lexical representation consists of the transcriptionist's and/or the researcher's interpretation of what is on the audio tape. Not only are the spoken words important, but also contextual meanings—pauses, periods, et cetera. Basically, this representation entails applying linguistic rules to the data, as well as detailing prosodic features and timing.

The topic representation involves splitting the lexical representation into short phrases, each of which is concerned with a single task topic. These phrases are called topic segments, and they become the units of analysis. This breakup of the protocols is achieved by applying grammatical and linguistic rules to the transcript.

The element representation is the first in which meaning is extracted from the protocols. Problem space relationships or occurrences are detailed. Knowledge elments (i.e., things the subject knows) and operator elements (i.e., data transformation mechanisms) are identified. In general, knowledge elements are the in- or outputs of operator elements. A third class of element specifies the relationship(s) between operator and knowledge elements, such as which type(s) of knowledge element(s) is (are) associated with a particular operator element. These relationship-specifying elements are known as indicator elements.

The next representation consists of analyzing operator and knowledge elements in terms of which inputs are associated with which operators and their outputs. The combination of an operator element with its in- and output knowledge elements is called an operator group. Operator groups become the nodes in the next representation—the problem behavior graph (PBG). Examples of operator groups are shown in Table 1.

As previously stated, the problem behavior graph is a dynamic representation of the processor attempting to solve the problem. The trace is essentially the PGB of the model. Additionally, the set of representations could be expanded to include the problem space, which is a necessary structure of the theory for analysis. Coding and model derivation procedures are addressed separately in following sections of the paper.

CODING

Coding techniques have been problematical for process tracing researchers. The primary issue is the lack of a systematic procedure for coding behavior. Many observers contend that the coding process is too subjective to offer valid, reliable results.

The description of the human problem solver as an information processing system [Newell and Simon, 1972] is a useful frame of reference when coding problem-solving behavior in task environments. Newell and Simon proposed that the human problem solver as a working mechanism is organized as a production system [Newell, 1973]. The productions, or condition(s)—action pairs, serve as control mechanisms structuring observed behavior. The observed behavior is a reflection of the program used to address the task, where the program is defined as "...a symbol structure... that would designate the sequence of elementary processes [productions] to be executed" [Newell and Simon, 1972].

TABLE 1

Operator Groups

Input Elements	Operator	Output Element(s)
Costs Sales	Increase	Decreasing Increasing
Sales Salaries	CI	Low High
Defense Contracts One Large Customer	Tag 1	Bad (A Negative)

Newell and Simon [1972, p. 29] list a set of elementary information processes sufficient to describe human problem-solving behavior. The included processes are: a) discrimination (contingent or alterable behavior) b) tests and comparisons, c) symbol creation (in working memory), d) writing symbol structures (in memory), e) reading and writing externally, f) designating symbol structures (e.g. "let symbol structure be x"), g) storing symbol structures (in long-term memory).

The first two processes are of primary interest in this paper since their output is generally reflected in observable task behavior. Further, their execution involves a transformation in the processor's knowledge with respect to the task. Such a change in knowledge is not generally implied by the execution of the balance of the listed elementary information processes; they are principally concerned with restructuring or retention of existing knowledge.

The above distinction was important since it was the basis for the definition of information use and process used in this study. Information (knowledge elements) was considered to be used if an operator was found to admit it as an input. Process was operationally defined in this research as the making of a comparison or the establishing of a relationship or link between previously made comparisons.[3] It was assumed that most processing behavior involves some type of comparison, either explicitly or implicitly. Processing behavior was viewed as a sequential series of comparisons, where the coding task involved designating the type of comparison made. The designation of type was based on the standard used for comparison; i.e., whether the standard was internal to the processor or external to the processor, qualitative or quantitative. Where necessary, links or relationships between these comparisons are established. Links may indicate that "a" is either related (cause by or causes) or not related to "b." A list of the operators (data transformers) used in this study appears below in Table 2. Operators were adapted from the set used by Bouwman [1978, 1980].

TABLE 2

List of Operators and Coding Devices Used

Type	Example or Meaning	Operation or Manipulation	Standard
Examine		Evaluation	—
Tag 1	Good, Bad	Impression (nonquantitative)	Internal
CI	High, Low	Impression (quantitative)	Internal
Compute	—	Calculation	—
Increase	Greater than, Less than,	Comparison (quantitative)	External
CA	Same as increase	Comparison (quantitative)	External
Trend	longer time	Comparison (quantitative)	External
Formulate Relation	Because, due to	Linking	—
Formulate Problem	Impression	Summarization	Either
—		—	—
Coding Devices			
Reading		Reading	—
Tag 2		Paraphrasing, talking, etc. Search activity	—

The above definition of process is consistent with Newell and Simon's [1972] description of knowledge states and operators. The knowledge state is defined as "the dynamic information about the task." The operator is defined as "(an) information process,...producing new states of knowledge from existing states of knowledge.'' The emphasis is on change, and implies comparison (i.e. new state implies comparison with old).

Further distinctions were also made. If the processor's behavior is viewed as a program, then behavior other than what was operationalized as process should be reflected in observed output. As a program is executed, two kinds of activity (activity is used broadly here) are generally observed. These were characterized as control activity and process activity. Control activity is that activity involving structure—goal, propositional, or other related statements. It is reflected in statements by the processors such as, ''I'm looking for the explanation of the extraordinary item...[4] Process activity involves actual data manipulations and is reflected in statements by the processors such as ''sales are increasing,'' etc. Control statements were therefore excluded from the primitive operator or process designation. They are coded Tag 2 in Table 2. Only activity related to the actual execution of procedures (data transformation) was designated as process or operator(s).

The act of reading was also excluded from the process or operator designation. Reading was assumed to be a passive act of information acquisition. While it is likley that some retention, learning or manipulation may occur during reading, the processes are not observable. Knowledge of use of these processes is available to observers only when some external indicator of their execution is given—the processor says or does something which implied their use. Further, operator use is not necessary for knowledge acquisition. Since the above external indicators imply a departure from the act of reading (given the characterization of humans as serial processors [Newell and Simon, 1972]), it was assumed that reading was excludable from process. The assumption is supported by research reviewed by Wickelgren [1981].

Use of the above scheme results in the coding process being quite general. It can be viewed as a sequential movement from one topic segment to another. At each, the following question is answered: What information exists in topic segment (x + 1) that did not exist at topic segment (x)? For example, a statement such as ''sales are increasing nicely'' implies two comparisons. One involves at least sales for year (x) with year (x + 1). The other involves a comparison to some internal standard for the rate of increase—high, low, etc.

Use of the above procedures produced raw agreement between the researcher and a naive coder of .91, and a Kappa Coefficient [Cohen, 1960] of .66. Further, most of the errors occurred in null situations, where no change occurred in a particular variable. Previous research indicates that such information is more likely to be ignored by processors, (such as a coder) [Nisbett and Ross, 1980]. Construction of separate flowchart models based on the coded data from both the researcher and the coder produced no major changes, and the output decision was the same for both sets of models.

The procedure outlined is also compatible with other coding schemes and levels of detail such as used in Payne [1976] and Waller [1981]. Delineations such as Einhorn and Hogarth's [1980] characterization of problem solving activity as consisting of information acquisition, information evaluation, and feedback phases are readily adaptible. The objective here is to demonstrate the generality of the underlying coding process.

Model Derivation

Models developed from the protocols are based on the PBG. The procedure flows from the characterization of processing behavior as a program. The approach adopted in this study was as follows. First, a preliminary flow diagram (protocol model) based strictly on the order followed by the processor was constructed. Components of the preliminary flow diagram were next grouped in a recursive fashion while maintaining processing order. Only those components that dealt with exactly the same aspect of some attribute of the subject firm were grouped together. For example, all of the subjects noted that "sales were increasing." They also noted that "sales were to a single customer—the government." These statements comprise two different components—one dealing with sales specifically, the other dealing with the clientele or customer base. They would not be grouped together. The objective of the grouping procedure was to establish the existence of subroutines, loops, or other recursive behavior in the protocols.

The final step was the establishing of the disposition of information by the processor. Again, the processor's actions were followed explicitly. In almost every case, as the processor processed a piece of information, he or she stated his or her view of the impact of the particular piece of information. In cases where this was not done and no implications could be inferred from other data, no disposition was made for the item (knowledge element).

Decision break points were depicted as occurring at the levels of data found in the information set. This was clearly not realistic. In the general case, one would need a set of cases over the entire range for each variable of interest, or theoretical and empirical support for imposing decision breakpoints in the model [e.g. Hogarth, 1974]. In this domain, such guidelines do not exist, and the research design precluded large numbers of cases. An example of a protocol and derived model appears in Figures 1 and 2.

Methodological Problems

Questions have been raised regarding the validity of results obtained using the process-tracing methodology. Primarily, these concerns have centered around the previously cited subjectivity of the coding process, the question of accessibility of mental processes for verbalization, and whether or not verbalization itself changed the ongoing mental processes. In a recent article, Nisbett and Wilson [1977] reviewed empirical evidence which purportedly demonstrated the relative inaccessibility of mental processes. They contended that individuals have no direct access to their mental processes and are often unaware of what they are doing;[5] their mental processes are often automatic and not subject to conscious control. As a result, verbal reports tend to be incomplete, sketchy and unreliable, particularly for familiar tasks.

The implications of their contentions are clearly serious if valid. However, Ericsson and Simon [1980] pointed out that Nisbett and Wilson's conclusions were based on retrospective, not concurrent, verbal reports. The evidence cited by Nisbett and Wilson also was collected during relatively uncontrolled debriefing sessions. None of the results came from studies designed explicitly to test the conclusions drawn.

FIGURE 1

Protocol Model of S4

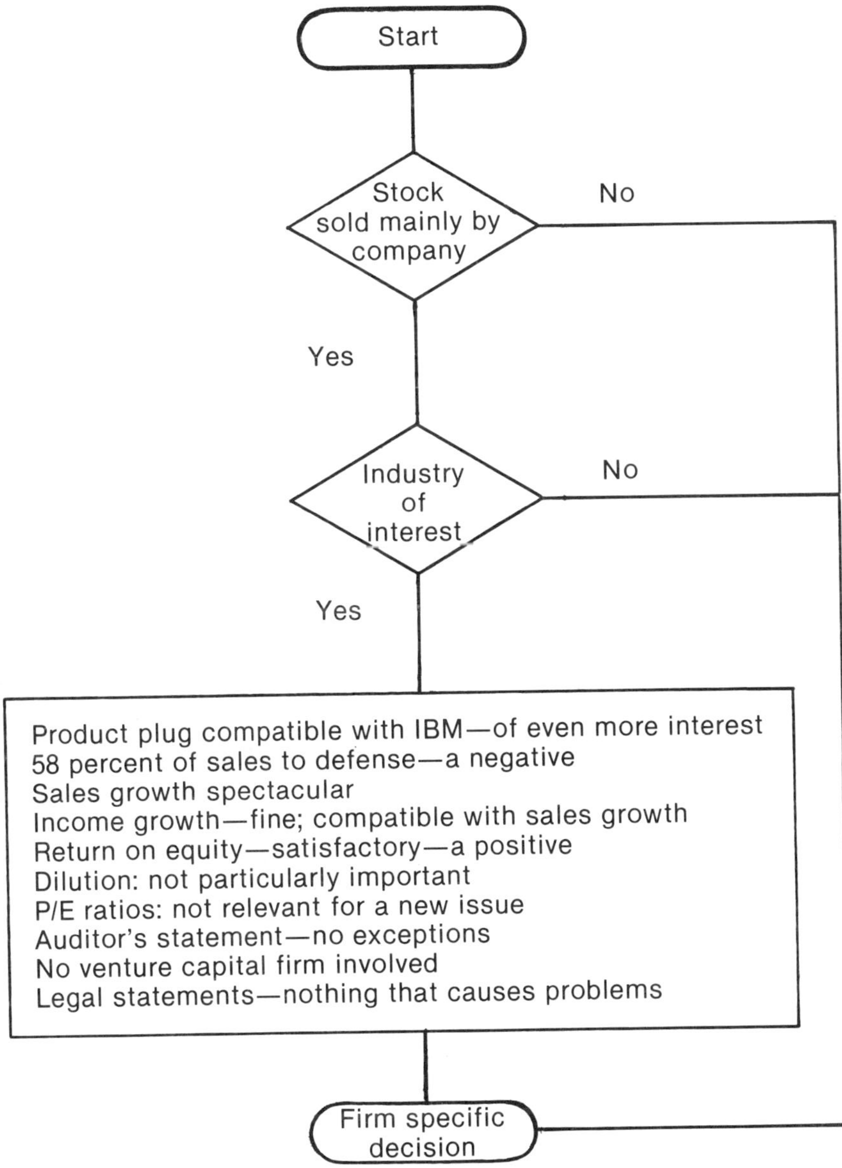

FIGURE 2
Derived Model of S4

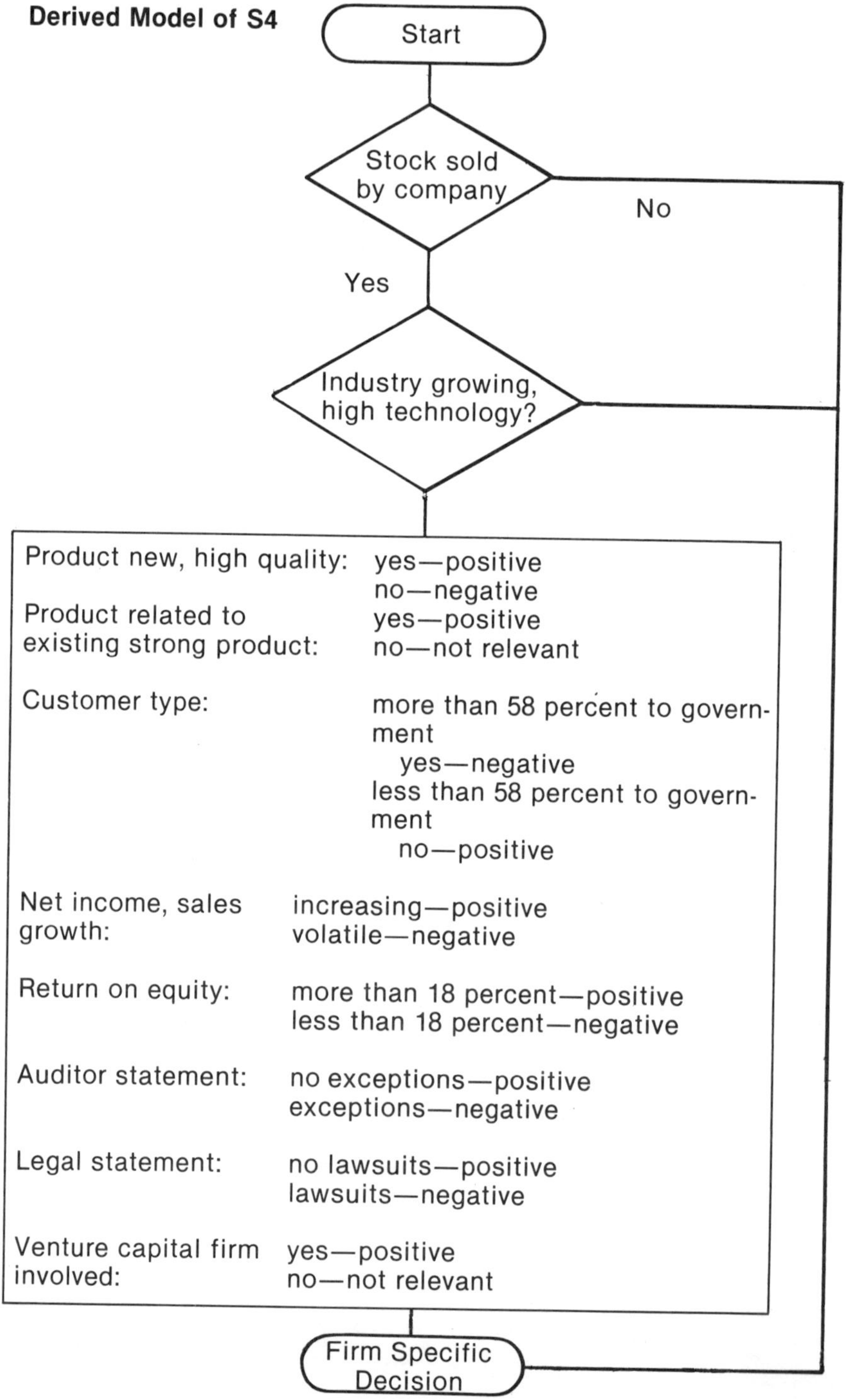

In addition, as pointed out by Mandler [1975], processes that become automatic over time due to overlearning generally have the feature of interruptibility. Specifically, "...structures that are not species specific and general but are the result of experience can be inspected and reorganized more or less easily," [Mandler, 1975, p. 245]. Should anything occur that disrupts a particular process, the process can be placed under conscious control. For example, driving a car over a familiar route is a task which tends to become automatic in nature. However, should anything occur which interrupts the ongoing behavior sequence, the task is generally returned to conscious control. Additionally, it is likely that in most complex or illstructured problems, the context is sufficiently different in each task that the processor retains some degree of conscious control. Automaticity generally occurs in tasks that are highly similar and repeated often [Shiffrin and Dumais, 1981; Norman and Bobrow, 1975]. Shiffrin and Dumais [1981] found that in inconsistent learning situations, little automatism occurred. However, further research is needed.

Another concern, which has not been often addressed, is the extent to which verbalization alters process. Ericsson and Simon's [1980] previously cited model offers evidence supporting the view that verbalization will not alter underlying mental processes under prescribed conditions. Nevertheless, the issue has not been definitively settled [Mandler, 1975]. Returning to the human-being-as-computer metaphor offers some insight to the problem. If one views the human processor as a limited capacity processing unit, then it is not difficult to envision situations in which the processing capacity may be taxed. However, the extent to which this may occur is not clear. A potential solution may be the extent to which the tasks attempted by processors are data and/or resource limited [Norman and Bobrow, 1975]. If task performance is resource limited (i.e. increasing the available resource would improve performance), then verbalization may alter the process if the total processing capacity is already in use. If the task is data limited, then no amount of additional resource above some critical level will change performance. It seems reasonable to assume that the more familiar a task is, the less likely it is to be resource limited. At any rate, Norman and Bobrow point out that in the general case, even if capacity is strained, catastrophic failures of the system do not occur. What is observed is a gradual decline in performance. The issue then becomes one of gauging the extent to which the potential change alters output.

Finally, concerns have also been raised about the lack of measures of efficiency and diagnosticity of information in process tracing models [Libby, 1981]. One view of a solution to this concern is that adopted by Clarkson [1962], using the Turing Machine analogy. Essentially, the premise is that human behavior is itself the ultimate standard of performance. To the extent that the process model (computer program) mimics in all observable respects its human counterpart, it is a success.[6] This view is limited in that it can only be applied to models reduced to a formal computer algorithm. And, even in the situation where the algorithm exists, the concerns raised are not directly addressed. Tuggle and Barron [1980] addressed the efficiency question in a recent article. They demonstrate a procedure which

TABLE 3

Ranking of Top Four Knowledge Elements Processed-Scoring Rule and Subject Results

		Ranking	
Subject	Knowledge Element	Scoring Rule	Subject (Debriefing)
S1			
	Growth Volatility	1	2
	Average Growth	2	—
	Competition	3	3
	Dividends	4	1
	Market Alternatives	—	4
S2			
	Origin of Shares	1	—
	One Large Customer	1	2
	New Issue	3	3
	Average Growth	5	—
	Single Product	5	1
	Industry Beta	—	4
S3			
	Product Line	1	1
	Margins	1	—
	One Large Customer	3	2
	Competition	3	—
S4			
	State of Market	1	2
	Origin Shares	3	1
	One Large Customer	3	—
	Average Growth	4	3
	Product	—	4

provides a logical framework for calibrating a model over time. The importance or diagnosticity issue is addressed in an appendix section of this paper.

Attempts to resolve some of the issues and concerns raised have led to several suggested solutions. The most often repeated of these is the contention that process tracing methodologies should be used in conjunction with other techniques, in a multi-method paradigm [Payne, et. al., 1978]. An illustrative and insightful example of the multimethod approach is offered by Einhorn, Kleinmutz and Kleinmutz [1979]. The multimethod approach is being adopted by increasing numbers of researchers.

CONCLUSION

This paper offers a potential framework for employing the process tracing paradigm. Problems and strengths of the methodology were addressed. The framework allows a definitional base which should depersonalize many of the inferences of process tracing researchers. However, as in most such frameworks, further research and testing is needed.

NOTES

[1]MacCrimmon and Taylor [1976] describe an ill-structured problem as one in which uncertainty exists (for the problem solver) relative to either the initial state, the goal state, or the transformations required to go from one state to the other. The solution obtained is not generally unique. A well structured problem is one for which an algorithm or standard operating procedure exists for moving from the initial state to the goal state. The solution is generally unique. The ill-structured versus well-structured distinction is not a dichotomy; it should be viewed as a continuum along which any problem environment may be placed [Simon and Hayes, 1976].

[2]This view is controversial. Researchers such as Anderson and Bower [1973] explicitly state that the model (program) is not the theory.

[3]This designation is concerned with process as a primitive, or smallest element of codeable behavior. For example, information search behavior is a more global concept since it may entail comparisons as well as other types of behavior. Programmed or algorithmic activity was also excluded from the process designation.

[4]This activity would be included in more global coding schemes such as information search.

[5]There are two issues here. The first is whether or not decisionmakers can accurately report what they are doing. The second issue is whether or not the behavior is appropriate, conditional on some standard of comparison.

[6]Newell and Simon adopt the Freudian position that individual behavior is deterministic [1972, p. 10]. In this framework, the individual models are errorless to the extent they are veridical representations.

REFERENCES

Bouwman, M.J., "Computer Simulation of Human Decision-Making in Accounting: The Analysis of Financial Statements," unpublished Ph.D. dissertation, Carnegie Mellon University, 1978.

_____________, "The Use of Accounting Information: Expert Versus Novice Behavior," unpublished manuscript, University of Oregon, 1980. Forthcoming in *Accounting, Organizations, and Society*.

Clarkson, G., *Portfolio Selection: A Simulation of Trust Investment* (Prentice-Hall, 1962).

Cohen, J., "A Coefficient of Agreement of Nominal Scales," *Educational and Psychological Measurement* (1960), pp. 37-46.

Ebbesen, E.B. and V.J. Konécni, "On the External Validity of Decisions Making Research: What Do We Know about Decisions in the Real World?" in *Cognitive Processes in Choice and Decision Behavior*. Edited by T.S. Wallsten. (Lawrence Erlbaum Associates, 1980), pp. 21-45.

Einhorn, H.J. and R.M. Hogarth, "Behavioral Decision Theory: Processes of Judgment and Choice," in *Annual Review of Psychology*. Edited by M. Rosenweig and L. Porter. (Annual Review, Inc., 1980), pp. 53-88.

Einhorn, H.J., D.M. Kleinmutz, and B. Kleinmutz, "Linear Regression and Process Tracing Models of Judgment," *Psychological Review* (1979), pp. 465-485.

Ericsson, K. and H. Simon, "Verbal Reports as Data," *Psycholgical Review* (1980), pp. 215-251.

Hayes, J.R. and H. Simon, "Understanding Complex Tax Instructions," in *Cognition and Instruction*. Edited by D. Klahr (Lawrence Erlbaum, 1976), pp. 269-289.

Hirschleifer, J., *Price Theory and Applications,* (Prentice Hall, 1976).

Hogarth, R., "The Process Tracing in Clinical Judgment," *Behavioral Science* (1974), pp. 298-313.

Just, M.A. and P.A. Carpenter, "Eye Fixations and Cognitive Processes," *Cognitive Psychology* (1976), pp. 441-481.

_______ , *Accounting and Human Information Processing: Theory and Applications* (Prentice-Hall, 1981).

MacCrimmon, K.R. and R.N. Taylor, "Decisionmaking and Problem Solving," in *Handbook of Industrial and Organizational Psychology*. Edited by M.D. Dunnette (Rand McNally, 1976), pp. 1397-1453.

Mandler, G., "Consciousness: Respectable, Useful, and Probably Necessary," in *Information Processing and Cognition: The Loyola Symposium*. Edited by R.L. Solas (Lawrence Erlbaum Associates, 1975), pp. 229-254.

Miller, G.A., "The Magical Number Seven, Plus or Minus Two," *Psychological Review* (1956), pp. 81-97.

Newell, A., "Production Systems: Models of Control Structures," in *Visual Information Processing*. Edited by W.G. Chase (Academic Press, 1973), pp. 463-526.

Newell, A. and H.A. Simon, *Human Problem Solving,* (Prentice-Hall, 1972).

Nisbett, R.E. and T.D. Wilson, "Telling More Than We Know: Verbal Reports on Mental Processes," *Psychological Review* (1977), pp. 231-257.

Nisbett, R.E. and L. Ross, *Human Inference: Strategies and Shortcomings of Social Judgment,* (Prentice-Hall, 1980.)

Norman, D.A. and D.B. Bobrow, "On Data Limited and Resource-Limited Processes, *Cognitive Psychology* (1975), pp.44-64.

Payne, J.W., "Analyzing Decision Behavior: The Magician's Audience," in *Cognitive Processes in Choice and Decision Behavior*. Edited by T.S. Wallsten (Lawrence Erlbaum Associates, 1980), pp. 69-76.

Payne, J.W., "Task Complexity and Contingent Processing in Decision-Making: An Information Search and Protocol Analysis," *Organizational Behavior and Human Performance* (1976), pp. 366-387.

Payne, J.W., M.L. Braunstein and J.S. Carroll, "Exploring Predecisional Behavior: An Alternative Approach to Decision Research," *Organizational Behavior and Human Performance* (1978), pp. 17-44.

Reilly, F.K., *Investment Analysis and Portfolio Management,* (The Dryden Press, 1979).

Shiffrin, R.M. and S.T. Dumais, "The Development of Automatism," in *Cognitive Skills and Their Acquisition*. Edited by J.R. Anderson (Lawrence Erlbaum Associates, 1981), pp. 111-140.

Simon, H.A., "Information Processing Models of Cognition," in *Annual Review of Psychology*. Edited by M. Rosenweig and L. Porter (Annual Reviews, Inc., 1979), pp. 363-393.

Simon, H.A. and J.R. Hayes, "Psychological Differences Among Problem Isomorphs," in *Models of Thought*. Edited by H. Simon (Prentice Hall, 1979), pp. 498-511.

Slovic, P., B. Fischhoff, and S. Lichtenstein, "Behavioral Decision Theory," in *Annual Review of Psychology*. Edited by M. Rosenweig and L. Porter (Annual Reviews, Inc., 1977), pp. 1-39.

Tuggle, F.D. and F.H. Barron, "On the Validation of Descriptive Models of Decision-making," *Acta Pychologica* (1980), pp. 197-210.

Tversky, A. and D. Kahneman, "Framing of Decisions and the Psychology of Choice," *Science* (1981), pp. 453-458.

Ungson, G.R., D.N. Braunstein, and P.D. Hall, "Managerial Information Processing: A Research Review," *Administrative Science Quarterly* (March 1981), pp. 116-133.

Waller, W.S., "A Schematic Model for Describing the Effects of Task Conditions on Probability Assessment: An Application Using Professional Auditors," unpublished Ph.D. dissertation, University of Washington, 1981.

Waterman, D.A. and A. Newell, "Protocol Analysis as a Task for Artificial Intelligence," *Artificial Intelligence* (1971), pp. 285-318.

Waterman, D.A. and A. Newell, "Pas II: In Interactive Task-Free Version of an Automatic Protocol Analysis System," *IEEE Transactions on Computers* (1976), pp. 402-413.

Wickelgren, W.A., "Human Learning and Memory," in *Annual Review of Psychology*. Edited by M. Rosenweig and L. Porter (Annual Reviews, Inc. 1981), pp. 21-52.

Wood, D.J., "Problem Solving—Development of Strategies," in *Strategies of Information Processing*. Edited by G. Underwood (Academic Press, 1978), pp. 329-355.

APPENDIX 1

On the Notion of Information Importance

The following outlines a preliminary scoring rule for estimating the importance of information. Derivation of the rule is explained below.

The importance of information in the linear model tradition has been measured in two general ways; variance accounted for, or some type of correlational statistic such as a beta or regression weight. Such measures are not generally available in process tracing studies. The following are proposed as indicators of importance in a process tracing framework:

1) An operator is derived for the knowledge element in question;
2) The time spent by the processor attending to the particular knowledge element;
3) The number of times the processor returns to the particular knowledge element during processing;
4) The processor says that the particular knowledge element is important—unsolicited.
5) The order in which the items are processed by the processor;
6) The number of lines spoken by the processor/subject relative to the particular knowledge element;
7) The knowledge element appears in the debriefing instrument.

Knowledge elements are assigned a score ranging from 0 to 3 on each dimension above. The knowledge elements are then ranked based on the obtained score. The ranking may then be compared to those obtained from linear model results or subjective rankings of the processor(s).

The rationale for the scoring was developed as follows. Item one implies that the processor, by the act of processing a knowledge element, imparts some level of importance to it. The completeness of the protocols is a critical issue for this item. As pointed out earlier, researchers have demonstrated that many processes become automatic as they become well learned, and thus unavailable for verbalization [Mandler, 1975; Nisbett and Wilson, 1977]. This would tend to imply that the protocols may be incomplete and therefore may not contain indications of the processors having attended to potentially important parts of a problem. However, most of the automaticity research results have been concerned with perceptual or programmable activities—vision, mental arithmetic, word completion, etc. None of the studies have looked at activities in ill-structured settings, where small changes in task variables may lead to alterations in processing [Einhorn and Hogarth, 1981]. And, as mentioned earlier [Mandler, 1975], in most nonperceptual tasks, the automatic processes are themselves interruptible, and therefore available for conscious examination and verbalization. Just and Carpenter [1976] also note that verbal protocols correlate well with eye movement data, which do tend to pick up perceptual processing. The debriefing session serves as a validity check on this item as items appearing in the debriefing session must have been attended to to be remembered (task specific items).

The time requirement is related to the fact that time can be viewed as a scarce or limited resource [Hirschleifer, 1976; Norman and Bobrow, 1975]. The time the processor spends processing each knowledge element can be viewed as the allocation of a resource. In addition, one must be concerned with the write times of long term memory, which Newell and Simon report to be on the order of 5k to 10k seconds per chunk, where k is in the number of familiar subpatterns in the chunk. The presumption is that more important items will be remembered. The debriefing list also acts as a validity check on this item.

The return of the processor to a particular item is related to the time notion. However, in general it would appear plausible to assume that if a processor returns to an item it is implicitly designated as important in some sense. As a minimum, it indicates that the processor desires to understand the item. Additionally, it is well known that rehearsal plays an important part in memorization [Wickelgren, 1981].

Processing order has traditionally been deemed to be an important factor. In the linear model, for example, processing order is a major determinant of variance accounted for by a particular cue, given some cue set (intercorrelated). However, as point out by Clarkson [1962], processing order is not necessarily of primary importance in many settings. The processor may may choose to process items in a different order by chance, because they are presented a certain way, or because it does not matter—all important elements will be processed regardless.

The lines spoken item should be correlated with time. However, this is not necessarily the case, as speech patterns vary across individuals. The appearance of an item on the debriefing questionnaire is viewed as an indication that it has been written in long term memory [Bouwman, 1980].

The scoring rule for the items is structured as outlined below. Items 1, 4, and 7 are scored either 0 or 1. Item 2 is scored as follows:0—10 seconds, 1 point; 11—20 seconds, 2 points; 21 or more seconds, 3 points. Item 3 is scored analogously: 1 return, 1 point; 2 returns, 2 points; 3 or more returns, 3 points. Item 5 is scored as follows: first knowledge element processed, 3 points; 2nd element, 2 points; 3rd or later, 1 point. Item 6 is scored in a similar fashion to item 3, except that lines are used instead of returns.

Three was chosen as the maximum score because, first, most linear modeling studies have indicated that 2 or 3 cues generally account for most of the variance across many task environments. Second, Just and Carpenter [1976] reported that most of the processes in verbal protocols take on the order of 5 to 10 seconds, a result also obtained in this study. Generally, time spent beyond this level was spent in justification procedures. Multiples of ten seconds thus was justifiable for the technique. Third, there was a desire to maintain parsimony. Finally, given that these measures are somewhat correlated, it was deemed unreasonable to arbitrarily allow any particular variable to vary a great deal and therefore dominate the results. The results of this procedure are demonstrated below for four subjects from this study in Table 3.

Richard G. File
University of Oklahoma

Discussant's Comments on:

"The Process Tracing Paradigm: A General View"

The paper by Anderson [1984] is best seen as a tutorial regarding the process tracing paradigm. If process tracing is limited to the development of computer models from concurrent verbal protocol analysis (VPA), the paper does a good job of reviewing this powerful and controversial research tool. However, since application of the paradigm is a relatively recent occurrence, I would like to review the other forms of the process tracing paradigm. Additionally, my comments expand on the methodological problems addressed by Anderson, and point out some limitations of his example study.

In addition to concurrent verbal protocol analysis, the process tracing paradigm encompasses retrospective and interpretive verbal protocol analysis (as well as eye movement studies and explicit information search studies). The retrospective approach requires the subject to analyze his thought processes over a single case, while the interpretive approach requires the subject to analyze and synthesize his thought processes over several cases. Both of these approaches require the subjects to remember what information was used, when, and how it was used.

Ericsson and Simon [1980] concluded that the inability of subjects to remember their thought processes was responsible for Nisbett and Wilson's [1977] contention that we have little access to our mental processes. Ericsson and Simon distinguish between short-term memory (STM) and long-term memory (LTM). STM has only limited capacity, and information may be stored there for possibly only a few seconds, but can be readily accessed. Therefore, collection of "after the fact" protocols causes a reliance on retrieval of information from LTM, which is not as easily accessed.

The researcher aids the subject in the retrieval of the protocol from LTM through the use of instructions, or questions, called "probes." These questions may be very general, or very specific. A general probe asks the subject to report everything about their decision process. If the probing takes place immediately after the task is completed, some of the process may still be in STM and recalled easily. This may, in turn, facilitate the retrieval of information from LTM. Because the retrieval process is variable, large portions of the decision process may go unreported.

Some researchers have attempted to elicit more of the decision process from LTM via directed or specific probes. However, specific probes have a demand characteristic. Subjects may indicate that they needed information because they were asked about it, when in fact they did not. Additionally, they may remember an associated process, rather than the process they are being questioned about. These problems of addressing LTM are thought to cause a loss of reliability in retrospective VPA studies, and hence the emphasis on concurrent VPA studies. Due to the high cost of concurrent VPA studies, further research needs to be undertaken to determine if and when retrospective VPA may be used effectively (perhaps in explaining ANOVA or regression results).

The automation of decision processes is often cited, [e.g., Nisbett and Wilson, 1977] as an additional reason for incomplete verbal protocals. As noted by Anderson, if the ongoing behavior sequence is interrupted, "the task is generally returned to conscious control." In a concurrent VPA scenario, the use of immediate, or concurrent, probes is a means to interrupt the behavior sequence. This returns the task to conscious control where the process may be accessed via VPA. However, care should be taken in formation of the probes. If the probe simply asks the subject to think aloud, it will have minimal impact on the decision process. However, if the probe asks the subject to *explain* his thought process, it could have a significant impact on the decision process [Ericsson and Simon, 1980].

The use of multiple measurement techniques has been frequently cited [e.g., Einhorn, Klienmuntz, and Kleinmuntz; 1979] as a means to control or test the validity of VPA. However, real decision tasks are characterized by Einhorn [1976] as:

(1) ill defined;
(2) information must be searched for;
(3) data is rarely perfectly reliable; and
(4) subject to a broad range of hypothesis.

This is the scenario in which VPA is at a comparative advantage. In order to utilize one of the alternative paradigms, (e.g., the lens model or decision theory) structure must be added to the task. The additional structure can in some situations lessen external validity, and hence the appropriateness of any protocol data collected. At best in these circumstances VPA could be used as a means of interpreting the results of the statistical or analytical analysis.

The form process tracing takes is driven by the question which the researcher wishes to address. According to Bouwman [1983] the analysis of verbal protocols may take four forms:

(1) *Scanning* is used when the researcher is interested in obtaining information to assist in interpreting other observations; e.g., the results of a lens model study,
(2) *Scoring,* or counting frequencies is used when the researcher is interested in specific well-defined groups of items,
(3) *Global modeling* is used when the researcher is interested in the form of the decision process, and

(4) *Computer simulation* is used when the researcher is interested in specifying each element of the decision process, and in testing his understanding of this process.

Anderson fails to mention the first three forms of VPA. These are in fact the form which VPA frequently takes due to the high cost of developing the computer program.

The example case is limited in several respects: (1) data coding methods, (2) depiction of decision break points as occurring at the levels of data found in the information set, and (3) failure to establish information use of data for which the use was not stated explicitly or could not be inferred by the data. Anderson relies on a comparison of the coding strategies of himself and a naive coder. This really does not address the problem of the objectivity of the coding schemes. A more complete solution would require the comparison of various coding schemes [Libby, 1981, pp. 94-95]. The other two problems could have been addressed through the use of retrospective probes. For example, Elstein, Shulman, and Sprafka [1978] conducted a study in which doctors attempted to diagnose a medical complaint as presented by a patient, who was in fact an actor. After the doctor interviewed the patient, obtaining the patient's history and symptomology, the patient left and was replaced by a "medical assistant." The "medical assistant" provided any clinical test data requested by the doctor. Each doctor was asked to think aloud during the examination and data analysis. These thoughts were recorded via a video tape. Later the doctor reviewed the video tape and tried to recall what he was thinking at each stage. A retrospective probe at this time could elicit data on both decision break points and information usage.

VPA is an important tool for the development of practical decision aids. The aids developed via VPA have an intuitive appeal as their form is seen by users as being similar to their own decision rules (i.e., lexicographic, conjunctive, disjunctive). Aids based on ANOVA implicitly use a compensatory decision rule, which many users perceive to be overly simplistic. This has led to a reluctance by many users to adopt these simple additive models. An example of the actual application of VPA has been the development of computer programs to simulate doctors' diagnostic behavior for a range of symptoms [e.g., Pauker, et al, 1976]. The use of VPA in medical research, and in some areas of medical practice, has been so pervasive that it has appeared in the popular literature about medicine. For example, Dr. Robin Cook's novel *Brain* incorporates VPA as a basic premise: First, as a computer program to read x-rays; and then, as a step in achieving true artificial intelligence.

In conclusion, I would like to quote from Ericsson and Simon [1980]:

> For more than half a century, and as the result of an unjustified extrapolation of a justified challenge to a particular mode of verbal reporting (introspection), the verbal reports of human subjects have been thought suspect as a source of evidence about cognitive processes. In this article we have undertaken to show that verbal reports, elicited with care and interpreted with full understanding of the circumstances under which they were obtained, are a valuable and thoroughly reliable source of informa-

tion about cognitive processes. It is time to abandon the careless charge of "introspection" as a means for disparaging such data. They describe human behavior that is as readily interpreted as any other human behavior. To omit them when we are carrying the "chain and transit of objective measurement" is only to mark as terra incognita large areas on the map of human cognition that we know perfectly well how to survey.

REFERENCES

Anderson, M.J., "The Process Tracing Paradigm: A General View," in S. Moriarity and E. Joyce (Eds.), *Decision Making and Accounting: Current Research,* (University of Oklahoma, Center for Economic and Management Research, 1984), pp. 158-172.

Bouwman, M.J., "Protocol Analysis in Accounting Research: Different Methods for Different Purposes," unpublished working paper, University of Oregon (March 1983).

Cook, R., *Brain,* (Putnam, 1981).

Einhorn, H.J., "Synthesis: Accounting and Behavioral Science," *Empirical Research in Accounting* (1976), pp. 196-206.

____________, D.N. Kleinmuntz, and B. Kleinmuntz, "Linear Regression and Process Tracing Models of Judgement," *Psychological Review* (1979), pp. 465-485.

Elstein, A.S., L.E. Shulman, and S.A. Sprafka, *Medical Problem Solving: An Analysis of Clinical Reasoning,* Harvard University (1978).

Ericsson, K.A. and H.A. Simon, "Verbal Reports as Data, "*Psychological Review* (May 1980), pp. 215-251.

Libby, R., *Accounting and Human Information Processing: Theory and Applications* (Prentice-Hall, 1981).

Nisbett, R.E. and T.D. Wilson, " Telling More Than We Know: Verbal Reports on Mental Processes," *Psychological Review* (May 1977), pp. 231-259.

Pauker, S.G., G. Gary, J. Kassirer, and W. Schwartz, "Towards the Simulation of Clinical Cognition: Taking a Present Illness Computer," *American Journal of Medicine* (1976), pp. 981-996.

Marinus J. Bouwman
University of Oregon

Discussant's Comments on:

"The Process Tracing Paradigm: A General View"

I wholeheartedly agree with Anderson's premise that more research is needed on predecisional behavior in solving real-life tasks. The ill-structured nature of such tasks, and the associated search for relevant information introduce dimensions that cannot be reproduced easily in the laboratory. In this context I like to refer to the intriguing bankruptcy prediction study of Abdel-khalik and El-Sheshai [1980], which suggests that the acquisition of the right information may have a greater impact on the final decision than the utilization of that information.

Anderson presents a good overview of the premier methodology used to study ill-structured decision making: the collection and analysis of concurrent, verbal protocols. I particularly like his attempt to link protocol codes explicitly to the "elementary information processes" of the underlying "human problem solving" theory of Newell and Simon [1972]. Another meaningful contribution is Anderson's operational definition of "importance" of information. Although I do not necessarily agree with the specific weights, the idea of evaluating importance through a combination of observable protocol characteristics is interesting and deserves further consideration. On the minus side, I find the discussion of the modeling phase rather confusing. It is also not very detailed and, more significantly, it fails to consider the relation between model type and research objective.

I will organize my comments along these three major issues: I will discuss protocol coding first, followed by information importance and modeling.

CODING PROTOCOLS

Anderson states that "coding techniques have been problematical for process tracing researchers," and that the "primary issue is the lack of a systematic procedure for coding behavior" (p. 160). I take exception to those statements. Researchers such as Newell and Simon [1972], Bouwman [1978, 1983], Stephens et al. [1980], and Biggs and Mock [forthcoming] report their coding procedures in considerable detail, and appear to have little difficulty in applying the codes systematically. That they developed different sets of codes is an entirely separate issue, and I will later argue that this does not impact coding validity.

Code Selection

The development of a coding procedure involves two separate aspects: (1) the selection of a set of codes, and (2) the assignment of those codes to individual protocol segments. Anderson's claim that the *selection* of a set of codes tends to be ad hoc, does have some validity. Consequently, his attempt to link the codes explicitly to the "elementary information processes" of Newell and Simon is an important step in the right direction. Newell and Simon's human problem solving theory [Newell and Simon, 1972] is frequently referred to as the theoretical basis of process tracing studies, yet those studies rarely build explicitly upon that basis.

At the same time, however, Anderson's set of codes falls considerably short of representing a complete set. If we examine his list of codes (Table 2) we see that most deal with *examination* of information, such as "comparing numbers," "evaluating a trend," and "comparing with an internal standard." There only are two reasoning codes, "linking" and "summarization." While this particular set of codes may be sufficient for certain tasks and certain research objectives, it falls short in cases where, for example, the *reasoning* activities are of primary interest. In those cases, more specific reasoning codes, such as "stating an assumption," "formulating a hypothesis," and "making an inference" are needed, and it is less obvious how these codes would tie uniquely and unambiguously to Newell and Simon's elementary information processes.

Another factor which limits the generality of Anderson's set of codes is his downplaying of control statements. Control statements represent the goals and sub-goals of the decision maker. Anderson groups these statements together into one overall category. I do not question that this was a wise thing to do in this specific task. Bouwman [1978] did the same thing in a similar financial analysis task. However, these tasks involved relatively "contained" amounts of information. As tasks become more complex and involve more extensive amounts of information, control statements acquire increased importance. In such cases, problem solving constitutes formulating and achieving a series of sub-goals, and identification of those sub-goals becomes the primary means to unravel decision making behavior [Bouwman et al., 1983].

A final issue that impacts the selection of codes is that different research objectives require different sets of codes. It is illustrative to compare the codes selected by Stephens et al. [1980], Biggs and Mock [forthcoming], and Bouwman et al. [1983]. All three studies employ basic examination, reasoning, and control codes, which attests to the common nature of the financial tasks that they studied. The number of codes, however, varied from 12 to 23, and there were many codes unique to each study. These differences can be explained by differences in research objectives. Stephens et al. wanted to develop a global model of a loan officer's decision making process. They employed a limited number of codes, 12, which were phrased in general terms. Biggs and Mock were interested in audit scope decisions, particularly in the formulation and selection of the final sample size for the required audit procedures. They employed specialized sample size codes such as the specification of a sample size heuristic, and the specification of a sample size. Bouwman et al. focussed on information usage of financial analysts:

what information was used, and what for? Consequently, their set of codes included many detailed examination codes, such as "compute trend," "compute number," and "compare," and many goal (control) codes such as "state goal," "state future goal," "get specific report," and "get specific item."

The point of this comparison is that one should expect different sets of codes for different tasks and different research objectives. Moreover, the selection of a particular set is much less critical than is generally believed. Different sets of codes simply provide different views of the same behavior. And although comparability is a worthwhile objective, it is more important to develop that view of behavior that most facilitates the investigation of the research questions one is trying to answer.

Code Assignment

The second coding issue involves the assignment of codes. Clearly, inconsistencies at this stage will undo the efforts that went into the selection of the codes. Anderson employs two coders, with different levels of coding skills, and compares their code assignments. This is a useful and important test, not only to establish the overall coding reliability, but also to identify those codes that are still ambiguous. Coding is an iterative process. Disagreements in code assignments can be resolved by adjusting the code set and by sharpening the definitions of the individual codes.

Coding reliability and consistency can be improved further through the use of the computer. Ericsson and Simon [1980] explored the potential of computerized, context-free coding. They developed a program that presents protocol lines on a screen in a random sequence, and that allows the coder to type in the code assignments. The immediately preceding and following protocol lines are available upon request. Sproull and Sproull [1981] developed extensive protocol manipulation software which, among others, allows the coder to list together all protocol lines that are assigned a specific code. This provides an easy check on whether similar codes indeed describe similar kinds of behavior. Computer software does not do anything magical that cannot be done manually. But it can take over a lot of burdensome clerical data manipulation, thereby freeing the coder to attend to the more critical consistency issues.

IMPORTANCE OF INFORMATION

The importance of information to the user has become a major issue in process tracing studies in accounting. The FASB's desire to provide information that is useful to decision makers, and the failure of questionnaire studies to uncover what decision makers really use, have spawned several protocol studies that address this issue [Stephens, 1980; Campbell, 1981; Bouwman et al., 1983]. The difficulty in assessing importance is that information is used for different purposes. Bouwman et al. observed in a financial analysis task that certain, predominantly accounting information is largely used for screening purposes, while other, predominantly product and market information is used for making the "positive" investment decision. One would expect different usage patterns for these different types of information. For example, information that is used for screening purposes needs to be examined only once, while information that is used to develop a "positive" case for the potential investment may be referred to a number of times. Yet, it is not necessarily obvious that the latter item is more important than the former, as would be suggested by Anderson's scoring method.

Despite these reservations, I think that the idea of combining a number of observable protocol characteristics is intriguing, and one that deserves further study. I would like to encourage attempts to automate this measurement of information importance, and to integrate it with the protocol coding and manipulation software described above. It would mean a big step towards reducing the cost of protocol analysis and improving the comparability of different protocol studies. I also welcome statistical analysis of the correlations between the various measures. I do not share the author's opinion that the present method is not biased towards any particular variable. If variables 2, 3 and 6 are highly correlated, which I suspect they are, they virtually determine the "importance" score. And although statistical analysis would not be easy given the limited number of protocols, it may be possible to increase the numbers by combining protocols from different tasks.

MODELING

Anderson's discussion of model derivation is minimal. The discussion is at a much more general level than that of the coding procedures. This reflects the much less structured nature of the modeling process. Modeling is often considered more art than science, and I think that there is an element of truth in that statement. Yet, as a researcher who has spent almost 10 years in the process tracing area, I consider the modeling phase much more critical than the coding phase. Coding relies on systematic application of formal rules. It is *analysis* in the pure sense of the word. Modeling, on the other hand, requires *interpretation.* It requires the researcher's judgment in stripping away that which is deemed irrelevant, and in representing the remaining behavior in a formalized framework.

I will not present a detailed treatise of modeling here. The interested reader is referred to Simon and Simon [1977], and Bouwman [1983] for two detailed descriptions of the modeling process. I will only stress that modeling can occur at different levels of detail, and from different points of view, resulting in different models that each serves its own purpose. Anderson's modeling, for example, is based on "operator groups," and represents a moderately detailed modeling approach. In addition, Anderson is interested in the examination of information. Consequently, his model provides many details regarding the examination process, particularly with respect to what information is used, and in what order. But the model provides little insight into the decision formulation.

Using Anderson's model as a baseline, modeling can move both to a more detailed and to a more aggregate level. If one wants a close look at the formulation of a decision, or if one wants to identify the specific knowledge that is used by the decision maker, detailed computer simulation is an appropriate vehicle. The development of a computer model forces the researcher to include all elements of the decision making process, including the decision maker's knowledge. Like Anderson's model, such a model would be based on the "operator groups" of the protocol. On the other hand, if one is interested in the overall decision making strategy, and in the heuristics used by the decision maker, a more global modeling approach will do. Global modeling focusses on larger sections of protocol, usually called episodes, that each are devoted to the attainment of a specific (higher level) goal [Bouwman et al., 1983].

CONCLUSION

Process tracing is an expensive methodology in terms of time and effort. It also is a methodology that is able to serve a large variety of objectives. Given this flexibility, it is crucial to determine carefully what it is that one wants to achieve, and, consequently, what level of protocol analysis best serves that purpose. The selection of the codes and the specific modeling approach follow from those decisions. Failure to give proper consideration to these issues is not irrevocable, but it is expensive. I commend Anderson for helping to clarify these issues, and I express the hope that his presentation will serve to sharpen the focus of future process tracing studies.

REFERENCES

Abdel-khalik, A. Rashad and K.M. El-Sheshai, "Information Choice and Utilization in an Experiment on Default Prediction," *Journal of Accounting Research* (Autumn 1980), pp. 325-342.

Biggs, S.F. and T.J. Mock, "An Investigation of Auditor Decision Processes in the Evaluation of Internal Controls and Audit Scope Decisions." *Journal of Accounting Research* (forthcoming).

Bouwman, M.J., "Financial Diagnosis: A Cognitive Model of the Processes Involved," Ph.D. Thesis, Graduate School of Industrial Administration, Carnegie-Mellon University (1978).

____________, "Human Diagnostic Reasoning by Computer: An Illustration from Financial Analysis," *Management Science* (June 1983), pp. 653-672.

____________, P.A. Frishkoff and P. Frishkoff, "Financial Analysts' Information Processing: A Protocol Analysis of the Screening Decision." Working Paper, University of Oregon (1983).

Campbell, J.E., "An Empirical Investigation of the Impact on the Decision Processes of Loan Officers of Separate Accounting Standards for Smaller and/or Closely Held Companies." Ph.D. thesis, The University of Tennessee (1981).

Ericsson, K. A. and H.A. Simon (private communication, 1980).

Newell, A. and H.A. Simon, *Human Problem Solving,* (Prentice-Hall, 1972).

Simon, D.P. and H.A. Simon, "Individual Differences in Solving Physics Problems," CIP Working Paper No. 342, Carnegie-Mellon University (September 1977).

Sproull, L.S. and R.F. Sproull, "Microethnography: A Research Strategy for Understanding Behavior in Organizations," Working Paper, Carnegie-Mellon University (January 1981).

Stephens, R.G., *Uses of Financial Information in Bank Lending Decisions,* (UMI Research Press, 1980).

____________, J.K. Shank and R. Bhaskar, "The Lending Decision: A New Perspective on the Role of Accounting Information," Working Paper 80-46, The Ohio State University (1980).

William F. Messier Jr.*
University of Florida
James V. Hansen
Brigham Young University

Expert Systems in Accounting and Auditing: A Framework and Review

INTRODUCTION

In the past twenty years much has been said and written about the interaction between man and machine. Sagan [1977, p. 211], for example, has commented that

> When all is said and done, the invention of writing must be reckoned not only as a brilliant innovation but as a surpassing good for humanity. And assuming that we survive long enough to use their inventions wisely, I believe the same will be said of the modern Thoths and Prometheuses who are today devising computers and programs at the edge of machine intelligence. The next major structural development in human intelligence is likely to be a partnership between intelligent humans and intelligent machines.

He states further that

> ...in reasonably restricted contexts the human use of artificial intelligence seems to be one of the two practicable major advances in human intelligence available in the near future.

While real progress over this time period has not achieved some of the early expectations,[1] research in one area of artificial intelligence (AI) recently has shown much promise. This area is referred to as knowledge-based,

**We would like to thank the Peat, Marwick, Mitchell Foundation for its support of our research on knowledge-based, expert systems. The views expressed herein are those of the authors and do not necessarily reflect the views of the Peat, Marwick, Mitchell Foundation. An earlier version of this paper was presented at the University of Florida's Center for Information Research and Departments of Computer and Information Sciences, and Electrical Engineering Lecture Series, the Southeast AAA Graduate Workshop and the University of Minnesota accounting workshop. Helpful comments were provided by Chris Dungan and Bob Michaelson.*

expert systems. This technology has started to leave the research laboratory for real-world application in numerous areas (e.g., medicine, agriculture, oil exploration, etc.) and has sparked interest in other areas where expert judgment is required.

Recently, practitioners and researchers in accounting and auditing have become interested in applying this technology to a number of problem domains.[2] To date two expert systems have been constructed and tested and two others are in various design and development stages. All of the existing systems rely on previously developed expert system software and their problem domains include: estate planning, assessing the allowance for bad debts, EDP auditing, and investigating analytical review fluctuations.

The remainder of the paper is divided into four sections. The first section presents a framework for expert systems and is intended to provide an overview for those readers unfamiliar with this area of research. The second section provides a detailed description of the expert system that is currently being developed to assist EDP auditors evaluate the reliability of advanced EDP systems. The third section contains a review of the other systems currently being developed in accounting and auditing domains. The final section contains some concluding comments.

A FRAMEWORK FOR EXPERT SYSTEMS[3]

Knowledge-based, expert systems are programs "that perform some specific task in a (problem) domain by combining methods of symbolic inference and representation with knowledge of that domain" [Nii, 1980]. They are referred to as "knowledge-based" because their performance depends heavily on facts and heuristics captured from experts [Stefik, *et al.* 1982]. In this section of the paper we will describe the nature of expertise, engineering issues which must be addressed in designing an expert system, the stages of development and the state of the art in expert systems, and a brief discussion of one well-known expert system: MYCIN [Shortliffe, 1976].

The Nature of Expertise

We might ask the question: "What type of problem domains require expert judgment?" One way of answering this question is to address the *structure* of the particular problem domain. We might classify problem domains along a continuum with *highly structured* and *highly unstructured* as the end points and *semistructured* as a mid-point. Tasks which are characterized by highly structured domains are well specified and usually have a unique solution. Problems that are amenable to operations research/management science applications would fall into this category. A good example would be EOQ inventory models. As we move along the continuum towards the unstructured (semi or highly) end we encounter tasks which are ill-defined and where more than one solution may be feasible. It is in this area where expertise plays a major role.

Expertise has been defined as a "demonstrated ability to efficiently perform a complex, perhaps ill-structured, task in a superior way (on specified dimensions) based on accumulated domain-specific knowledge and inference/judgment procedures" [Wright, 1983]. Stefik, *et al.* [1982] suggest that the following generic tasks characterize expert behavior: interpretation, diagnosis, monitoring, prediction, planning, and design. Expertise enters into the execution of these tasks as a result of what Davis [1982] refers to as "compiled experience." For example, in the medical field much of a physician's expertise arises from "the large collection of empirical associations he accumulates by dint of experience in the field" (p. 4). In other words, an expert physician builds up rules or heuristics over time about a particular clinical problem as a result of exposure to numerous medical cases. In domains of this type current expert system technology may prove to be useful.[4]

Duda and Gaschnig [1981, p. 262] suggest the following prerequisites for the success of an expert system:

1. There must be one human expert acknowledged to perform the task well.
2. The primary source of the expert's exceptional performance must be special knowledge, judgment, and experience.
3. The expert must be able to explain the special knowledge and experience and the methods used to apply them to particular problems.
4. The task must have a well-bounded domain of application.

It is worthwhile to briefly examine the range of behaviors exhibited by experts since they have implications for some of the engineering principles used in expert systems. In performing a particular task experts typically: (1) solve the problem, (2) explain the results, (3) learn from the decision, (4) restructure their knowledge, (5) change or break rules when necessary, and (6) seek assistance when the problem is beyond their expertise [Davis, 1982]. To date only the first three behaviors have been examined in depth and implemented in viable expert systems. MYCIN, for example, can reach a medical conclusion (assuming sufficient data), explain how it arrived at the conclusion (prints out the rules used), and learns new rules from its interaction with the expert.[5] The other three have not been explored but represent important behaviors exhibited by experts in various problem domains.

Engineering Issues

Before presenting each of the engineering issues in detail Feigenbaum [1977] noted two important insights from previous research. First, from the work conducted to date it is clear that the problem solving power exhibited by experts results from their *specific domain knowledge* rather than from some general problem solving abilities. As a result there has been a shift from general problem solvers (e.g. Newell and Simon [1972]) to how to represent large amounts of domain specific knowledge for effective use. The second insight is that the knowledge an expert brings to a task "is largely heuristic knowledge, experiential, uncertain...in lieu of facts and rigor" [p. 1017]. In many instances the expert is unable to express much of this knowledge. This domain specific knowledge can be identified, however, through interaction with a "knowledge engineer" on a number of sample problems.[6]

In designing an expert system a number of important themes or issues must be considered. The ones discussed here were suggested by Feigenbaum [1977] and Davis [1982] and were codified from their summary and review of a number of expert systems.

Representing Knowledge as Rules. One of the most common ways of representing the expert's knowledge is in the form of IF-THEN rules (also referred to as situation—action rules or production rules). The rules typically capture the heuristic reasoning that characterizes the expert's decision making (i.e. "chunks" of domain specific knowledge). Such rules have the following general form:

IF: antecedent_1
.
.
.
antecedent_m
THEN: consequent_1 with certainty factor CF_1
.
.
.
consequent_n with certainty factor CF_n

The antecedents are the patterns (e.g., symptoms) that are matched against the input data, and the consequents are the actions to be performed or conclusions reached if the antecedents are matched. In many rules the evidence supports the conclusion with less than certainty. In these cases numerical values (certainty factors in MYCIN) are assigned by the expert to each rule to indicate the degree or belief to which the evidence supports the conclusion. Most existing expert systems contain hundreds of such rules. These rules are connected to each other in the form of networks which represents a substantial body of knowledge. Following is an example of a rule taken from MYCIN [Shortliffe, 1976, p. 107]:

IF: 1) THE STAIN OF THE ORGANISM IS GRAMNEG, AND
2) THE MORPHOLOGY OF THE ORGANISM IS ROD, AND
3) THE AEROBICITY OF THE ORGANISM IS AEROBIC
THEN: THERE IS STRONGLY SUGGESTIVE EVIDENCE (.8) THAT THE CLASS OF THE ORGANISM IS ENTEROBACTERIACEAE.

Generation and Test. Behavioral studies of experts [e.g., Elstein, *et al.* 1978; Biggs and Mock, 1981] support the notion that in making a judgment experts usually develop a hypothesis about the state of nature and then gather and examine evidence to see if it is consistent with the hypothesis. This generate-and-test strategy (also referred to as control strategy) is found in most expert systems but in a variety of forms. Two examples of generate-and-test strategies are forward and backward chaining. In forward chaining the rules are scanned until one is found whose antecedents match the evidence (input data). The rule(s) is applied and the process continued until either a goal state is reached or no applicable rules are found. With backward chaining a goal is selected and the rules are searched for consequents which match the goal. When the antecedents for a rule match the existing facts the rule is applied. If no rules are matched the system will query the user. Newell and Simon [1976] have suggested that generate-and-test is a law of AI.

Flexibility. Few of the problem domains that experts operate in are static. Thus, it is important to be able to change the knowledge base (rules) as the expert's understanding of the problem domain changes. The previously described rule based approach allows for such flexibility. By storing the knowledge in small chunks (individual rules) it is quite easy to add, remove, or change the rules (knowledge) in the system.[7] The necessity to maintain flexibility has led to an important architectural principle: separate the knowledge base (set of rules) from the inference engine (rule interpreter). Following this approach allows easy maintenance of the knowledge base.

Explanation. An important consideration in any expert system is the ability to explain how it reached its conclusion(s). Gorry [1973] pointed out the need for such a capability based on his work with Bayesian decision programs. He found that statistical decision theory performed quite well in many judgment situations but that the program's inability to explain how it arrived at a conclusion limited its implementation and acceptance. In other words, we would expect experts to be more willing to accept the system's advice if they are able to understand the system's decision process. It's not important, however, that the expert system possess the same psychological reasoning model but only that the model be understandable to the expert(s) familiar with the problem [Buchanan, 1982].

Stages of Development and State of the Art

Davis [1982, p. 10] has listed seven stages to developing an expert system:

1. System design.
2. System development.
3. Formal evaluation of performance.
4. Formal evaluation of acceptance.
5. Extended use in prototype environment.
6. Development of maintenance plans.
7. System release.

A detailed discussion of each of these steps is beyond the scope of this paper and would not be fruitful since the detail of each step is typically unique to the system. To date, however, very few systems have progressed beyond stage 3. DENDRAL [Feigenbaum, *et al.* 1971] and PROSPECTOR [Duda, *et al.* 1980] are currently being used commercially.[8] In fact, PROSPECTOR was recently credited with a major discovery of molybdenum [Cambell, *et al.* 1982]. These and other successes (e.g., MYCIN) have been one of the reasons for the increased interest in expert systems. However, before optimism spreads too quickly, the reader should be reminded of the effort required to build such systems. For reasonably well understood problem domains Davis [1982] estimates that it requires at least five man-years to develop a system that is robust.

Given the previous discussions let's examine the current state of the art in expert systems. The following characteristics summarize what can currently be done [Buchanan, 1982; Davis, 1982]:

- narrow domain of expertise.
- limited language for knowledge representation.

- limited (stylized) input/output languages.
- stylized explanation of line of reasoning.
- one expert as knowledge base "czar."

Expert systems have to deal with relatively narrow domains of expertise mainly because current technology places limits on the size of the knowledge base. Current knowledge representation languages are also limited to simple frameworks (e.g. object hierarchy or production rules). Many times the experts will find it difficult to express knowledge relationships with such a framework.

Since the natural language problem [Winograd, 1972] has still not been solved, expert systems are straddled with very stylized and inflexible input/output languages. These are usually keyword parsing of input and template-generated production of text for output [Davis, 1982]. For example, MYCIN has a limited dictionary and menu of question options for interaction with the user. Similarly, the system's explanation of its line of reasoning is also limited. The answer to the user's question "How did you arrive at that conclusion?" is a display of the rules used in arriving at the goal. Examples of this are provided later in the paper.

Current technology does not allow the use of multiple experts because there is no way of reconciling differing and conflicting views. So while it is helpful to have several experts contributing to the knowledge base, a single "czar" must be responsible for monitoring changes. This points out an important constraint for builders of expert systems: There must be an expert available and willing to spend time developing and debugging the knowledge base [Buchanan, 1982; Nii, 1980].

MYCIN: A Physician Consultation System

MYCIN [Shortliffe, 1976] is a consultation program which assists physicians in diagnosing and treating infectious diseases. In terms of our earlier discussion of structured/unstructured decisions, MYCIN is directed at a problem domain that falls towards the highly unstructured end of the continuum.

One reason for discussing a system like MYCIN is that we believe that there is a direct analogy between the way a physician diagnoses a disease and the way an auditor "diagnoses" the state of a client's accounting systems and financial statements. An examination of some recent research in medical decision making [Elstein, *et al.* 1978] discloses a good deal of similarity between physician and auditor decision making.

Figure 1 provides an overview of the MYCIN program. Basically the way the system works is as follows: The physician begins an interactive session with the Consultation subprogram. Patient specific data is entered by the physician and MYCIN uses its knowledge base to process the patient data and decide what questions to ask the physician. The dynamic data base stores a record of the consultation. When MYCIN has completed asking questions it provides a recommendation and passes to the Explanation subprogram. Here the physician may ask additional questions and request that MYCIN explain its recommendation. As mentioned previously this is an important feature because the physician is not only provided with a recommendation but he is able to follow the reasoning processes of MYCIN.

FIGURE 1
Overview of the MYCIN System

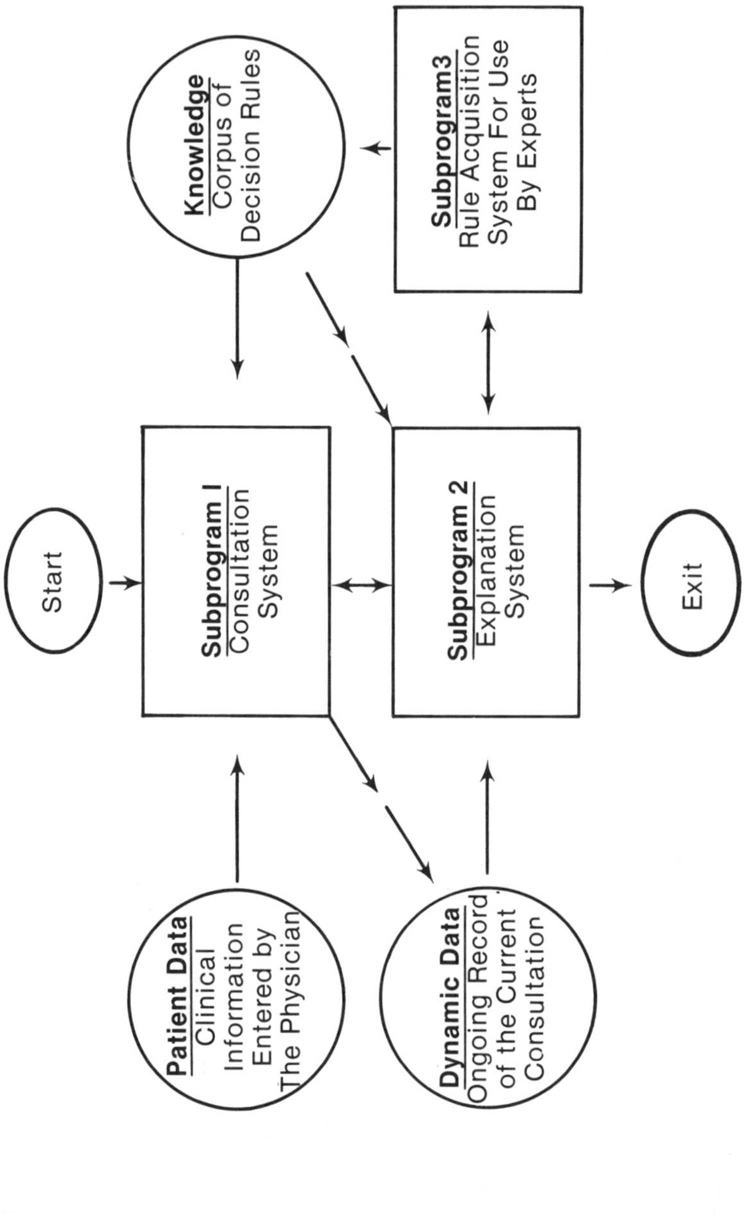

AN EXPERT SYSTEM FOR AUDITING ADVANCED COMPUTER SYSTEMS

In this section we discuss the system that we are currently developing which will assist EDP auditors in evaluating the reliability of advanced computer systems. We have described the complexity of this decision process and the need for decision support elsewhere [Hansen and Messier, 1982]. The EDP auditing problem domain appears to meet the prerequisites for an expert system discussed earlier. There are experts in the field that perform this task well. All of the major public accounting firms use computer audit specialists and it is apparent that the source of their expertise comes from specialized knowledge and training, and exposure to companies with advanced computer systems. Peat, Marwick International, for example, has three levels of computer audit specialists and requires that Senior Computer Audit Specialists (highest level of training) be included in the audit teams for all clients with complex computer applications [Elliott, 1983]. Based on our preliminary interview [Hansen and Messier, 1981] and protocol work, experts in computer auditing are capable of expressing their special knowledge and experience. Finally, we have some reservations about whether the entire area of computer auditing is "well bounded" given the rapid changes in technology.[9] We are convinced, however, that certain subareas of this domain are capable of being defined as evidenced by the work described here.

We will focus our discussion in this section on two areas: the expert system software and construction of the knowledge base. This will be followed by a sample interactive session with the current prototype. For more detailed information on the current system the reader is referred to Hansen and Messier [1983a].

Expert System Software

The expert system software used in the current project is called AL/X (Advice Language/X) [Paterson, 1981]. AL/X is based on the PROSPECTOR system [Duda, *et al.* 1980] and was originally developed to diagnose the underlying causes of oil platform shutdowns. AL/X has since been used for expert systems in a number of other problem domains.[10]

The system consists of two separate components: the knowledge base (rules) and the inference engine (rule interpreter). The knowledge base contains the IF-THEN rules provided by the experts to solve the problem. The rules are collected in an inference network (i.e. decision tree) and form the evidence-hypothesis relationships which represent the problem domain. The inference engine contains the analytical framework for generating and explaining advice to the user.

The underlying model used in the AL/X inference engine is based on the subjective Bayesian updating method suggested by Duda, *et al.* [1976] for rule-based expert systems. A discussion of the mathematics of their approach is beyond the scope of the current paper.[11] For current purposes keep in mind that it is the expert that provides both the rules and the likelihood ratios that indicate the strength of the rules. AL/X is capable of accommodating uncertainty in both evidence and rules. This is accomplished by attaching degrees of belief to spaces (nodes in the inference net) and by specifying the type of link (arc) that connects the spaces.

Spaces and Degrees of Belief. Spaces represent the hypothesis or evidence (intermediate hypotheses) in AL/X. Each space in the inference network is assigned "a prior degree of belief (by the expert) which expresses how likely the hypothesis is given no evidence whatever" [Paterson, 1981, p. 5]. A degree of belief is a number in the range of -100 to 100 where a positive degree indicates that the hypothesis is more likely to be true and a negative number indicates it is more likely to be false. A degree of belief of zero indicates that the hypothesis is equally likely or unlikely, i.e. probability of 0.5.

The degree of belief in a hypothesis, H, is defined as

$$\text{Degree (H)} = 10 \log_{10} (\text{odds (H)}) = 10 \log_{10} \frac{P(H)}{1-P(H)}$$

Conversion between the degree scale and the more familiar probability scale is made relatively easily by using the formula.[12]

Links. The links in the inference network determine how the other hypotheses are updated. The two major types of links in AL/X are logical and Bayesian links.

Logical Links. With logical links the degree of belief of a hypothesis is completely determined by the degrees of the evidence which define it. There are three types of logical links: conjunction (and), disjunction (or), and negation (not). If *all* the evidence must be true for a hypothesis to be true, then the hypothesis should be represented by an "and" space. The degree of belief of an "and" space is defined to be the *minimum* of the degrees of its evidence. If a hypothesis is true if *any* of its evidence is true then the hypothesis should be represented by an "or" space. The degree of belief of an "or" space is defined to be the *maximum* of the degrees of its evidence. A "not" space simply negates the degree of belief of its evidence [Paterson, 1981]. These rules of logical combination follow the theory of approximate or inexact reasoning proposed by Zadeh [1979]:

$$\text{degree } (a_1 \text{ and } a_2 \text{ and } \ldots \text{ and } a_n) = \min \{\text{degree}(a_1), \text{degree}(a_2), \ldots, \text{degree}(a_n)\}$$

$$\text{degree } (a_1 \text{ or } a_2 \text{ or } \ldots \text{ or } a_n) = \max \{\text{degree}(a_1), \text{degree}(a_2), \ldots, \text{degree}(a_n)\}$$

$$\text{degree (not a)} = -\ \text{degree(a)}$$

Bayesian Links. A Bayesian link is one that can be informally stated as "if (to some degree) evidence then (to some degree) hypothesis." The degree to which the evidence effects the hypothesis is given by two parameters: the positive weight (pw) and the negative weight (nw) of the link. These express the effect of the evidence on the hypothesis being true and false, respectively. These weights are provided by the expert at the time the system is being designed.

Auditor Interaction. The auditor uses the expert system interactively by responding to a series of questions intended to assist in arriving at well-founded conclusions regarding a particular problem. The auditor is assumed to possess some audit evidence, e.g., description of the internal control system or test results relating to the system being audited.

AL/X chooses a goal hypothesis and asks all the relevant questions related to that goal. The goal chosen is the one thought to be most likely (i.e. the one with the highest degrees of belief). The user normally responds to a question by providing a certainty factor: a number in the range −5 to 5. A certainty factor is a measure of subjective certainty where 5 indicates the evidence is present, −5 indicates the evidence is not present, and zero indicates no information about the evidence. Certainty factors are a different scale of measurement than degrees of belief. A certainty factor of 5 or −5 corresponds to the equivalent maximum degree of belief, 100 and −100, respectively. A certainty factor of zero leaves the degrees of belief at their prior value. For any certainty factor other than 5, −5, 0,

> ...linear interpolation is done on probability values. A positive certainty factor involves interpolating between the prior probability and 1. A negative certainty factor involves interpolating between zero and the prior probability. The resulting probability value is then converted back to a degree value [Paterson, 1981, p. 18].

The effects of this response then updates the degrees of belief for all spaces for which the question (evidencc) was relevant.

When AL/X has asked, and received responses to, all of the questions in the expert system, it provides a report on the likelihood of the truth of the hypothesis which is being investigated. A example of such a report appears below:

Investigated goals with degree > = 0.0 are:
The control system is adequate and functioning well (RELIABILITY).
Prior degree was 0.0. Current degree is 2.0[13]

In this example, prior to the questioning, RELIABILITY was assumed to be as likely true as false, that is, to have a prior degree of belief of 0.0. The system is reporting to the auditor that his responses to the questions asked by the system have increased the likelihood of the truth of the hypothesis called RELIABILITY from 0.0 to 2.0 on the degree scale.

Constructing the Knowledge Base

The success of an expert system depends heavily on the knowledge engineer capturing the expert's expertise. Johnson [1983] has proposed three means for representing expertise. The first way he suggests is referred to as "reconstructed methods" of reasoning. By this he means "rules for how a task might be done that seem plausible to a practitioner or group practitioners in some domain of problem solving" [p. 81]. The second way of describing expertise is based upon observing the performance of an individual or group of individuals doing the task. He refers to this as "authentic methods" of reasoning and suggests the use of process tracing techniques for observation purposes. The third way of representing expertise is through the use of "mechanical optimation methods" which include techniques such as regression analyses and Bayesian inference.

We are still in the very early stages of development with our expert system. The development of the knowledge base is a long and tedious task. As was mentioned previously, Davis [1982] has estimated that in reasonably complex problem domains that it takes approximately five man-years to construct an expert system that begins to be robust. Some of the more familiar expert systems have taken much longer to develop.[14]

The current prototype only contains "reconstructed" expertise and includes rules solely related to access controls in a distributed processing system. Figure 2 contains the inference met that is currently in the system. The names which appear at the nodes (some of which are cryptic) are defined in the expert system data base. The rules included in the current knowledge base were derived from the EDP internal control questionnaires of two major public accounting firms.

The authors and Stan Biggs have recently conducted a protocol study using three EDP auditors from a major public accounting firm. The data is currently being analyzed. Our purposes in conducting this experiment were two fold. First, since there is very little research available on the decision processes of EDP auditors we felt it was necessary to obtain some descriptive information about how EDP auditors made decisions in this problem domain. Second, we hoped that the experiment would provide us with some of the decision rules used by EDP auditors. This latter purpose is in line with Johnson's [1983] "authentic" approach to representing expertise.

In addition to constructing a decision aid that may be useful to experts, the process of building an expert system provides many additional benefits. In order to develop the knowledge base and inference network the researchers must thoroughly examine and understand the problem domain. The EDP audit decision-making process has not been examined in great detail. The work by Abdel-khalik, *et al.* [1983], Davis and Weber [1983], and Weber [1980] represent some preliminary efforts. In constructing the knowledge base for the current system we have examined the EDP audit materials of a number of major public accounting firms and conducted the previously mentioned protocol study. These two studies have provided us with valuable insight into this important problem area.

As we have examined the EDP audit problem domain we have noted a number of issues and conducted research in those areas [Hansen and Messier, 1983b, c, d]. Similar contributions would be forthcoming to other researchers who choose to examine important problem domains in detail. Our point here is that construction of an expert system forces the researcher to understand the problem and that this process contributes to our knowledge.

A Sample Interactive Session

Exhibit 1 contains an example of a typical session with the auditor's decision making being supported by the expert system. We remind the reader that an actual analysis of an advanced EDP system involves many more

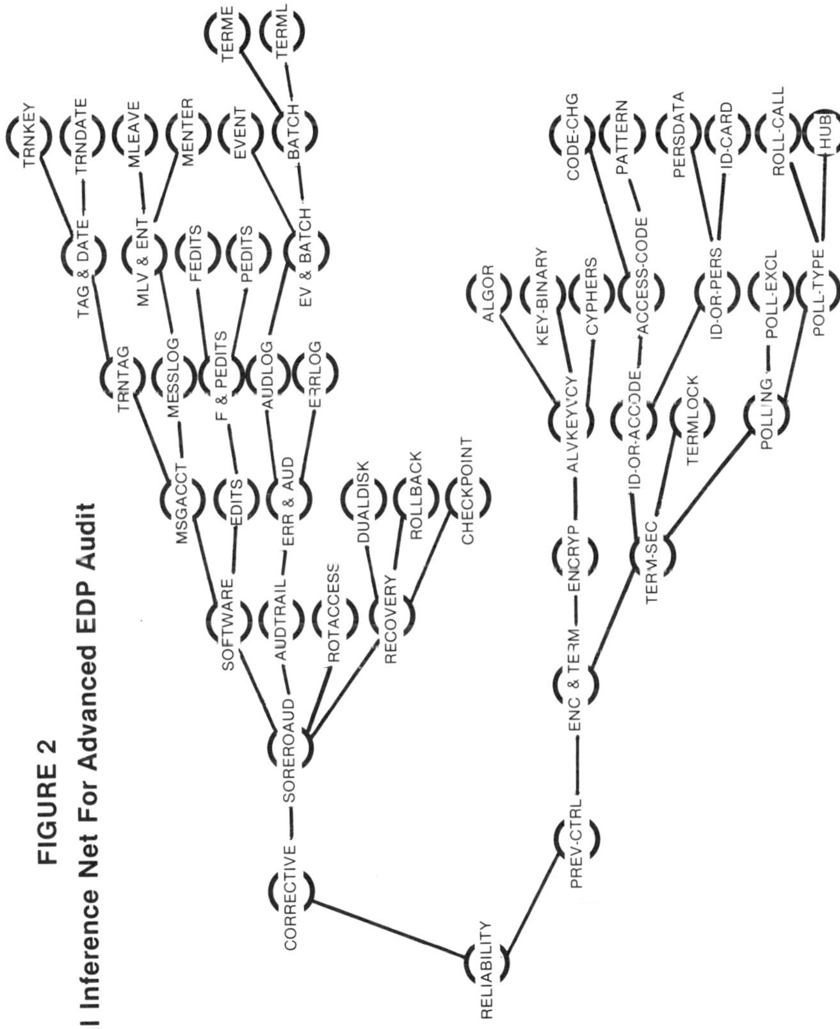

FIGURE 2
Partial Inference Net For Advanced EDP Audit

rules than are currently contained in the system. We have simply tried to capture some preliminary elements of the process at this time. The underlined numerical values represent a hypothetical EDP auditor's responses (certainty factors) to the questions.

EXHIBIT 1

Sample Session With Expert System

How certain are you that access controls are rotated on a regular basis?

<u>1</u>

How certain are you that all outgoing messages are logged?

<u>1</u>

How certain are you that all incoming messages are logged?

.<u>5</u>

How certain are you that transactions are written to dual disks as a backup precaution?

<u>2</u>

How certain are you that a log of all errors and when they are corrected is maintained?

<u>3</u>

How certain are you that mode of process is event?

<u>5</u>

How certain are you that transactions are entered in batch mode from terminals; these are batched prior to entry?

<u>3</u>

How certain are you that transactions are identified by transaction type?

<u>2</u>

How certain are you that each transaction is identified by date and terminal of origin?

<u>1</u>

How certain are you that front end edits are complete and sufficient?

<u>1</u>

How certain are you that processing edits are complete and sufficient?

.<u>2</u>

How certain are you that all master records having activity against them are captured in pre-image form?

.<u>4</u>

EXHIBIT 1 (continued)

How certain are you that transactions are entered as they occur but are batched by the computer?

1

How certain are you that access code is changed frequently?

3

How certain are you that code pattern is developed at random and is of sufficient length?

4

How certain are you that cyphers are used as a form of encryption?

. 1

How certain are you that checkpoints are used as a recovery strategy?

3

How certain are you that keys and binary addition are used for encryption?

1

How certain are you that algorithms are used for encryption?

1

How certain are you that the terminal is lockable with keys issued to only authorized users?

2

How certain are you that out of service terminals are not polled?

1

How certain are you that id-card is used for user identification?

3

How certain are you that terminals pass along the polling message?

3

How certain are you that personal data is used for user identification?

1

How certain are you that terminals are polled in rotation?

2

After considering all significant questions, the degree that the control system is adequate and functioning well (RELIABILITY) initially was 0.0. It is now 2.0.
There are no more significant questions for the current goal.

Investigated goals with degree of belief > = 0.0 are: The control system is adequate and functioning well (RELIABILITY). Prior degree was 0.0. Current degree is 2.0.

(end)

We earlier cited Gorry's arguments that a useful program must be able to explain how it arrives at a conclusion. In Exhibit 2, the EDP auditor has been asked how certain he is that access controls are rotated on a regular basis. Instead of immediately providing a numerical response the EDP auditor may want to know why the expert system asked this question. By entering "c" he will be provided a review of the chain of reasoning from the nearest goal to the current question. Thus, the auditor can examine the system's reasoning process.

EXHIBIT 2

Explanation of Reasoning Process

```
(begin)
    How certain are you that access controls are rotated on a
        regular basis?
        c
        access controls are rotated on a regular basis
        (rotaccess)
        with degree 1.0
        is evidence for
        software, rotation of access, recovery measures, and
        audit trail are satisfactory (soreroaud)
        with degree 0.5
        which is evidence for (pw = 1.0   nw = -1.0)
        corrective controls are adequate (corrective)
        with degree 1.5
        which is evidence for (pw = 1.0   nw = -1.0)
        the control system is adequate and functioning well
        (compliance) with
        degree 0.0
(end)
```

The auditor may also wish to know why a question is asked (enters "w"). Exhibit 3 presents two examples of such queries. Note that the response is only a template representation of the rule.

EXPERT SYSTEMS IN ACCOUNTING AND AUDITING

In this section we briefly review two expert systems that have been developed or are undergoing development in accounting and auditing. We are aware of one other system that is currently in the very early stages of development [Braun and Chandler, 1982] that is intended to assist auditors with analytical review procedures. No information about the system, however, is available at this time. The application of this technology is relatively new and as a result little research in this area exists.

EXHIBIT 3

Examples of Query and Explanation Capability

```
(begin)
    How certain are you that access controls are rotated on a
    regular basis?
    5

    How certain are you that all outgoing messages are logged?
    w
    This question is asked to find out whether or not
       the message log includes both entering and leaving
       messages
       (mlv&ent)
       which has current degree 1.0
    How certain are you that transactions are written to
       dual disks as a backup precaution?

    w
    This question is asked to find out whether or not
       recovery measures are adequate (recovery)
       which has current degree 0.5 (pw = 1.0   nw = -1.0)

(end)
```

Tax Advisor

TAX ADVISOR [Michaelsen, 1982] is a system whose problem domain is estate planning. The "system's goal is to make recommendations, based on projections of future events, for tax-related actions that will approximately maximize the wealth that an individual transfers at death (p. 3)." The rules used in the system were initially developed by the designer based on his personal experience and current textbooks on estate planning. Michaelson refined the system in two ways prior to testing. First, three tax experts were allowed to experiment with the system and communicate their criticisms. Second, a pilot study of the verification test was conducted. Michaelson concluded that if someone is knowledgeable in expert systems *and* the problem domain that a "successful expert system (could be developed) at a lower cost than is possible using conventional means [p. 18].

TAX ADVISOR uses EMYCIN[15] [van Melle, 1981] for implementation of its structure. The system attempts to mimic the deductive process of a tax consultant. The consultation involves four basic steps: (1) the client is screened to see if tax consultation would be beneficial, (2) client data is obtained, (3) client investment portfolio is reviewed for conformity to his/her preferences, and (4) planning categories are reviewed to see if the client has needs or opportunities in these areas (e.g. provision for retirement, gifts, etc.). Once the system decides that one of the categories may prove beneficial to the client, the system proceeds down the goal tree for specific recommendations.

The system is currently not capable of handling all estate planning contingencies.[16] In order to keep the project manageable the designer limited the breadth of the system by limiting the types of clients it could serve.

The system was verified using the same "blind" procedure used on MYCIN [Yu, *et al.* 1979]. Two experts from public accounting firms ran two estate planning cases on TAX ADVISOR and recorded its recommendations.[17] Two other experts then served as judges by evaluating the recommendations made by TAX ADVISOR and those made originally by the firm. The judges only expressed opinions as to the acceptability of the recommendations. The results are shown in Table 1. Two items are noteworthy: (1) None of TAX ADVISOR's recommendations were considered unacceptable and (2) the "human" expert made more recommendations. Michaelson does not perform any statistical tests but concluded that TAX ADVISOR performed as well as the tax expert.

TABLE 1

Expert System Evaluation Results

	Number of Recommendations Rated		
	Equivalent	Acceptable	Unacceptable
Tax Advisor			
Case 1	2	1	0
Case 2	4	4	0
Human Expert			
Case 1	4	2	0
Case 2	6	3	0

Comments by the experts who used TAX ADVISOR indicated that in its current state of development use by experts was unlikely. Apparently, the robustness (limitations) of the current prototype affected their evaluation. The experts did comment that they could see at least two potential uses for TAX ADVISOR. One would be for "general practitioners" who must occasionally make estate planning decisions, and secondly, as an educational device for formal classroom education. Future extensions of TAX ADVISOR call for expanding the breadth of the system and improving its consultation capabilities.

Auditor

AUDITOR [Dungan and Chandler, 1980; Dungan 1983] is an expert system which assists an auditor in assessing the adequacy of a company's allowance for bad debts. The knowledge base was constructed by:

1. eliciting from expert auditors a list of factors (cues) that are important in examining the allowance for bad debts,
2. transforming these cues into rules of the form IF (EVIDENCE CUE): THEN, to a certain extent (HYPOTHESIS)
3. polling auditors on the relative weights of the effect of each of these factors,
4. transforming the relative weights into system parameters,
5. inserting rules using the AND and NOT connectives to express relationships suggested by the auditors, and
6. refining and validating.

Considerable consensus was found among the auditors in their relative weighting of the factors.

This information was assembled in rule form for use in AL/X. The system was refined through interaction with the expert auditors and the system's performance was tested using real and hypothetical cases.

The system was validated in two ways. First, different auditors from the same firm of the ones who participated in building the system operated the model against ten cases taken from audit working papers. Agreement with the human expert was about 90 percent. Second, two other expert auditors, from a different CPA firm, one serving as a user of the system and the other as a "blind" validator, evaluated eleven real world cases. Agreement was again very high, 91 percent. Dungan [1983] concluded that "the validations were supportive of a belief that the system contained the rules and weights utilized by auditors in their evaluation of trade accounts receivable."

CONCLUDING COMMENTS

There is a growing interest in auditing and accounting in developing expert systems. We had two purposes in preparing this paper. First, we wanted to present an overview of expert systems. The goals of this discussion were to indicate the types of problem domains where expert systems might be appropriate, to discuss important design and development issues, and to point out that expert systems are still in an embryonic stage. Second, we wanted to review the work that is currently ongoing in accounting and auditing on expert systems. As our review points out all of this work is heavily dependent on "technologies" developed by AI researchers. It is our hope that this paper may encourage others to pursue research in expert systems.

NOTES

[1]Simon [1965], for example, suggested that most management tasks would be programmed by 1975. This prediction has proven to be overly optimistic.

[2]An indication of this interest is the fact that all of the systems discussed in this paper were funded through Peat, Marwick, Mitchell Foundation's Research Opportunities in Auditing Program.

[3]Much of the discussion in this section is based on five recent and excellent articles which deal with expert systems: Buchanan [1982], Davis [1982], Duda and Shortliffe [1983], Feigenbaum [1977] and Stefik *et al.* [1982]. The reader is referred to these articles for more details on expert systems.

[4]See Messier [forthcoming] for evidence of experience effects in a complex judgment task in auditing.

[5]TEIRESIAS [Davis and Lenat, 1982] has been coupled to MYCIN and allows for the modification of old rules or the acquisition of new rules.

[6]For an excellent discussion of knowledge engineering the reader is referred to Nii [1980].

[7]See Hansen and Messier [1982] for an example of how "modularity" allows for easy maintenance of the knowledge base.

[8]See Duda and Shortliffe [1983] for a list of current expert systems and their related problem domains.

[9]The reader is referred to a recent book by Feigenbaum and McCorduck [1983] which discusses the Japanese fifth generation computers which are planned for the 1990s. It's interesting to note that their fifth generation machines rely extensively on expert system software.

[10]AL/X can be leased on an annual basis from Intelligent Terminals, Ltd.

[11]The reader is referred to Duda, *et al.* [1976] or Hansen and Messier [1983a] for more detail.

[12]From an auditor's perspective and assuming conservative probabilities (e.g. .01 and .99) for the truth or falsity of a hypothesis, the effective range for degrees of belief is -20 to 20. The following data show this relationship:

Degrees	*Probability (approx)*
-20	.01
-10	.10
0	.50
10	.90
20	.99

[13]The equivalent probability is easily recaptured since

$$p = \frac{0}{0+1}.$$

In this case

$$\begin{aligned} \text{degree (H)} &= 10 \log_{10}(0(\text{H})) = 2 \\ \log_{10}(0(\text{H})) &= .2 \\ 0(\text{H}) &= 1.58 \\ p &= \frac{1.58}{2.58} = .61. \end{aligned}$$

[14]See Figure 10 in Davis [1982] for an estimate of the man-years that were required to build some of the more well known expert systems [e.g. MYCIN, PROSPECTOR, etc.].

[15]EMYCIN ("Essential MYCIN") is the basic MYCIN structure with the medical knowledge removed.

[16]Four areas are specifically excluded but considered for future inclusion: (1) clients who own a controlling interest in a business, (2) clients who are already deceased, (3) clients whose estates are less than $175,000, and (4) clients who own material community property.

[17]Note that a number of different recommendations are possible *and* feasible for each case.

REFERENCES

Abdel-khalik, A.R., D.A. Snowball and J.H. Wragge, "The Effects of Certain Audit Control Variables on the Planning of External Audit Programs" *The Accounting Review* (April 1983), pp. 215-227.

Bailey, A.D., Jr, J. Gerlach, R.P. McAfee and A.B. Whinston, "TICOM II: The Internal Control Language" in *Internal Control and the Impact of the Foreign Corrupt Practices Act.* Edited by A.R. Abdel-khalik. (University Presses of Florida, 1982a).

__________, G.L. Duke, J. Gerlach, C. Ko, R. Meservy and A.B. Whinston, "Internal Control Evaluation by Computer—TICOM III," working paper, University of Minnesota, (1982b).

Biggs, S.F. and T.J. Mock, "An Investigation of Auditor Decision Processes in the Evaluation of Internal Controls and Audit Scope Decisions," Working Paper No. 25, University of Southern California, (July 1981).

Braun, H.M. and J.S. Chandler, "Development of an Expert System to Assist Auditors in the Investigation of Analytical Review Fluctuations" research proposal, University of Illinois, (1982).

Buchanan, B.G., "New Research on Expert Systems" in *Machine Intelligence 10.* Edited by J.E. Hayes, D. Michie and Y-H Pao, (1982).

Campbell, A.N., V.F. Hollister, R.O. Duda, and P.E. Hart, "Recognition of a Hidden Mineral Deposit by an Artificial Intelligence Program" *Science* (September 1982), pp. 927-929.

Davis, R., "Expert Systems: Where are We? and Where Do We Go from Here?" *AI Magazine* (Spring 1982), pp. 3-22.

________ and D.B. Lenat, *Knowledge—Based Systems in Artificial Intelligence* (McGraw-Hill, 1982).

Davis, B.G. and R. Weber, *Auditing Advanced EDP Systems: A Survey of Practice and Development of a Theory.* (The Management Information Systems Research Center, 1983).

Duda, R.O., P.E. Hart and N.J. Nilsson, "Subjective Bayesian Methods for Rule-Based Inference Systems" *Proceedings of the 1976 National Computer Conference* (1976), pp. 1075-1082.

Duda, R.O. and J.G. Gaschnig and P.E. Hart, "Model Design in the PROSPECTOR Consultant System for Mineral Exploration" in *Expert Systems in the Microelectronic Age.* Edited by D. Michie. (Edinburgh University Press, 1980).

Duda, R.O. and J.G. Gaschnig, "Knowledge-Based Expert Systems Come of Age" *Byte* (September 1981), pp. 238-281.

Duda, R.O. and E.H. Shortliffe, "Expert Systems Research" *Science* (April 1983), pp. 261-268.

Dungan, C., *A Model of an Audit Judgment in the Form of an Expert System.* Unpublished Ph.D. Dissertation. University of Illinois, Urbana-Champaign, (1983).

Dungan, C. and J. Chandler, "Development of Knowledge—Based Expert Systems to Model Auditors' Decision Processes," research proposal, University of Illinois, (1980).

Elliott, R.K., "Unique Audit Methods: Peat, Marwick International" *Auditing: A Journal of Practice and Theory* (Spring 1983), pp. 1-12.

Elstein, A.S., L.E. Shulman and S.A. Sprafka. *Medical Problem Solving: An Analysis of Clinical Reasoning* (Harvard University Press, 1978).

Feigenbaum, E.A., "The Art of Artificial Intelligence: I. Themes and Case Studies of Knowledge Engineering" *Proceedings of the Fifth International Joint Conference on Artificial Intelligence* (1977), pp. 1014-1029.

____________, B.G. Buchanan and J. Lederberg, "On Generality and Problem Solving: A Case Study Using the DENDRAL Program" in *Machine Intelligence 6.* Edited by B. Meltzer and D. Michie (American Elsevier, 1971).

Feigenbaum, E.A. and P. McCorduck. *The Fifth Generation* (Addison-Wesley Publishing Company, 1983).

Gorry, G.A., "Computer-Assisted Clinical Decision-Making" *Methods of Information in Medicine* (1973), pp. 45-51.

Hansen, J.V. and W.F. Messier, Jr., "The Feasibility of Using Artificial Intelligence Techniques for EDP Auditing" A Report to Peat, Marwick, Mitchell & Co. (December 1981).

_________ and _________, "Expert Systems for Decision Support in EDP Auditing," *International Journal of Computer and Information Sciences* (1982), pp. 357-379.

_________ and _________, "A Knowledge-Based, Expert System for Auditing Advanced Computer Systems" ARC working paper 83-6, University of Florida (August 1983a).

_________ and _________, "Scheduling the Monitoring of EDP Controls in Online Systems" *International Journal of Computer and Information Sciences* (1983b), pp. 35-46.

_________ and _________, "A Model for Scheduling the Monitoring of Internal Control in Advanced EDP Systems" *International Journal of Systems Science* (1983c), in press.

_________ and _________, "Decision Support for EDP-Auditing" under review at *The Communications of the Association of Computing Machinery* (1983d).

_________, _________, and S.F. Biggs, "Software Development for Implementation Testing of Artificial Intelligence Methods in EDP Auditing" research proposal, University of Florida, (1981).

Johnson, P.E., "What Kind of Expert Should a System Be?" *The Journal of Medicine and Philosophy* (1983), pp. 77-97.

Messier, W.F. Jr., "The Effect of Experience and Firm Type on Materiality/Disclosure Judgments" *Journal of Accounting Research* (forthcoming).

Michaelson, R.H., "An Expert System for Federal Tax Planning" working paper, University of Nebraska, (1982).

Newell A. and H.A. Simon, *Human Problem Solving* (Prentice-Hall, Inc., 1972).

_________ and _________, "Computer Science as Empirical Inquiry: Symbols and Search" *Communications of the ACM* (1976), pp. 113-126.

Nii, H.P., "An Introduction to Knowledge Engineering, Blackboard Model, and AGE" Heuristic Programming Project Report No. HPP-80-29, Stanford University, (March 1980).

Paterson, A., *AL/X User Manual* (Intelligent Terminals Ltd., 1981).

Sagan, C., *The Dragons of Eden* (Random House, 1977).

Shortliffe, E.H., *Computer-Based Medical Consultations: MYCIN* (American Elsevier Publishing Co., Inc., 1976).

Simon, H.A., *The Shape of Automation for Men and Management* (Harper & Row, 1965).

Stefik, M., J. Aikins, R. Balzer, J. Benoit, L. Birnbaum, F. Hayes-Roth and E. Sacerdoti, "The Organization of Expert Systems, A Tutorial" *Artificial Intelligence* (March 1982), pp. 135-174.

van Melle, W.J., *System Aids in Constructing Consultation Programs* (UMI Research Press, 1981).

Weber, R., "Some Characteristics of the Free Recall of Computer Controls by EDP Auditors" *Journal of Accounting Research* (Spring 1980), pp. 214-241.

Winograd, T., *Understanding Natural Language* (Academic Press, 1972).

Wright, W.F., "Professional Judgment, Expertise and Auditing Research" Presentation at the Audit Judgment Symposium, University of Southern California, (February 1983).

Yu, V.L., L.M. Fagan, S.M. Wraith, W.J. Clancey, A.C. Scott, J. Hannigan, R.L. Blum, B.G. Buchanan and S.N. Cohen, "Antimicrobial Selection by a Computer: A Blinded Evaluation by Infectious Diseases Experts" *Journal of the American Medical Association* (September 21, 1979), pp. 1279-1282.

Zadeh, L., "A Theory of Approximate Reasoning." *Machine Intelligence 9*. Edited by J.E. Hayes, D. Michie and L. Mikulich (Halsted Press, 1979).

Jesse F. Dillard
Ohio State University

Discussant's Comments on:

"Expert Systems in Accounting and Auditing: A Framework and Review"

INTRODUCTION

As was requested, I will restrict my comments to the topics of future research and alternative approaches to expert system applications in accounting and auditing. The future research is nearly endless both from extending the applications in the areas being investigated as well as the new areas in which this methodology can be applied. For example, I am currently involved with several projects directed toward this area:

- Accounting education and basic accounting learning
- Expert system feasibility for military procurement
- Audit judgment in opinion formulation.

You will see many more areas in accounting and auditing being investigated using some semblance of Artificial Intelligence methodology. What I would like to direct my comments toward in this discussion is related to both future research and alternative approaches. More specifically, I want to propose an expanded approach to that apparently taken by Hansen and Messier in the preceding paper.

LITERATURE REVIEW

The first portion of the paper merely summarized several reviews of the expert systems area. Obviously the area is more extensive than presented here. I strongly recommend *Building Expert Systems* by Hayes-Roth, Waterman and Lenat [1983] for any one interested in this area. The point made strongly here and in much of the other AI literature is the importance of understanding the problem being investigated and the enormous time required to build expert systems. Also, one is struck by the infancy of the field in trying to simulate expert human behavior.

This leads us to the need for evaluation criteria for expert systems. Several lists are presented by several authors, but I would like to present a set proposed by Bobrow [1975] in his discussion of representation:

- How do objects and relationships in the world correspond to the units and relations encoded in the expert system?

- In what ways do the operations in the system correspond to actions in the world?
- How can system knowledge be used in mapping the world state?
- How can information be added to the system without further external input?
- How are units linked to provide access to appropriate knowledge?
- How are two structures compared for equality and similarity?
- What knowledge does a system have to have about its own structure and operation?

These are very fundamental issues that are not explicitly addressed by Messier and Hansen, or many others currently involved in constructing expert systems. However, these issues are at the heart of the problem of constructing expert systems for real world applications. We should be more sensitive to the basic research issues than is currently the case. Better expert systems will be the result.

As I said, these criteria are not currently being used. What are being used? I fear we are again falling into the predictive accuracy trap. Are we trying to explain human behavior or predict the outcome? And which of these is appropriate under what circumstances?

From a short run application perspective, predictive accuracy is the appropriate criteria. Prediction of bankruptcy is a good example of this. Linear models using a limited number of cues have been shown to be very good predictors of bankruptcy. Two observations can be made from the expert systems perspective. First, there is little about the behavior of the human expert that can be encoded into an AI system for carrying out the task. Second, if the task can be carried out by an algorithm then there is no need to build an expert system to do it. In other words, predictive accuracy provides little in the way of designing expert systems.

The approach taken by Messier and Hansen has the propensity to provide greater insight into the actual decision making process. However, I'm a little concerned that they not be caught in the prediction syndrome. Prediction is a necessary but not sufficient condition for explaining expert behavior.

BUILDING EXPERT SYSTEMS

Knowledge based expert systems are being developed for several accounting and auditing related tasks (See references). Results from current AI research suggests that the actual heuristics and problem solving processes used by human experts provide the most promising avenues for the development of system architecture [Hayes-Roth *et al,* 1983].

Constructing knowledge based AI systems is viewed as a three stage process requiring many persons years of work. The first stage is the specification of the task and the design of a system architecture based on the analysis. The result of the first stage is a knowledge based decision support system. This stage is carried out by identifying the task and human experts within the area and representing the human knowledge in such a way that it can be understood and encoded into a computer system. The decision hierarchy, decision points and linkages are identified. This results in a specific description of the task and information processing that is required. The structure is encoded in an information organization program that represents, organizes and links the decision frames or episodes. Ideally, there would be one frame representing each decision required. This frame would be linked to all other relevant frames, required data bases and prior decision results.

Software systems for organizing knowledge in this way are currently available. Thus, the development required is inserting and organizing the contents of the system. The resulting system provides a detailed description of the decision process. It identifies the types of data bases and prior information used and the sequence of use. It identifies the requisite analytic capabilities needed to carry out the task and the point at which they are utilized. It identifies the decisions that must be made in carrying out the task, their sequence and their relationship to prior and/or future decisions. The resulting system is a detailed outline of the task. It provides a means for testing the proposed structure in online, interactive sessions with human experts. The intelligence in this first stage system is the decision structure, its sequence, hierarchy and component linkages which provide the framework for building a sophisticated knowledge based expert system.

The second stage modifies the structure constructed in the first phase through intensive testing with human experts and comparisons of predictions from historical cases. In effect, the first stage results, i.e., a prototype system, is viewed as a set of hypotheses to be tested. As the structure is refined, it is also made more "intelligent." The first stage system confronts the user with the decisions that must be made but requires that the user actually carry out the logical processes. The decisions are broken down into their lowest components so that the decision maker makes many intermediate decisions that will be combined by the system into the final decision required. This is intelligence only in the sense that the intermediate decisions are aggregated, formatted and presented to the decision maker. The intermediate decisions will begin to be "compiled." That is, all the steps will not have to be carried out by the user. The system will have the capability of inferring the needed result. Prior work indicates that this requires the implementation and encoding of decision heuristics as well as the availability of requisite data bases. System interfaces with requisite data bases and other decision support facilities can present a major impediment in constructing AI system [Chandrasekaran, *et al,* 1983].

The third stage in developing AI systems involves the construction of an expert system which contains extensive reasoning, learning and language capabilities and which can be applied to more expanded audit tasks and situations. No AI system currently meets all these objectives in any domain. It is, however, a goal which appears not too far beyond our grasp.

CONCLUSION

The following discussion is not meant as an indictment of the Messier and Hansen work. Theirs is a courageous attempt at an extremely complex task. Their objective is to provide assistance to practitioners in the area of EDP auditing and to carry on research that will be funded by practitioners. Thus, predictive accuracy is the appropriate criteria for evaluating the research. They have started their research project somewhere between stage one and stage two. I do not think this bodes well for long run development of their expert system.

There is, I believe, a need for more basic research into the behavior of expert decision makers. The central determinant of effective use of knowledge is how it is organized. Issues of representation should come after the organizational structure of knowledge that is needed for problem solving has been clarified.

As more audit related expert systems are built, we should become more mindful of system interfacing. The audit task can be viewed as a series of intermediate decisions which are made by different people. These systems could be viewed as specialists in their areas and would be consulted in forming the audit opinion similar to the consultation of medical specialists during a diagnostic evaluation of a patient. Expert systems are being designed to carry out the tasks of these specialists. Thought needs to be given as to how these specialists should interact with one another and how they should interface with the "opinion" expert. [See Dillard *et al,* 1983] for amplification.

REFERENCES

Bobrow, D.G., "Dimensions in Representation," in D.G. Bobrow and A. Collins (editors), *Representation and Understanding* (Academic Press, Inc., 1975), pp. 1-33.

Braun, H.M., "An Application of Expert Systems to Study the Decision Process Used by Analytical Review Information for Audit Decisions," Dissertation Proposal (University of Illinois, 1983).

Chandrasekaran, B., J.F. Dillard and K. Ramakrishna, *The Design of an Expert System for Contract Price Analysis,* Technical Report I and II, Department of Computer and Information Science, The Ohio State University (April 1983).

Dillard, J.F., J.F. Mutchler and K. Ramakrishna, "Knowledge Based Expert Systems for Audit Opinion Decisions," The Ohio State University, (1983).

Dillard, J.F., K. Ramakrishna, and B. Chandrasekaran, "Expert Systems for Price Analysis: A Feasibility Study," in *Federal Acquisition Research Symposium,* U.S. Air Force, (December, 1983).

J.V. Hansen and W.F. Messier, "Expert Systems for Decision Support in EDP Auditing," *International Journal of Computer and Information Sciences* (1982), pp. 357-379.

Hayes-Roth, F., D.A. Waterman and D.B. Lenat, "An Overview of Expert Systems," in F. Hayes-Roth, D.A. Waterman and D.B. Lenat (editors), *Building Expert Systems* (Addison-Wesley, 1983), pp. 3-30.

Messier, W.F., Jr. and J.V. Hansen, "Expert Systems in Accounting and Auditing: A Framework and Review," in S. Moriarity and E. Joyce (Eds.) *Decision Making and Accounting: Current Research,* (University of Oklahoma, Center for Economic and Management Research, 1984), pp. 182-202.

Michaelson, R.H., *A Knowledge-Based System for Individual Income and Transfer Tax Planning.* Ph.D. thesis, University of Illinois (1982).

Ramakrishna, K., J.F. Dillard, T.G. Harrison, and B. Chandrasekaran. "An Intelligent Manual for Price Analysis," in *Federal Acquisition Research Symposium,* U.S. Air Force, (December 1983).

William F. Wright
Peat, Marwick, Mitchell & Co.

Discussant's Comments on:

"Expert Systems in Accounting and Auditing: A Framework and Review"

EXPERT SYSTEMS RESEARCH IN AUDITING

Since the Messier and Hansen paper is an overview of expert systems research and a description of their in-process system, my comments will be quite general. I will discuss the possible contribution of expert systems in auditing, and consider the meaning of expertise in "semi-structured" audit contexts. I will then concentrate on knowledge acquisition during the development of an expert system.

THE NEED FOR EXPERT SYSTEMS RESEARCH IN AUDITING

Effective and efficient audits, and the training of auditors to provide for quality auditing, require that auditing judgment expertise be applied as frequently and as thoroughly as possible. It therefore is important to know what expert auditors do when they evaluate available evidence and determine risk assessments, materiality judgments, analytical review procedures, and, most importantly, the appropriate audit opinion in the circumstances. Given awareness of what experts do in different situations, decision aids such as expert systems can be developed to make the expertise available for all audits.

Understanding and modeling expertise in "semi-structured" audit decision contexts, and manifesting the expertise in the form of a computer program (e.g. a knowledge-based, expert system), is a contemporary research topic in auditing research, as well as psychology and artificial intelligence. The basic idea is to understand how experts formulate and solve complicated, semi-structured problems.

Understanding how expert auditors perform professional judgment tasks and manifesting this knowledge in a computer program, can provide several important benefits:

(1) Supporting experienced auditors in the field by providing a computer-based decision aid that, e.g., recalls ways to structure a problem, indicates pertinent sources of evidence and provides an evaluation of the evidence in the form of a preliminary judgment;

(2) Top-level expertise can be transferred via the expert system to less-experienced staff personnel at multiple locations;
(3) Since the design of an expert system requires complete specification of an expert's knowledge and reasoning processes, the system can be used for staff training purposes to simulate audit situations and permit new auditors to understand what to do in those situations;
(4) Documentation of audit judgments will be facilitated since the expert system will print out its reasoning in structured sentences with degrees of support for the possible audit judgments. The auditor may augment, or override, the program output when and where necessary and include this in the audit documentation.

The above benefits indicate that both the effectiveness (quality of audit judgments) and efficiency (overall effort/cost required) of audit judgments can be enhanced by the development of an expertise model and a knowledge-based, expert system.

Nature of Expertise in Professional Judgment Situations

Judgment expertise may be defined as follows:

> A demonstrated ability to efficiently perform a complex, perhaps semi-structured, task in a superior way (on specified dimensions) based on accumulated domain-specific knowledge and inference/judgment procedures.

The study of expertise is to understand how experts subjectively structure problems and inference tasks, search for, and use, information and generate judgments. The judgment formulation process (information search, lines of reasoning, number and type of hypotheses generated and considered) may be different for expert vs. novice auditors.[1] Typically considerable domain-specific knowledge (facts and rules only for a specific type of task) is used by experts; use of domain-specific knowledge is the essence of superior professional judgment [Chi, Glaser & Rees, 1981].

The following semi-structured audit situations are contexts where audit expertise is extremely important and expert systems could be developed:

a) Auditing EDP systems (the context selected by Messier and Hansen);
b) Design of a set of efficient audit procedures to yield sufficient evidence to support an audit opinion;
c) Assessment of the inherent risk for statement assertions, e.g. the probability of an undetected material error in a specific account balance, absent any internal controls, and other audit risks [see Kinney, 1983];
d) Generation, and particularly, interpretation of the results from analytical review procedures relative to management's results [Libby, 1983];
e) Assessment of the effectiveness and reliability of internal controls over assets and information flows [Mock and Willingham, 1983], possibly including formal and informal controls;
f) Evaluation of the validity of the "going concern" assumption;
g) A decision concerning the type and extent of disclosure of current contingencies (e.g. an ongoing legal dispute);

h) Most importantly (and ambitiously), subjective aggregation of all of the available evidence into an audit opinion on the financial statements (including possible qualifications and disclosures).

Given the judgment process employed by an auditor, superior performance must be observed if one is to be an expert. Performance dimensions include:

1. Accuracy of audit judgments, predictions and/or decisions given actual outcomes (preferably over a large number of trials). Consensus is presently used as a surrogate given the absence of outcome evidence; e.g. when evaluating the quality of internal control judgments;
2. Degree of random error in judgment processes and eventual judgments;
3. Amount of time needed to complete the decision process [Hayes-Roth, Waterman and Lenat, 1983, pp. 44-45];
4. Degree of learning from types of feedback [Einhorn, 1980].

Given the typical lack of a judgment accuracy measure (i.e. actual results or outcomes) in many audit situations, validating that a person is an expert can be a problem. Some indirect criteria include:

1) The nature and importance of an individual's position in an organization (e.g. Messier and Hansen's selection of senior EDP audit specialists),
2) Number of years of experience (and what type of experience),
3) The person's degree of recognition outside his/her organization and among his/her peers.

The above are (correlated) indirect measures of expertise. Messier and Hansen have, in effect, selected criteria 1 and 2 as their standards for expertise. While this selection is quite reasonable, the authors should attempt to validate that the audit specialists actually possess expert ability in performing the task. Messier and Hansen indicate the builder of an expert system must select a single knowledge base "czar" to guide development of the system; validation of the ability of the knowledge czar is particularly important.

KNOWLEDGE ACQUISITION RESEARCH AND EXPERT SYSTEMS

The basis for expert systems research is "knowledge acquisition," i.e. elicitation and representation of expert knowledge, including models of how knowledge is organized (the knowledge base) and description of heuristic inference procedures used in a specific problem-solving context. Very detailed knowledge depiction is required; this forces the expert to think through the problem in a precise and thorough manner. This codification of non-textbook knowledge (e.g. in the form of a "decision tree" model of the knowledge and heuristics) is a major benefit of the development of an expert system. Provision of this knowledge for EDP auditing will be an important contribution from the Messier and Hansen system development process.

When discussing computer models of expert cognition, two distinct approaches are feasible:

1)The perspective of a cognitive psychologist trying to understand and explicitly model cognitive functioning, including perception, memory, inference, learning and other aspects of cognition [e.g. Anderson, 1976] or

2) the perspective of the computer scientist attempting to determine how experts solve difficult problems, including what knowledge an expert possesses and how that knowledge is used, with the intention of using the information (and other sources) to build a system.

The two perspectives can be thought of as the first being concerned with "models of the mind" vs. what sources of information will result in expert performance of the computer program. An illustrative example is that researchers modeling cognitive functioning would explicitly model cognitive heuristics that lead to known biases in judgment [Kahneman, Slovic & Tversky, 1982; Tversky and Kahneman, 1974] while builders of expert systems would want to eliminate any known biases when they design the knowledge base for the system.

Knowledge Acquisition: A Productive Role for Multiple Knowledge Elicitation Methods

The typical practice in the development of an expert system (including the Messier and Hansen system) is for a knowledge engineer to work with one expert over a period of time, using interviews and perhaps verbal protocol analysis [Anderson, 1983; Biggs and Mock, 1983] to develop the knowledge information for the system. Input from other experts may be obtained but one person supervises and mediates the generation of the knowledge base. A potential major weakness of current knowledge engineering efforts is this dependence on one expert (a knowledge "czar") to ultimately reconcile and synthesize knowledge information from multiple experts and other sources; the extreme case is where only one expert is consulted. With a "knowledge czar," the knowledge information will be viewed from one person's perspective, i.e. one subjective representation of the problem and a single knowledge base. Given concern for both the effectiveness and efficiency of the knowledge elicitation process, one would like to incorporate the "best" abilities of multiple experts, particularly if different experts are relatively more competent at different aspects of the same judgment task (e.g. structuring the problem vs. information selection vs. weighting and combining of information into a judgment): As noted by Messier and Hansen, current practice does not allow for optimal integration of the knowledge of multiple experts.

Knowledge acquisition efforts can be more productive and efficient if multiple methods from the behavioral decision theory literature [Einhorn and Hogarth, 1981; Slovic, Fischhoff and Lichtenstein, 1977; Pitz and Sachs, 1983] are employed based on the relative strengths of the different methods [Slovic & Lichtenstein, 1971; Wright, 1982], i.e. the optimal mix of research methodologies to best elicit evidence on the nature of audit expertise [cf. Einhorn, Kleinmuntz and Kleinmuntz, 1979; Payne, 1976]. The idea is to match specific research methodologies [Ashton, 1982; Libby,

1981] to different aspects of the knowledge acquisition process, e.g.

a) descriptive process tracing methods such as concurrent verbal protocol analysis [Anderson, 1983] and information display boards [Payne, 1976] to obtain detailed data on cognitive processes and information search leading to a judgment or decision;
b) lens model/policy capturing methods [Ashton, 1974; Libby, 1975; Wright, 1979, 1982] to model (at an abstract/aggregate level) how a specific judgment (a subgoal) is generated, including relative cue weights for information variables. This approach would be particularly helpful if evidence is desired from multiple experts concerning both the judgment and relative cue weights;
c) subjective probability (Bayesian) methods for explicit elicitation of subjective uncertainty [e.g. Solomon, 1982; Solomon, et al., 1982; Crosby, 1980, 1981] and consideration of how prior evidence (prior probabilities) and case-specific evidence (data likelihoods) are integrated into subgoal judgments [Borgida & Brekke, 1981; Wright, 1983]. Subjective probabilities could be explicitly compared and reconciled with "degrees of belief" and "certainty factors" [see Messier and Hansen], using procedures designed to permit reconciliation of subjective probabilities elicited using different probability encoding methods [e.g. Spetzler & Stael von Holstein, 1975-also Fischhoff, 1982]. (Several systems, including Messier and Hansen use Bayesian concepts as a general framework.);
d) methods from cognitive psychology (analysis of free or cued recall data [Weber, 1980], responses to materials differing in the context and/or background, etc.) designed to provide data on use of memory, learning, the effects of context on information use and judgments, etc. [see Anderson, 1980].

The general idea here, relative to current knowledge acquisition practice, including the procedure discussed by Messier and Hansen, is to "fine tune" interview and verbal protocol results using a portfolio of the available research methods.

CONCLUSION

Messier and Hansen have selected an important aspect of auditing that is relatively unstructured, with the available expertise being both scarce and evolving as computer technology advances rapidly. They are proceeding conscientiously with an ambitious project, given the complexity of the task domain. I expect Messier and Hansen will provide a workable system for the purposes indicated at the start of this comment, no doubt providing refinements of the expert systems methodology along the way.

NOTES

[1]Libby [1981, pp. 78-98] summarizes research results on the structure of "expert" memory, as well as its role in what seems to be two areas where expert and novice auditors may differ—the direction of information search and the selection of alternative decision rules. Suggestions for auditing research are also provided.

REFERENCES

Anderson, J.R., *Cognitive Psychology and Its Implications* (W.H. Freeman, 1980).

__________, *Language, Memory and Thought* (L. Erlbaum, 1976).

Anderson, M.J., "The Process Tracing Paradigm: A General View," in S. Moriarity and E. Joyce (Eds.), *Decision Making and Accounting: Current Research,* (University of Oklahoma, Center for Economic and Management Research, 1984), pp. 158-172.

Ashton, R.H., *Human Information Processing in Accounting.* Studies in Accounting Research #17 (American Accounting Association, 1982).

Ashton, R.H., "Cue Utilization and Expert Judgments: A Comparison of Independent Auditors with Other Judges," *Journal of Applied Psychology* (1974), pp. 437-444.

Biggs, S.F. and T.J. Mock, "An Investigation of Auditor Decision Processes in the Evaluation of Internal Controls and Audit Scope Decisions," *Journal of Accounting Research* (1983), pp. 234-255.

Borgida, E. and N. Brekke, "The Base Rate Fallacy in Attribution and Prediction," in J.H. Harvey, W.J. Ickes and R.F. Kidd (Eds.), *New Directions in Attribution Research* (L. Erlbaum, 1981).

Chi, M.T.H., R. Glasser and E. Rees, "Expertise in Problem Solving," Learning Research and Development Center, #1981/3, University of Pittsburg, (1981).

Crosby, M.A., "Implications of Prior Probability Elicitation Auditor Sample Size Decisions," *Journal of Accounting Research* (1980), pp. 585-593.

Crosby, M.A., "Bayesian Statistics in Auditing: A Comparison of Probability Elicitation Techniques," *The Accounting Review* (1981), pp. 355-365.

Einhorn, H.J., "Learning from Experience and Suboptimal Rules in Decision Making," in Thomas S. Wallsten (Ed.), *Cognitive Processes in Choice and Decision Behavior* (L. Erlbaum, 1980), pp. 1-20.

Einhorn, H.J. and R.M. Hogarth, "Behavioral Decision Theory: Processes of Judgment and Choice," *Annual Review of Psychology* (1981), pp. 53-88.

Einhorn, H.J., D.N. Kleinmuntz, and B. Kleinmuntz, "Linear Regression *and* Process-Tracing Models of Judgment," *Psychological Review* (1979), pp. 465-485.

Fischhoff, B., "Debiasing," in D. Kahneman, P. Slovic, and A. Tversky, (Eds.), *Judgment under Uncertainty: Heuristics and Biases* (Cambridge University Press, 1982).

Hayes-Roth, F., D.A. Waterman, and D.B. Lenat, (Eds.), *Building Expert Systems* (Addison-Wesley, 1983).

Kahneman, D., P. Slovic, and A. Tversky, (Eds.), *Judgment under Uncertainty: Heuristics and Biases* (Cambridge University Press, 1982).

Kinney, W.R., Jr., "A Note on Compounding Probabilities in Auditing," *Auditing: A Journal of Practice & Theory* (1983), pp. 13-22.

Libby, R., "The Use of Simulated Decision Makers in Information Evaluation," *The Accounting Review* (1975), pp. 475-489.

Libby, R., *Accounting and Human Information Processing: Theory and Applications* (1981).

Libby, R., "Availability and the Generation of Hypotheses in Analytical Review," unpublished manuscript, University of Michigan (April 1983).

Messier, W.F., Jr. and J.V. Hansen, "Expert Systems in Accounting and Auditing: A Framework and Review," in S. Moriarity and E. Joyce (Eds.) *Decision Making and Accounting: Current Research,* (University of Oklahoma, Center for Economic and Management Research, 1984), pp. 182-202.

Mock, T.J. and J. Willingham, "An Improved Method of Documenting and Evaluating A System of Internal Accounting Controls," *Auditing: A Journal of Practice & Theory* (1983), pp. 91-99.

Payne, J.W., "Task Complexity and Contingent Processing in Decision Making: An Information Search and Protocol Analysis," *Organizational Behavior and Human Performance* (1976), pp. 366-387.

Payne, J.W., "Contingent Decision Behavior," *Psychological Bulletin* (1982), pp. 382-402.

Pitz, G.F. and N.J. Sachs, "Judgment and Decision: Theory and Application," unpublished paper, Southern Illinois University at Carbondale (1983).

Slovic, P., B. Fischhoff, and S. Lichtenstein, "Behavioral Decision Theory," *Annual Review of Psychology* (1977), pp. 1-39.

Slovic, P. and S. Lichtenstein, "Comparison of Bayesian and Regression Approaches to the Study of Information Processing in Judgment," *Organizational Behavior and Human Performance* (1971), pp. 649-744.

Solomon, I., "Probability Assessment by Individual Auditors and Audit Teams: An Empirical Investigation," *Journal of Accounting Research* (1982), Part II, pp. 689-710.

Solomon, I., J.L. Krogstad, M.B. Romney, & L.A. Tomassini, "Auditors Prior Probability Distributions for Account Balances," *Accounting, Organizations and Society* (1982), pp. 27-41.

Spetzler, C.S. and C.-A.S. Stael von Holstein, "Probability Encoding in Decision Analysis," *Management Science* (1975), pp. 340-358.

Tversky, A. and D. Kahneman, "Judgment Under Uncertainty: Heuristics and Biases," *Science* (1974), pp. 1124-1131.

Weber, R., "Some Characteristics of the Free Recall of Computer Controls by EDP Auditors," *Journal of Accounting Research* (1980), pp. 214-241.

Wright, W.F., "Properties of Judgment Models in a Financial Setting," *Organizational Behavior and Human Performance* (1979), pp. 73-85.

Wright, W.F., "Comparison of the Lens and Subjective Probability Paradigms for Financial Research Purposes," *Accounting, Organizations and Society* (1982), pp. 65-75.

Wright, W.F., "An Empirical Test of a Bayesian Decision Support Procedure in a Financial Context," *Proceedings of the Fourth International Conference on Information Systems,* Society for Information Management: Houston, Texas (1983), pp. 241-250.

Edward J. Joyce
University of Minnesota

The Implications of the Information Processing Paradigm for Decision Research in Accounting

In the 1970's it was quite fashionable for decision researchers to demean human cognitive abilities. Hundreds of studies of human judgment had consistently demonstrated low achievement and systematic non-Bayesian behavior.[1] Most of these studies were conducted within the paradigm of Brunswik's lens model [Brunswik, 1952]. The latter was formulated when the dominant influence in psychology was neobehaviorism. Neobehaviorists were profoundly antimentalistic. Concepts such as thinking, mind, and consciousness were considered "unscientific" because they referred to unobservables.[2,3] To neobehaviorists, the mind was merely a black box between objectively measurable inputs and outputs. They made no attempt, at any level of abstraction, to infer cognitive processes.

Thus in the early 1950's, when Egon Brunswik formulated the lens model, no body of theory on cognitive processes existed. Brunswik related cues (inputs) to judgments (outputs) using simple mathematical transformations.

For accountants interested in decision research, the appeal of this paradigm was twofold. First, accounting is an applied discipline interested in improving both the quality of accounting numbers and decisions made therewith. The lens model literature not only indicated that there was plenty of room for improvement in decision making, but it also offered suggestions on how to bring about this improvement (e.g., bootstrapping, PIP systems, actuarial prediction). Second, the black box treatment of cognitive processes obviated mastering a vast body of psychological theory.

INFORMATION PROCESSING PARADIGM

In recent years, neobehaviorism has been replaced as the dominant psychological paradigm by the information processing approach. Contrary to the tenets of neobehaviorism, information processing researchers theorize about how, at least at a logical level, the mind works. They draw on an analogy between the mind and a computer. Information processing researchers put cognitive processes between information and judgment much like computer scientists put flowcharts between computer input and output [Lachman *et. al.,* 1979].

The information processing paradigm is beginning to change decision researchers' views of human cognitive abilities. Whereas lens model studies focus on cognitive deficiencies or errors (relative to a Bayesian posterior or an environmental criterion), information processing research is concerned with cognitive *abilities.* Some of these abilities are awesome. Perhaps most awesome is language acquisition and use. By age 6, the typical child exhibits a facility with language that is many orders of magnitude above the most impressive current natural language computer programs.

Implications of Information Processing Paradigm

In recent years, decision research in accounting has become more descriptive and somewhat less normative in character. I attribute this to two major factors. First, researchers are more skeptical of the "normativeness" of normative models. Normative models are built for very simple worlds; decision researchers in accounting are interested in making generalizations about behavior in very complex ones. As Einhorn and Hogarth [1981] point out, an inconsistency between human behavior and the output of a normative model may be due to the inappropriateness of the model rather than to the inappropriateness of the behavior. Second, information processing research is having a large impact on decision research in all domains. The information processing paradigm is a *descriptive* paradigm. It is primarily concerned with *how* people think rather than *how well* they think.

Lens model research has always had an ad hoc flavor. There was little theoretical basis for many of the hypothesis tests conducted. I attribute this to the influence of neobehaviorism on the lens model paradigm. Neobehaviorism did not permit psychologists to theorize about mental processes.

Information processing psychology is concerned with little else but the generation and validation of theories about mental processes. I therefore expect decision research in accounting to have a stronger theoretical basis.

I also expect decision researchers in accounting to pay more attention to context and expertise in the design of experiments. We've known for years that seemingly trivial variations in context could profoundly influence decision behavior, yet we had little to offer in the way of explanation. The information processing paradigm posits a long term memory as part of an information processing system. The psychological research thus far indicates that the interaction between the contents and organization of long term memory and context affect perception, attention, coding, information processing, and decision making. This suggests the importance of studying experts in realistic tasks if one wishes to generalize to expert decision making in the real world.

PSYCHOLOGY VERSUS ECONOMICS

As mentioned above, information processing psychologists conduct research which is more descriptive in nature, and hold human cognitive abilities in more esteem, than do lens model researchers. This may serve the useful function of lessening the misunderstandings that have developed between applied economists and decision researchers.

To many applied economists, "cognitive constraints," "cognitive limitations," or "cognitive biases" imply "irrational" behavior. Understandably unwilling to give up an assumption about human behavior (i.e., rationality) which serves as an underpinning of economic theory, they have not been appreciative of the decision research literature.

Is the notion of a cognitive bias or constraint inconsistent with rational human behavior? Some people think so. I do not. Suppose an athlete is offered a prize of $1 billion if he runs a mile in under 3 minutes anytime in the next year. Is he irrational if he fails to do it? Clearly not. No athlete is physically capable (given current running "technology") of running a mile so quickly. He is not irrational for failing to do something he is incapable of doing, regardless of the incentive. He is physically limited.

The resistance to *cognitive* limitations, I suspect, is rooted in the notion that humans are remarkably adaptive and inventive. What I don't know today I might be able to learn tomorrow. Particularly if I feel it is in my interest to do so. If I am suffering from a cognitive bias that hurts my performance, I may find it in my interest to overcome it.

I believe that humans do learn, but I feel that the difficulty of doing so is grossly underestimated by many applied economists. The real world is not a very good laboratory. It does not conveniently stop so that we can change one variable and see what happens. Before I can overcome a bias, I first have to know that I am biased. How do I find out that I am in a world where treatment effects [Einhorn, 1980] and multicollinearity are the rule? Even the most carefully conducted laboratory experiments cannot rule out all plausible rival hypotheses. If experts in acquiring knowledge have difficulties under the most carefully controlled conditions, it's reasonable to expect people in the real world will have even more difficulty.

How prevalent are the cognitive biases people will have to overcome? Information processing psychologists believe that many human abilities are innate. For example, at present the only satisfactory explanation of human language acquisition and use is that people are "prewired" for language. (Prewiring is analogous to read only memory in computers.) Innate language ability was undoubtedly selected for in human evolution, and serves an important function today.

We are doubtless prewired in other ways as well. In some cases the prewiring is probably functional for the sorts of decision problems we face today. In other cases it may not be. Today we are rarely killed by errors in our judgment or denied the opportunity to pass our prewiring along to our progeny. Natural selection plays little role in civilized societies.

Thus a brain optimally prewired for survival in prehistoric times is unlikely to be optimally prewired for life in today's world. We undoubtedly *learn* to compensate for the more obvious problems. (Our brains are not 100 percent prewired.) I view the role of decision research as identifying the less obvious problems and devising means to cope with them. Decision research exists because individuals do not have the wherewithal to do these things on their own.

NOTES

[1]For reviews of this literature, see Slovic and Lichtenstein [1971] and Slovic, Fischhoff, and Lichtenstein [197].

[2]Lachman, Lachman, and Butterfield [1979, Ch. 2] contains an excellent comparison of neobehaviorism with other psychology paradigms.

[3]Note that physicists, arguably the most "scientific" of scientists, have long relied on unobservables such as electrons, quarks, and photons.

REFERENCES

Brunswik, E., *The Conceptual Framework of Psychology.* (University of Chicago Press, 1952).

Einhorn, H. and R. Hogarth, "Behavioral Decision Theory: Processes of Judgment and Choice." *Journal of Accounting Research* (Spring 1981), pp. 1-31.

Einhorn, H., "Learning from Experience and Suboptimal Rules in Decision Making." In *Cognitive Processes in Choice and Decision Behavior,* T. Wallsten (ed.), (Erlbaum, 1980).

Lachman, R., J. Lachman, and E. Butterfield, *Cognitive Psychology and Information Processing: An Introduction.* Hillsdale, NJ: Erlbaum, 1979.

Slovic, P., B. Fischhoff, and S. Lichtenstein, "Behavioral Decision Theory." *Annual Review of Psychology* (1977), pp. 1-39.

Slovic, P. and S. Lichtenstein, "Comparison of Bayesian and Regression Approaches to the Study of Information Processing in Judgment." *Organizational Behavior and Human Performance* (November 1971), pp. 649-744.